PASSION IN EXILE

In the spirit of rugby
Kindest regards
Peter Bills.

PASSION IN EXILE

100 Years of London Irish RFC

PETER BILLS

Foreword by Spike Milligan

MAINSTREAM
PUBLISHING

EDINBURGH AND LONDON

First published in Great Britain in 1998 by
MAINSTREAM PUBLISHING COMPANY (EDINBURGH) LTD
7 Albany Street
Edinburgh EH1 3UG

ISBN 1 84018 132 X

A catalogue record for this book is available from the British Library

Typeset in Palatino
Printed and bound in Great Britain by Butler and Tanner Ltd, Frome

This book is dedicated to the people of Ireland, many of whom on both sides of the Irish Sea have offered me such wonderful hospitality, help and kindness through the years. As this book was being written, the large majority voted for peace and a future for their children after years of anguish and sorrow. Perhaps the story of this rugby club, which has always offered friendship to all Irish men and women whatever their background, will inspire people throughout Ireland on their chosen path ahead.

Contents

Acknowledgements

'Been asked to write the history of the club, eh? Ah, yer poor bugger, come and have a pint.'

Not for nothing are the Irish known for their sense of humour. And hospitality. Great thing was, while I was supping pints of the black stuff in assorted locations where London Irishmen, past and present, might be lurking, the stories would emerge. Funny thing, that. And the characters.

From day one, the fact that the Irish welcome all comers with a firm handshake with one hand and a glass for their other hand was undeniable. How else to explain the fact that London Irish, one of the world's great rugby clubs in the true sense, asked an Englishman to write their centenary history and commissioned a Scottish-based company to publish it?

I am indebted to so many people at London Irish and in Ireland for their wonderful friendship and assistance. Jim O'Hara, a long-time servant of the club, read my manuscript and made many valuable suggestions, as did David Banks, the then commercial director, Michael Flatley (no, not that one), the press officer, and Michael Gibson, another loyal servant. Kieran McCarthy, who has become an institution at the club in the eyes of most of London rugby, similarly contributed much useful advice. In the early stages, Chuck Nelson, the then chief executive, also offered help and encouragement.

And London Irish members everywhere, past and present, gave me much of their time and some wonderful yarns to embellish the pages that follow. Men like the sprightly Albert Hill, 82 years young and quaffing his pint or two at the Royal Cinque Ports golf club on the Kent coast, Len Dinneen and Jim Sheehan near Limerick, Des O'Brien in Scotland and Al Moroney, until two in the morning at Jury's Hotel in Dublin. To name just four. In the course of my research, I caught up with another 46 London Irish members, supporters or followers, and almost every one was only too willing to help.

But I could doubtless have found another hundred or two, willing and able to recount days of yore. For this is a club which possesses a vibrancy, a heartbeat, a passion and an intrigue which it would be hard to match elsewhere. But in the short time I was allotted to research and write this book, I did my best.

It may be altogether too presumptuous to call it 'the definitive history of

London Irish'. I'm quite sure someone else could reach that extra hundred followers and elicit similarly wondrous yarns for another publication at some time in the future. If they do, I'll be among the first to buy a copy and enjoy it, because writing this book was essentially one hell of a pleasure. Physically tiring and mentally enervating, to be sure – but, above all else, a delight. Because, for me, this club, its servants and the people who have graced its premises are the epitome of what a real rugby club should be like. Play hard, party long and late, welcome strangers warmly and never take yourself or the game too seriously.

Of course, professionalism renders that philosophy silly and outdated. But I wonder whether it does not strike closer to the hearts of most true rugby followers than any Super 12, English Premiership, Tri-Nations or other supremely professional rugby contest, because the pleasure principle underpinned this fantastic game for a hundred years and more. And few clubs offer friends and foe alike such a pleasurable experience as an afternoon down at Sunbury to see the London Irish.

Finally, no book is produced successfully without the huge contribution of publisher, production staff and agent. Bill Campbell, Cathy Mineards and the rest of the staff at Mainstream were all marvellously supportive, as was John Pawsey.

To one and all, a warm thank you.

PETER BILLS
Tunbridge Wells, Kent
October 1998

Foreword
by Spike Milligan
(Or the Confessions of a Rugger Bugger)

Rugby is a game for big buggers; if you're not a big bugger, you get hurt. I wasn't a big bugger but I was a fast bugger and therefore I avoided the big buggers. If I thought I was going to be tackled by a 'big 'un' I would drop the ball by accident so that the big bugger couldn't tackle me. Or I would simply knock on, which would force the blind referee to blow his whistle, which would stop play and therefore stop the big buggers tackling this small bugger. Sometimes, to avoid one of those tackles, I would accidentally step into touch, which would immediately result in a line-out for more of the big buggers. The small ones were, of course, not involved.

Those, briefly, are the basic rules of rugby.

I remember London Irish before the war, when I played in their 'B' team. I'd been playing for two or three years on the wing for the London Polytechnic, and there was this head-hunter named Curran. He said, 'Listen, you're pretty fast, would you like to play for London Irish?' I said, 'Yes, of course.' So I played four or five games for the 'B' team, one of them on a field somewhere in Slough. There was just a tin hut for a changing-room and a bloody dripping tap for water! We came off the field covered in mud and only had this tap to clean up. Most of us just went straight to the pub.

I thought I was good enough to play in the 1sts at the Irish. After all, you had to be Irish to play; you couldn't have Italians or Germans in the team. But then I had to stop playing because the bloody war came, and I got transferred to a rugby-playing battery.

The Sergeant-Major at the battery was Welsh, and rugby mad. 'If that Hitler and Mussolini had been good players, I'd have used them in my bloody team,' he said one day. Wasn't joking, either. I loved the Welsh for their passion for the game.

After the war I went to Wales, and I used to go and watch the valley games. The fire, that was it, the fire. They went out there and forgot everything else. The

Irish have the same fire. And London Irish have still got that Irish spirit. They never think they are going to lose, that is why they are so unpredictable. The tackling in my day was ferocious. I've never seen anything like it.

I remember the drinking was colossal down there before the war. I couldn't keep up with it and once said to the barman, 'Look, I can't drink all this bloody Guinness – I'll have some wine.' The bugger shouted down the bar, 'A glass of white wine for Mrs Milligan!'

My best tackle would have to be long after I retired from the game. I was in Dublin for an Ireland international against the All Blacks, and that great wing forward Ian Kirkpatrick was the New Zealand captain. We were having a few drinks after the game and I saw this giant of a man standing at the other end of the bar. I was filled with a sense that this would probably be the last chance I had in my whole life to tackle an All Black. So I launched myself across the room with a shout, clearing a path to the giant, and hit him below the thigh, bringing him down to the floor. He took it very well, really. Big buggers tend to take tackles well.

SPIKE

Preface

The cups are everywhere at this rugby club: on desks, in the bar, on dressing-room benches, in the press room . . .

Some are half-filled with coffee, others the dregs of cold, discarded tea, abandoned in a silent Saturday-night dressing-room.

If you regard the only cups of merit as being of the glittering silver variety, your criterion for achievement being a piece of inexpensive silverware, then the story of London Irish Rugby Football Club may be of little interest to you. Better, in all probability, to head west from the location of this club to the great Limerick club of Shannon, or, indeed, to the province of Munster, renowned winners through the years of the Inter-Provincial Championship. Perhaps, also, to the English spa town of Bath, or to Leicester in the English Midlands, where polished cups are shown off in swank display cabinets into which supporters gawp, as though looking at caged animals in a zoo.

But should a rugby club's heritage be judged solely on its collection of cups? Is not the motivation of trophies by its very nature largely a materialistic activity? In 1738, six years before the end of his life, Alexander Pope wrote with delicious sarcasm on the subject:

> *Our Gen'rals now, retir'd to their estates,*
> *Hang their old trophies o'er the garden gates,*
> *In life's cool ev'ning satiate of applause.*

For there's the rub. Ought not a club's heritage to focus, rather, upon its human element, the characters it has spawned and who have contributed richly to its annals: extroverts and extremists, the wily and the shrewd, the coy and the cunning, the brave-hearted, the loyal, the grand, the modest, the devoted servants who have comprised so rich a tapestry of life in a simple sporting club? Is not the human spirit, in adversity as much as in triumph, the intrinsic soul of any gathering, any club of such kind?

Pioneers! The first London Irish team, season 1898–99, captained by R.S.V. Dyas (middle row, with ball). On his left is Louis Magee.

CHAPTER ONE

A Dream Realised

'They bore within their breasts the grief
That fame can never heal –
The deep, unutterable woe
Which none save exiles feel.'

W.E. AYTOUN, 1813–65

The peace of the country graveyard is broken only by the wind, whistling conspiratorially through the tall, leaning trees across the lane, and the cawing of the rooks as they descend from their nests and strut arrogantly beside the silent stones. Loneliness is all about this silent graveyard down the lane from the village . . .

* * * * *

At the final whistle, there is bedlam. Complete strangers embrace one another, excited children leap in delight, pints are ordered by the score in the packed bars. The music starts, and the party begins as the players are hugged and jostled in excitement as they leave the field . . .

* * * * *

Rugby attaches these two scenes, 100 years apart, like an umbilical cord. One man, one player, links two such vastly different worlds. Today, 12 or 15 miles into the countryside north-west of Dublin, it is possible to find the resting place of Louis Magee. His memorial, proud and erect among many others, is in a simple country graveyard a mile and a half down the deserted lane from the village of Dunboyne in Co. Meath. The house where he lived much of his life stands, sentry-like, beside the green in the centre of the small village. The gravestone reads simply:

In loving memory of Louis Magee, died 5 May 1945.
Also his wife Catherine, died 8 March 1956.
Brian Magee, died 15 February 1970.

Also his wife Patricia, died 10 March 1990
and their daughter Brona Mary Magee, died 12 September 1995.

RIP
St Joseph pray for us.

Simple lives, simple memorials. No mention of so full a life.

When the first seeds were sown of a rugby club named London Irish, one hundred years ago this autumn, little was as we know it in our modern world. Imagine, for example, the role played by one rugby player, L.M. Magee, in the birth of the London Irish club.

Magee, born in Rathmines, Dublin, on 26 May 1875, married in 1903 and was to father twelve children, seven boys and five girls. His was a fulfilling life in every sense. Ireland rugby international, British Isles rugby player in South Africa in 1896, champion player of the Irish club Bective Rangers. And a crucial inspiration behind the creation of London Irish.

On the eve of the anniversary of his birth, they raised the roof with excitement long into the night at London Irish. Their future had been secured in the Premiership; they had retained their place among the élite of the English game after a match of taut nerves and tense emotions in a play-off against the Yorkshire club Rotherham. The world, the game and the club had changed immeasurably in the course of those years.

Magee was without question one of Ireland's dozen top stars in the oval-ball code. During his near-decade of stardom from 1895 to 1904 he played on ten winning sides and skippered the national XV nine times in three successive seasons. He also starred in two scoreless draws, one of them – against Scotland in 1896 – denying Ireland the Triple Crown. When Ireland did capture that mythical trophy at Cardiff in 1899 after a gap of five years, Magee played a big part in the achievement.

A contemporary account stated:

Unlike the majority of the Irish players who found it difficult to get valuable match practice because of the small number of clubs functioning at the time, Magee had wide experience of the strategy of the game. A remarkably fit man through middle age, Magee, who also studied in Edinburgh and represented Edinburgh Wanderers, in later years was to be employed as a veterinary surgeon in the Department of Agriculture.

Others, such as James A. Manning, like Magee a pupil of Clongowes Wood College in Ireland, were said to be instrumental 'in starting it [the new athletic club in London] and bringing it to a successful issue'. But many had put their heads together to establish the necessary paperwork. For the view had been expressed on both sides of the Irish Sea that a sporting club for Irishmen in London was badly needed. London Scottish had been formed in 1878, London Welsh some seven years later in 1885. Both had offered their countrymen a home away from home in London, a place to visit and enjoy while their professional employment or any other reason required absence from their homeland.

It was 1898 – just two years away from entry into what would prove to be a staggering, rip-roaring, war-torn, invention-rich century. The century of all centuries, in many respects. Thomas Hardy was publishing his *Wessex Poems* and Oscar Wilde saw into print *The Ballad of Reading Gaol*. The Boer War was about to break out in the South Africa Louis Magee and his fellow British Isles players had visited only two years earlier, winning the Test series 3–1.

Outside-half Magee had played in all four Test matches on that tour, but for the Magee family back in Dublin the second and fourth Tests were of particular moment: brother Jim, although he was never to win a rugby cap for Ireland, had appeared with Louis in the British Isles teams. (Another brother, Joe, played for Ireland with Louis against England in 1895.)

Two of Louis and Jim's 1896 British Isles team-mates from Ireland, Tom Crean and Robert Johnston, would return to South Africa within a couple of years on a very different mission: to fight in the Boer War. With a distinguished outcome, too: both won the Victoria Cross, the highest military decoration, for valour.

In London, Irishmen came together to form their own club, the London Irish Rugby Football Club. At that first meeting in central London, the following officers were appointed:

- President: Lord Russell of Killowen, formerly Sir Charles Russell, whose title changed in 1894 when he became Lord Chief Justice. He was the representative for Dundalk between 1880 and 1885 and then Hackney South from 1885 to 1894.
- Vice-president: Lord Castletown
  Other officials were as follows:
- Lord MacNaughten
- The Hon. Horace Plunkett, MP for Dublin South 1892–1900
- Sir Thomas Grattan Esmonde, MP for Dublin County South 1885–92, Kerry West 1892–1900 and North Wexford 1900–18
- Edward Carson QC, MP for Dublin University 1892–1918 and Belfast (Duncairn) 1918–21
- Justin H. McCarthy, MP for Athlone 1884–85 and Newry 1885–92
- B.C. Molloy, MP for King's County 1880–85 and Birr 1885–1900
- T. Harrington, MP for Westmeath 1883–85 and Dublin (Harbour) 1885–1910

- W.E. Redmond, MP for Wexford 1883–85, North Fermanagh 1885–92 and Clare East 1892–1917
- David Arnott Esq.

I am indebted to Jim O'Hara for the following information on this founding group.

'A unique feature of this group is the large number of MPs who played a role in the formation of the club. Even more fascinating is the fact that of the six members of Parliament, five of them were members of the Home Rule party, founded earlier by Isaac Butt and Charles Parnell, while the sixth, Edward Carson, was a Unionist, as well as being a leading barrister. A few years earlier, Carson had been the prosecuting counsel at the trial of his fellow Dubliner Oscar Wilde in London, and he was later, of course, to become the leader of the Ulster Unionists in their fight against Home Rule for Ireland.

'Willie Redmond was the brother of John Redmond, who became undisputed leader of the Home Rule party in 1900 and was later killed in action on the Western Front, having joined the British Army in answer to his brother's call to do so.

'Despite the wide disparity in political views amongst this intriguing group of powerful personalities, this common sense of Irishness and love of rugby were the bonds that held them together. Thus, from its very inception, London Irish was to provide a welcoming home and hospitable meeting place for all Irish people, regardless of creed or politics.'

All worthy servants, to be sure, with a commendable sense of determination to ensure that the new club became a success. But the name of Magee was to be critical to the fledgling club's early years. A veterinary surgeon, Magee had gone to London in 1898 to pursue medical studies for his career. His rugby reputation was already secure: as a Bective Rangers player he had played in Ireland's championship-winning side of 1896, and he was captain of his country when Ireland took the Triple Crown and the championship in 1899. Magee was to represent his country 27 times between 1895 and 1904 as a shrewd, visionary outside-half, and he played a key role in both attack and defence in Ireland's triumphs of that era.

To the new London Irish club, he was a vital recruit and a potent magnet. Magee might have been seduced by the entreaties of other more established clubs in London, but his decision to represent London Irish set up a trend for Irishmen coming to London and joining the club that lasted, by and large, for almost an entire century, until the advent of professionalism.

But in mid-September 1898, when he first joined London Irish, Magee remained a player with Bective Rangers back in Ireland, and thus showed an astonishing commitment to a game which became the centrepiece of his sporting life. Magee, one of four brothers from a sporting family, would on Fridays board the boat train in London for the North Wales coast and Holyhead, and survive the atrocities the Irish Sea regularly inflicted upon its poor victims before arrival in the port of Dublin. He would then go out and play for Bective on the Saturday afternoon. A night at home would be followed by the same routine, in reverse. There were no cars to whisk him away to swish airports for the 45-minute flight to London. Instead, the journey would last the entire night and spew up – a crude but perhaps appropriate phrase in this context – an exhausted traveller on a London railway station platform around breakfast time on Monday morning.

By late September, as the 1898–99 season began, London Irish were ready. There are no reports of fanfares or Guinness specials in the bar afterwards, nor of Irish dancing music long into the night. Rather, we are told that the imposing sight of the well-built Lord Russell of Killowen, who attended the first game together with Sir Rowland Hill of the Rugby Football Union, one of the leading legislators of that era, and Capt. The Hon. Southwell-Fitzgerald, administered a suitably grand sense to the occasion.

Lord Russell greeted all who had shaken, shuddered and rattled their way out on the trams through the leafy London suburbs to reach the ground, promising to do all within his powers to make London Irish one of the most famous sporting clubs in London.

The first match was played on 1 October 1898 against the Hammersmith club (long since defunct) at Herne Hill Athletic Ground in south-east London, the first of many grounds where the club resided over the years. Through the enterprise of Lord Russell and Martin Doyle and the generous assistance of the Irish Rugby Union, the new club had negotiated a five-year lease at the Herne Hill ground. The ground would later host the London Welsh club after the Irish had moved on.

That first game, which Lord Russell started by kicking off, was won by London Irish by eight points to three. The team for that opening match was led by an army officer, R.S.V. Dyas, who was to go through two world wars and then become president of London Irish for the 1946–47 season. In that first ever London Irish team was Martin Doyle, who was also honorary secretary and a man who would become one of the stalwarts of the club, serving them in a variety of roles over an equally long period of time. Capt. The Hon. Southwell-Fitzgerald became honorary treasurer.

There is a photograph of the team from that first season, the classic, quintessential portrait of sporting men of the era, backs ramrod straight, presenting themselves before a cameraman shrouded in black cloth and about to activate his still-curious machine. Men like the Rev. J.R. James MA, who played in the first London Irish side and later became chairman, in the 1930s. All seem matter-of-fact in manner, delightfully oblivious to the long legacy they were establishing; sadly, they were oblivious, too, to the imminence of a terrible war that would tear Europe apart within 15 years. Elegant, fashionable moustaches are ubiquitous in the photograph; so, too, are the long shorts and traditional rugger boots. The ball resembles more a medicine ball, that torturous weapon with which cruel masters used to inflict painful retribution upon naughty schoolboys during gymnasium classes.

In a picture taken the following season, with Magee having replaced Dyas as captain, behind the good men and true on the pavilion balcony are precious reminders of a bygone age: a bearded gentleman in a bowler, a lady in a smart bonnet, small boys with neckerchiefs and caps at jaunty angles. Beside three boys stands a man in a flat cap alongside a lady, perhaps a family brought to a game by the presence of a participating brother or son.

Louis Magee was installed at once as vice-captain to Dyas in 1898, and he appeared for the first time in a match against Saracens which resulted in a 3–3

The second season, with Magee (seated, centre) now captain. Martin Doyle is standing, extreme right.

draw, a penalty goal apiece. Some weeks later, at the end of October, the Wasps club, which had been formed 31 years earlier in 1867, consented to a fixture with the new club south of the Thames. The Wasps players were doubtless offered a similar blithe assurance concerning their task to the poor, hapless infantry of the 1st London Rifle Brigade on the Somme a few years later – 'Success is assured and casualties are expected to be ten per cent.' Who encountered the greater surprise, whether from German guns or Irish rugby players, is unrecorded, but it would seem a safe bet to say that the men of Wasps were astonished to suffer a 9–8 defeat, three tries to a goal and a try.

As with any new club, the work which went on behind the scenes was considerable. A newspaper report of unknown origin from that time states: 'Prominent Irish people living in the London area endeavoured to persuade everybody they knew who had any Irish links, however tenuous, to join the club, if not as a player then as a social member.'

The report says of Magee:

He was regarded by very many, because of his friendly and helpful disposition, as one of the outstanding personalities in rugby football, and gave at once, by joining, a special prestige to the London Irish club. Because of his style of play and his unique skills, he could always attract a crowd to any game in which he took part, and soon his presence brought spectators to Herne Hill or the other grounds in which London Irish were playing.

Beyond dispute, Magee's presence opened the door to fixtures with most of London's leading clubs of that period: Blackheath, Rosslyn Park, Saracens and Wasps. There was, too, that early fixture against London Welsh, the first of what would become one of the highlights of the club's season. It took place on 19 November 1898 at a new ground being tried by the Welsh Exiles – Cambrian Park, Hampstead, next to Hampstead Cricket Club. It attracted a most healthy crowd of nearly 1,000. Irish won that first ever 'exiles international' by a goal to a try (5–3), despite the fact that, according to one report, the Welsh had been strengthened specially for that match by two players from Newport and two from Aberavon. As for the Irish, they ended that momentous first year of 1898 by defeating Southwark by two tries to nil on Saturday, 10 December. Magee's play was said to be 'brilliant'.

The New Year, the last of the century, saw continued good form and promising trends for London Irish RFC. At Herne Hill in January, a second match against Wasps, played in appalling conditions following heavy rain, ended 0–0.

Meanwhile, over in Dublin, the committee of the Irish Rugby Football Union were, for the first but by no means the last time, dithering over how to react to the new club in London. A motion was proposed stating that 'no Irishman resident in London be eligible for an international cap who is not a member of and does not play for the London Irish'. Somewhat laconically, a contemporary report states: 'The proposal was not pursued.' It would be only the first of very many times that the issue of London Irish would cause furrowed brows within IRFU committees back in Dublin. But, 100 years later, the IRFU would move close to an even more draconian ruling, suggesting to some players that playing their rugby in London rather than in their homeland might be detrimental to their international career. Attitudes towards the new club in London swung dramatically during the course of those hundred years.

Louis Magee had other fish to fry that year. Returning to Dublin, he helped Ireland defeat England 6–0 at Lansdowne Road on 6 February 1899. In their fourth successive victory over England, the Irish scored a try and a penalty goal, the latter being kicked by the outside-half who was by now Ireland's captain. London Irish, without Magee for one club match back in London, promptly lost it, 11–3.

On 24 March 1899, the *Belfast Newsletter* carried a report of a dinner held in London, under the title 'London Irish Rugby Football Club'. It stated:

> *The first annual dinner of this club, formed in September last, was held in the Café Florio, Rupert Street, Piccadilly, on 21st inst., about seventy gentlemen assembling, under the presidency of Mr David T. Arnott.*
>
> *The chairman commented upon the marvellous strides which rugby football has made in Ireland . . . He concluded by proposing the health of the Irish Rugby Union, coupling the toast with the name of Mr Magee . . .*
>
> *Honour was afterwards done to the English Rugby Union, on the proposition of Mr Bulger, Mr Rowland-Hill replying. The last speaker said the Irishman had an intense love of the game, played it fairly and squarely and, if beaten, was the first to congratulate his opponents.*

Appropriately, within less than a season of joining the club, Magee was made London Irish's first team captain. The club was truly on its way.

CHAPTER TWO

Little Strides, Small Steps

'Tall oaks from little acorns grow.'

DAVID EVERETT, 1769–1813

Given the nightmares that fixture secretaries and team secretaries have endured down the years in finding 15 men sober enough, sane enough and prepared to leave the woman's bedroom on a Saturday for an afternoon's sporting exercise playing for one of their club's junior teams, it was a notable achievement of the newly created London club to establish so quickly more than just one side.

In its first season, membership reached 100 and London Irish boasted three teams, a magnificent achievement which says much about the commendable early organisation at the club. There was some substantial opposition to meet early on, too, such as Harlequins, whom the Irish played for the first time on 3 November 1900 in a game at Herne Hill which produced a 5–0 victory for the Irish.

The following month, on 8 December 1900, London Irish were the first visitors to yet another ground tried out by London Welsh, Lower Welsh Harp in Hendon – it was their tenth ground in just 12 years. The match attracted what a report of the time described as a 'very large' crowd, around 1,500. London Welsh visited Herne Hill, first home of the Irish, on 27 January 1900.

All clubs of that period had much to do in establishing themselves, and we are told that the Walsh brothers, G.C. and J.N. Walsh, were instrumental in assisting the likes of Dyas, Magee and the committee in providing London Irish with so sound an early structure. J.N. Walsh is photographed in a team group of the club's 'A' team in season 1904–05, standing on a forlorn London heath in front of two stark trees which look like early examples of the flora on the Somme after the guns had opened for business in 1916.

In season 1903–04, the club's 'B' team played 21 matches, winning 16 and drawing one, with just four defeats. Points for registered 221, points against 60. It suggested a strength in depth which was unusual for clubs in their formative years and, more importantly, set a proud tradition for the exploits of the 'B' XV at London Irish that was to last to the present day.

By 1902, the London Irish 1st XV had become a formidable team, good enough to defeat all the London clubs they met. Magee was now captain and a true inspiration, and his name and repute had spread far across the Irish Sea to rugby circles on the mainland. One report states: 'Because of his style of play and his unique skills, he could always attract a crowd to any game in which he took part.'

By then, too, Irish had made the first of what would prove to be several moves. The lease had expired at Herne Hill and the club tried new accommodation at Stamford Bridge in 1904, then known as the London Athletic Ground. London's Queen's Club was next stop, then to Wandsworth Common to share with London Welsh. Why so many moves? There is a chance they weren't paying the rent, but it isn't the likeliest reason. The new club needed as good a base as possible, and its early committeemen and officials felt the need to maintain a search for that ideal location. Trying out several different venues seemed as good an idea as any.

Season 1905–06 was played at The Uplands, Blackhorse Lane, Walthamstow, in north-east London, on the road out to Epping Forest and Essex. In those days, the London sprawl was comparatively modest, and Walthamstow was a pleasant enough, almost rural venue. But it didn't satisfy London Irish for very long. By 1907–08, the club had continued the game of musical chairs by moving back south of the river, to the quaintly named Laurel Brook, Rutland Park, Perry Hill, near Catford, in south-east London. They were to settle there until the dark clouds of war began to build and playing rugger became of rather diminished importance in the minds of young men.

In 1904, Louis Magee played for Ireland for the 27th and last time, while back at London Irish, Martin Doyle had taken over as full-time honorary secretary, the first year of a long tenure. The impressive fixture list indicated a club on a healthy footing. The big London hospitals like St Thomas's, St Bart's, Guy's and the London, all powerful rugger sides in those days, were on the fixture card, together with the likes of London Welsh, Rosslyn Park, Harlequins, Bedford, Coventry, Blackheath, London Scottish, Oxford University and Richmond. The season opened late, on Saturday, 7 October (joy of joys, compared with these times of grotesquely congested fixture lists!), and finished on 17 March. A Christmas tour of Wales took place, with matches played against Pontypridd in the Rhondda on 23 December, Maesteg up the valleys on Christmas Day, and Pontypool on Boxing Day.

A forward, J.J. Rahilly, was club captain that season, another forward, H.M. Rooker, skippered the seconds, and a three-quarter, M.R. Gardner, led the thirds. The club had instigated, from its inception, the award of an annual honours cap for good play to a forward and a back from each XV. The tradition is continued

The London Irish 'A' team, 1904–05.

to this day, with ties having replaced caps after the Second World War. Familiar names from that era such as R.S.V. Dyas, J.N. Walsh, J.J. Rahilly and H.M. Rooker all received the handsome green-and-cream velvet cap with the shamrock proudly embossed on the front and 'London Irish RFC' written in gold braiding on the front panel, with the year of the award on the peak. A gold-braid tassel completed the elegant cap. One name is missing from the list of honours cap awards, however: one Louis Magee. A curious omission, it might seem – except that in 1901 a special cap was awarded to Magee and in 1906 to Martin Doyle, 'in recognition of their valuable services to the club since its formation'.

By 1905, Magee, Dyas and J.N. Walsh had become vice-presidents of the club, further acknowledgement of their already-fine service. The club already boasted 20 life members, among them Dyas, Doyle, the Rev. J.R. James and one Jeremiah MacMahon, who had taken over as honorary treasurer and who was to prove himself a valuable servant to the club in the following years. So much so, in fact, that at the end of the 1913–14 season he, too, received a special award with the same citation as Magee and Doyle.

Membership subscriptions for 1905 were ten shillings, with a fee of five pounds for life membership. Honorary members paid a subscription of five

A 1906–07 London Irish side, some resplendent in caps.

shillings per year, which included admission to the ground for all matches but did not give the right to vote at meetings.

Season 1907–08 began earlier for the players, on 5 October, to accommodate an increased fixture list which reflected the burgeoning strength and reputation of the club. In the 1905–06 season, Irish had had 26 fixtures; in 1907–08 it was up to 32. The good news from the players' point of view was that they had Christmas Day off – their Christmas tour that year began at Swansea on Boxing Day, continued at Pontypool the following day and finished at Merthyr the day after that.

In 1908–09, another Welsh-based club was added to the London Irish fixture list for the first time. 'Llanelly', as their name was spelt in contemporary accounts, were played in West Wales on 24 December, the match ending in a victory for the home side.

Of 28 matches played that season, there were 15 wins and 13 defeats. Results were erratic, with some encouraging wins interspersed with heavy defeats, such as the 34–0 thrashing Harlequins handed out at Catford in November 1908. The following year, under the captaincy of J.W.B. Milligan, the 1st XV met Bristol for the first time. The match took place in the West Country on Christmas Day, with another visit to Swansea two days later. Little strides, small steps.

In season 1909–10, the general difficulty of fulfilling certain fixtures at the lower levels became apparent, with six of the scheduled 27 3rd XV matches scratched. For this information, we are indebted to one B.J. Delany, captain of the 3rd XV in season 1910–11, who won the honours cap for forwards in that side for season 1909–10. Delany was one of those indubitable servants of a sports club who recorded meticulous details for future generations. Whatever, the information is contained in beautifully preserved tiny stiff cardboard-backed fixture cards spanning the years 1905 to 1912.

On 17 December 1910, Irish played Harlequins for the first time at Twickenham, the Quins having previously appeared at Wandsworth. That year, too, Neath became another Welsh club added to the fixture list as part of the Christmas tour of Wales, along with Llanelly.

Delany's 3rd XV had a fine season that year, winning 19 of its games, losing just three and drawing one. Wins by 45 points to nil over Beckenham and a 46–0 victory over the Civil Service were the highlights of their season. Also in this 1910–11 season, London Irish were for the first time able to put out four teams.

By season 1911–12, the Rev. J.R. James had replaced the Hon. Charles Russell as club president. But men who had been loyal and valued servants in

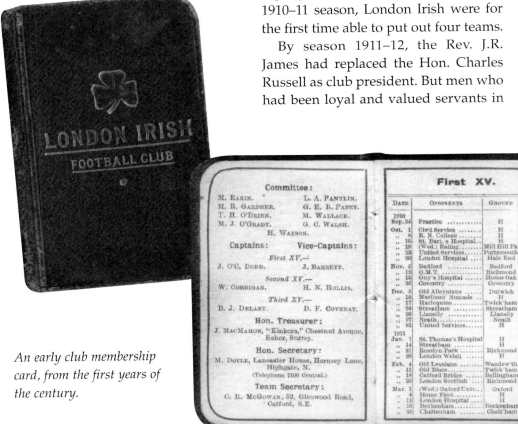

An early club membership card, from the first years of the century.

the first ten years of the club's history were still contributing in a variety of ways: men like K.D'A. Houston and J.N. Walsh, who had played together in the 'A's of 1904–05, Dyas and Magee, J.W.B. Milligan, F.S. Forde, C.R. McGowan, A.S. Lawlor and the Rev. R.J. Rothwell, who had been awarded the 1st XV honours cap in season 1907–08. A club, especially in its formative years, stands or falls on the contribution such men can make, and the fact that the Irish were so successful in establishing their club at an early stage was due to the generous efforts of men such as these.

In 1911, the 31st and final fixture of the season saw London Irish break more new ground with a fixture in France against Le Havre. But Irishmen would be crossing the English Channel for altogether different reasons within a very short time, the coming of the First World War drawing a curtain over the activities of sports clubs like London Irish once the 1913–14 season had ended (with the Irish having that season fielded a 5th XV for the first time). In a sense, war in 1914 meant that those charged with running the club could reflect upon and analyse the first 15 hectic, most successful years of London Irish. But against the

An Irish side from the 1913–14 season, the last before that fateful year of 1914.

28

backdrop of a war as disastrous as the 1914–18 conflict proved to be, all other considerations paled into insignificance. London Irish Rugby Club, like the rest, had to be mothballed as the savage conflict began just across the Channel.

In a very real sense, Irish rugby was afflicted by two crucial conflicts from 1914 onwards. Not only the Great War – 'the war to end all wars', as someone once unwisely dubbed it – but the Easter Rising of 1916 in Ireland precipitated death, injury and severe disruption to sport involving Irishmen of the time.

Not until 1923, when the Irish Free State was established on a firm foundation, did peace truly break for most Irishmen. London Irish RFC might have seemed somewhat remote from the latter conflict, yet, as events continued, it undoubtedly affected their chances of attracting more players from home.

For sure, many London Irish members lost their lives in the 1914–18 war. The Irish Regiments took many London-based Irishmen, and there are stories of foot soldiers in one of them dribbling a ball before them as they walked into battle at Loos in 1915.

For one famous man of the club, Jack Nelson, there were some extraordinary experiences. Nelson, who was to become Colonel J.E. Nelson OBE, MC, BA, survived some harrowing wartime emotions. In later life, he served in the Second World War, attached to the War Office in London. In February 1949 he was made Lieutenant-Colonel and later that year he became Colonel Nelson. His journey from a simple Lance-Corporal had been extraordinary.

In his retirement, Jack Nelson was a cheerful, breezy character who was as bright as a button. He was still active, a real gentleman well into his 80s. He became one of the most avid followers of London Irish and used to attend almost every home match. His love for the club provided one of his chief pleasures in later years and, indeed, he was on his way to the club one Saturday, sitting on the bar stool of his favourite pub near his Kensington home, eating a sandwich and drinking a pint of beer before journeying to see them play, when he suddenly died.

The survivors and the newcomers: the Exiles' 1st XV, season 1920–21. C.R. McGowan, seated third from right, is the captain.

CHAPTER THREE

A Happy Brotherhood

"Tis from high life, high characters are drawn.'

ALEXANDER POPE, 1688–1744

Recapturing much of a mood for sporting contests after the bloody war which had just wreaked havoc across Europe was no straightforward task and took some time. Although war ended in November 1918, the Treaty of Versailles was not signed by Germany and the Allies until June 1919. Back in London, the sense of shock at the enormous loss of life was prolonged; there was a feeling of hopelessness at so much carnage. All clubs had lost members, players and supporters, and establishing sport on an organised, regular basis drifted into the early 1920s.

Contemporary accounts of that time at London Irish are limited. As Bill Morgan, about whom much will be said in this and later chapters, wrote in a ledger soon after the Second World War had ended in 1945: 'On taking over . . . during the 1945–46 season . . . no records were available in this respect as they were destroyed by the bombing during the 1939–45 war.' Or at least, what previous officers of the club hadn't managed to lose, Hitler could be blamed for wrecking.

But we do know that for London Irish it was almost like beginning again. What is also clear is that, but for the efforts of men like C.R. McGowan, who came from Derry, and Jeremiah MacMahon, from Kerry (the Derryman and the Kerryman), who provided what one subsequent report described as 'energetic leadership', the club would have struggled even more. But difficult times at such clubs call for outstanding characters, and London Irish were fortunate to find a man of much charisma on the field, too: S.J. 'Cags' Cagney, a powerful forward who would later go on to win 13 caps for Ireland from 1925 to 1929 until a knee injury ended his international career. He was the first Irish international to emerge purely from the London Irish club, as opposed to others like Magee who had been capped while with their previous clubs.

The club managed to field only a 1st XV in season 1919–20. It was not until the following year, season 1920–21, that they could muster sufficient numbers to play three sides, a 1st XV, an 'A' XV and a 'B' XV. Little is known of the immediate post-war teams except that, in that first season, P.O. Norton won the honours cap for back play and G.N. Cracknell for the forwards. On 4 October 1919, there was a poignant reminder of the earliest times in the club's history when Irish returned to Herne Hill and the renowned cycle track at Burbage Road, Dulwich, which was the London County Athletic Ground where they had started out, for a fixture against London Welsh. By then, of course, Irish had moved on, but now London Welsh had gone to the same ground and were to remain there, apart from a single season at Surbiton, until they settled at Old Deer Park in 1957.

McGowan's role through the 1920s was crucial. He was team captain for the club's Christmas tour in 1920 and was still leader for season 1921–22. Solid and wiry with a neatly clipped moustache, he was a man with a businesslike manner, as befitted a military figure (he was eventually to become an army major) intent on accepting the next challenge, whatever it might be. P.J. Kelly was his vice-captain and took over as leader for the 1923–24 season. Alongside Kelly in the 1921–22 team photograph is J.P. Townsley, wearing a club shirt torn halfway down the front as though the irate family dog had just released it from its jaws. Kit was clearly in short supply in those days.

By 1924–25, C.R. McGowan had swapped a club shirt for blazer, brogues and tie in the team photograph, in his new role as honorary secretary. P.J. Kelly was captain that season and Townsley had meantime acquired a shirt in one piece. Cagney took over the captaincy in 1925–26 and held it for most of the remainder of the 1920s. The team photo that year includes, with a rather nice touch, all those unsung, hard-working heroes of the club who so rarely appear in the spotlight, together in the back row of the team picture. They are F.S. Forde (vice-president), J. MacMahon (hon. treasurer), C.R. McGowan (hon. secretary), M. Doyle (vice-president) and A. O'Carroll (hon. secretary).

It is possible to trace the life and times of the quintessential rugby clubman, such as Martin Doyle, through a club's collection of fraying, ageing, sepia-tinted photographs from years gone by. Doyle had begun as a first-team player when the club had been founded just before the turn of the century. He doubtless filled in thereafter in the junior sides before finally bowing to Anno Domini and hanging up his boots. By the mid-1920s, he stands proud and contented as club secretary for the 1st XV photograph, clad in what looks like a thick Donegal tweed coat. His thick, black, bushy handlebar moustache had, by then, been a familiar sight at the London Irish club for the best part of a quarter of a century.

In 1928, when London Irish went to Cork to play Cork Constitution at Mardyke, Doyle is seen sporting very smart plus fours, waistcoat, jacket and flat tweed cap. All he would appear to lack for the classic pose is a golf club in one hand, but clearly middle age has arrived. The years stand still for no man.

R. Segrave-Daly, a former captain of Downside school, had been in the side back in 1919–1920 but then went abroad for a time. He returned to London and the club in time for the 1925–26 season and is seated beside Cagney, the new skipper. Segrave-Daly also captained the Irish in 1926, and that year, at the County Ground, Southampton, he helped London Irish to a 13–6 win over Trojans, the Hampshire club, during which Bill Morgan achieved the unlikely feat for a front-row forward of dropping a goal. Cagney had been in the side as early as the 1920–21 season, when he won the honours cap for forwards, and he was to prove an inspired choice as leader.

But it was a mixture of energy on the field and determination and application off it, in the committee rooms, that helped London Irish regain its feet after the war and make real progress in the first half of the 1920s. Queen's University, Belfast, had produced an outstandingly talented centre, George (G.V.) Stephenson, one of the best Ireland has ever known. He made his debut for his country in 1920 against France and went on to win 42 caps between then and 1930. When he came to London to pursue medical studies at the London Hospital, he soon formed an association with London Irish, although his appearances for the club were restricted to a smattering, because of hospital and international commitments. Stephenson became London Irish's second captain of the Irish national side, after the great Louis Magee.

In the 1920s, the club had found a home at Norbiton, but it was to prove no more than temporary. Yet despite the continuing lack of a long-term base, and the difficulties of establishing teams with consistent personnel, the name and reputation of London Irish continued to grow. Two fixtures in the space of three years reflected that fact. Leicester met them for the first time, at Welford Road, on 20 January 1923, beating the visitors 22–3. Then, on Boxing Day 1926, London Irish played at Cardiff for the first time, going down 12–6 to a below-strength home side who were resting several key players for a match the following day against the New Zealand Maoris.

One of modern-day rugby's lost arts was a notable feature of the London Irish game in those times: the dribble. Not at 11 p.m. on a Saturday evening by tired and emotional men after a long, hard night at the bar, but during the match. A report from the 1927 game that London Irish lost 12–6 at Bedford states: 'Play was always lively and interesting. The Bedford pack did well in the scrums but the Irishmen dribbled finely, especially Morgan.'

London Irish's traditional force up front, alas seldom matched by the backs, was mentioned 'in dispatches' after a heavy 25–3 defeat at London Welsh in 1926. The report read: 'The Irish forwards gave a fine exhibition, more than holding their own both in the scrum and in the loose.' But the ability of the Welsh backs to pass so accurately even with a slippery ball in the heavy rain was the key factor. Also in 1926, a 19–5 victory for Irish over United Services, Portsmouth, mentioned 'the smart handling and dribbling of the Irish forwards' as a feature of the match.

By the mid-1920s, London Irish had a member of the famous Beamish stout-brewing family from Cork in their ranks, Victor, who was to stay only a season or two before being posted to an RAF base in the Midlands and joining Leicester for the 1926–27 season. Victor (F.V.), who was to lose his life while on active service in 1942, was an Ulster forward, had two Irish trials and was a reserve for the Irish XV. He is photographed in the London Irish team line-up for a match against Wanderers at Lansdowne Road, Dublin, in 1924, and also in a game they played against North of Ireland, in Belfast, on the same trip. London Irish beat Wanderers 14–3, and other players in that side included P.J. Kelly at outside-half, C.J.S. O'Malley at scrum-half and the Hilliard brothers.

Cagney, fresh-faced with powerful features and hair swept back, was an imposing character. For the match against Wanderers, he was resplendent in his famous scrum cap.

The Beamish family was to make a marvellous contribution to rugby football and become renowned as one of Ireland's greatest rugby families. The family produced four brothers and two sisters, all the brothers serving nobly in the RAF

The London Irish side which played Wanderers at Lansdowne Road in 1924.

during the Second World War. George (G.R.) Beamish, born in Dunmanway, Co. Cork, on 29 April 1905, was educated at Coleraine Academical Institute and played for Leicester when he was stationed in the Midlands in the early years after he came to England, beginning in 1924–25 when he won the first of what would be 25 caps for Ireland. In 1930, he toured Australia and New Zealand with F.D. Prentice's British Lions, playing in all five internationals on the tour (four were lost, a narrow 6–3 victory over New Zealand at Dunedin the only exception) and earning much praise and respect from the triumphant New Zealanders.

Another Beamish brother, the youngest, Cecil, who had represented Queen's, Belfast, as a fine, bustling forward, also went on to play for the Leicester and London Irish clubs and became an international golfer. In season 1933–34, Charles (C.E. St J.) Beamish also represented Leicester and joined his brother George in the Irish pack for the 1933 season internationals against Wales and Scotland. He was awarded the DFC in 1940 and retired from the RAF in 1948, as a Group Captain.

George was the most famous of the Beamish brothers. He was the biggest man in the 1930 Lions pack at 6ft 1in and around 16 stone. He was described by his colleagues as a No. 8 forward with tremendous powers of application.

Eugene O'Davy, who made 34 successive appearances for Ireland in the same era as Beamish and later became president of the IRFU, said of George Beamish, 'He gave great confidence, and his players looked up to him both as a captain and as a forward. Off the field, he was a quiet, serious-minded sort of man, but very likeable.'

In 1930, George Beamish joined London Irish. His was a name with the allure to the club of Louis Magee and G.V. Stephenson before him. Two years later, he was to captain the Ireland team which shared the championship of 1932. In his war years a decade later, George Beamish was a Battle of Britain pilot who made history by becoming the first RAF officer to be promoted to Air Commodore. He was awarded the CBE in 1942 and KCB in 1955. Just to fill in all the spare time he doubtless had on his hands, given his myriad talents, he became RAF officers' golf champion in 1925 and RAF heavyweight boxing champion in 1929. He also played in the Leicestershire/East Midlands side at Welford Road which was the only side to beat Benny Osler's 1931–32 South Africans. A commentator at that game described the Springboks as 'giants', but continued, 'No one could dwarf the huge Beamish.'

His sister Kathleen, a delightful old lady now in her 78th year, remembers the love her brother always had for the game. 'I do remember how keen he was about rugby. I can recall going to see Ireland play some internationals with George in the team. I was living in the north of Ireland at the time and it was a special day out for all of us at our school when we went to watch the rugby internationals. [Ireland were still playing some of their home internationals in the championship at Belfast, especially against Wales, up until 1950, after which all major internationals were held in Dublin.]

'George was 15 years older than me and was mostly out of Ireland until his retirement, when he came home.' Air Marshal Sir George Beamish went back to Ireland and Co. Donegal in 1959 and died, unexpectedly, at Castlerock, Co. Londonderry, in November 1967 at the age of 62.

In November 1925, a newspaper report chronicled 'The Progress of London Irish'. It read:

> *London Irish have got together a splendid fifteen this season, and the club's success is enhanced by the tremendous enthusiasm of the members. So far, six matches have been won out of eight played, 103 points being scored and only 41 given away. S.J. Cagney, the international, is a splendid skipper and more than one of his men should catch the selectors' eyes this campaign. I hear that the likeliest man for a trial is W. Morgan, who is a typical Irish forward and has been playing finely all the season.*

In 1926, the London Irish Annual Dinner was held – the usual quiet evening of modest consumption with everyone off home early for a good night's sleep. A newspaper report stated:

The Rev. W.P. [sic] James, who received an enthusiastic welcome, presided at the annual dinner of the London Irish 'Rugger' club on Saturday evening, supported by Cecil Walsh, R.S.V. Dyas, C.R. McGowan, J.B. Quin, J. Macmahon, M.P. Slattery, F. Ruthven of the London Scottish and S.J. Cagney, George Beamish and W. Morgan, the well-known players.

It was a most enjoyable evening, in which reference was made to the continual enthusiasm and support of 'Padre' James, the excellent work of McGowan, MacMahon and others, and the prominent part played by Cagney, the captain, in the effort made by Ireland to win the International Championship.

R.S.V. Dyas, the first captain of the club, was

IRISH RUGBY FOOTBALL UNION,
17, WESTMORELAND STREET,
DUBLIN.

DEAR SIR,

You have been selected to play for Ireland

v.   at

on

Please let me know at once if you will be able to play. You travel

Should you incur any expenses properly chargeable to the Union, please furnish your account to the Hon. Treasurer on the annexed form on your return.

Yours truly,
G.F. RUXTON,
Hon. Sec.

Bill Morgan's invitation to appear in the Irish trial, 1927.

welcomed by the present generation, who had heard many legends connected with this famous player who, although weighing over 13 stone, played at scrum-half.

The London Irish have had an excellent season on their new ground at Motspur Park and the future of the club appears bright indeed.

It is somewhat enlightening (and comforting) to read newspaper cuttings more than 70 years old expressing concerns regarding fixture-list difficulties and congestions. Given the considerable angst which dogged the 1997–98 season in English rugby, the following report by C.W. Packford in *The Sporting Life* of Wednesday, 16 November 1927 might be interesting:

In connection with these very attractive games – the Surrey and Kent match was equally exciting – and after my remarks in the last article, it is gratifying to know that next season a real effort will be made to play the chief encounters in the South-Eastern Division on Saturdays instead of in midweek.

There is nothing definitely settled yet, but I shall be surprised if the 1927–28 season does not witness certain weekends allotted for the meetings of Kent, Surrey, Middlesex and Hampshire. It can be easily done if arrangements are made in sufficient time so that the leading clubs are able to arrange their fixtures to prevent their chief engagements clashing with the county games.

County rugby at that time was the only step up, the sole bridge between club and international rugby. The major players were all involved, Middlesex fielding a team containing eight internationals for their county game against Hampshire at Teddington on the afternoon of Wednesday, 24 October 1928. A few of them weren't bad players, either: G.V. Stephenson of Ireland, W.W. Wakefield and R. Cove-Smith of England, other England internationals in Sir T.G. Devitt of Blackheath (pity the poor centre inside him: 'Would Sir like the ball now; would it be convenient, Sir?'), H.C. Laird, R.S. Spong and W.E. Tucker, also of Blackheath. Bill Morgan, who by then had had the first of his Irish trials back in 1926, was among distinguished company. Hampshire, who lost the match 17–3, included in their side J.D. Clinch, who won 30 caps for Ireland between 1923 and 1931.

The *Daily News* reported:

It was a hard and exciting game in which many players enhanced their reputation. S.J. Cagney, R. Cove-Smith, W. Morgan and George Stephenson for Middlesex, and G.M. Sladen, J.D. Clinch and R.G. Forbes-Robinson for Hampshire were particularly conspicuous.

In 1927, the 28th Annual Dinner of London Irish RFC was held at the Cock Tavern, a well-known watering-hole for many of the fourth estate down the years. A report states that with the Rev. J.R. James MA (president) in the chair, it proved a very successful one.

Dr Read proposed the toast of 'The Club' in the course of his speech, congratulating the captain S.J. Cagney on being capped for Ireland. He also emphasised the value of training. The captain, in his reply, expressed indebtedness to W. Morgan, who had capably carried out the duties during his own enforced absence from the field.

Mr J. MacMahon (hon. treasurer) submitted 'The Visitors and Press', acknowledged by Col. Pilkington of the Royal Irish Rifles, whose headquarters they had been permitted to use for training purposes.

By 1926, London Irish had moved again, to what was to become the BBC ground at Motspur Park, a venue also used by the Worcester Park Polo Club. It was the latest move by a club which had become somewhat peripatetic. That season, there was a 6–0 home win over London Welsh, arguably the most prized scalp the Irish sought in their season, especially after the 3–0 defeat Welsh had inflicted upon them in the fixture earlier that season at Herne Hill, where London Welsh were by now settled.

Among other results that season, London Irish beat London Scottish 9–0 at Richmond but, under the captaincy of Bill Morgan, lost 5–3 at home to Guy's Hospital. A report of that match confirms the type of rugby being played by the Irish at that time:

The Irish forwards, playing with their traditional spirit, maintained a tremendous pace until near the end of a gruelling struggle. They were great spoilers in the loose and in the scrums they wheeled cleverly and broke up quickly. Their hard tackling was sure 'and more than once, by picking the ball off the feet of the Guy's forwards, they turned an opponent's dribble to their own advantage. The Irish eight overshadowed the Hospital's pack.

In November, a match was organised at Lansdowne Road, Dublin, between the Lansdowne club and an Anglo-Irish XV which was a kind of unofficial trial game. The match became a regular inclusion on the fixture list and was regarded as a trial game for any Irish players wishing to make their point to the Irish selectors, who generally did not travel out of Ireland when assessing likely players for the international side.

The game attracted considerable interest and a large crowd. Unfortunately, it also happened to coincide with the weekend of a terrific storm which raged

*Dinner at Jury's after the 1926 unofficial
Irish trial game.*

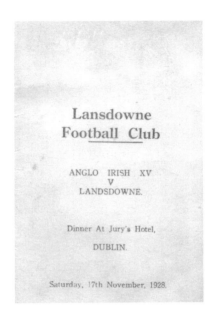

Lansdowne
Football Club

ANGLO IRISH XV
V
LANDSDOWNE.

Dinner At Jury's Hotel,

DUBLIN.

Saturday, 17th November, 1928.

across the Irish Sea and inflicted unspeakably vile sufferings and torment on any human beings foolhardy enough to be making the boat trip that Friday night. London Irish contributed ten players to the Anglos' XV: J. Egan, the full-back; T.W. King, the right wing who also played for Oxford University at that time; T.J. Ryan, who was studying at St Bart's Hospital, at centre; and G.S. Barry at scrum-half. Up front, Cagney, Morgan, M.C. Buckley, Victor and Cecil Beamish plus H. Anderson made up the remainder. George Beamish, selected to play, was unable to get there because the weather meant he missed a vital connection on his journey. But his aura was such that a commentator wrote after Lansdowne's 27–5 win:

The visiting side were at a disadvantage all through, with the result that individuals who might under other circumstances have had the chance of showing their capabilities to advantage were denied the opportunity. Had Beamish been playing the pack would likely have beaten the Lansdowne eight; the visiting backs would have had more chances and men such as D.F. Ryan and T.W. King would likely have shown up in a different light. These were the two backs who struck us as being the most likely aspirants to international honours.

Alas for the speedy King, although a frequent try-scorer for London Irish in club rugby, he was never to win an Irish cap. Meanwhile, T.J. Ryan suffered an early injury in the game which meant the Anglos played for more than three-quarters of the match with only 14 players, E.D. Gyles coming out of the pack to take his place in the three-quarters. Morgan scored the visitors' try, but one Irish newspaper called the whole affair 'a débâcle'.

London Irish were once more in Wales for Christmas 1928, losing 9–5 (three tries to a goal) to Llanelly on Christmas Day and then going down 16–0 to Cardiff on Boxing Day. Such fixtures were hugely popular in those days, an 8,000 crowd attending the Cardiff game; today, matches on Christmas Day would seem anathema.

At Llanelly, the running of C. Gummer, the Irish right wing, was especially meritorious. A report of the match stated that Gummer was the most prominent man on the field, bringing off a number of fine runs in which he displayed a refreshing turn of speed. He would certainly have scored two tries – and possibly more – but for the unerring tackling of A. Davies.

London Irish remained in West Wales overnight before catching the morning train east to Cardiff for the Boxing Day match. In our times, when coaches complain of too much rugby for the leading players, it is a statistic of revealing dimensions that London Irish fielded 13 members of their team at Llanelly the next day in Cardiff. The Welsh club themselves had met Pontypool in Cardiff on Christmas Eve and would entertain Watsonians the day after London Irish's visit. That season, 1928–29, Cardiff had a staggering 80 matches on their fixture list.

The official programme for the Cardiff game – price two pence – contained revealing notes as a prelude to the game:

> *Our guests today, however, are very fortunate in having such a player and captain as S.G. [sic] Cagney, one of those fiery international forwards who is capable of making his presence felt in every game he participates in. Up to the end of last season, Cagney had appeared for Ireland on nine occasions and he is again chosen to play against France on the last day of this month. He will be supported in the pack by W. Morgan, who has played in the Irish Trials and for the county of Middlesex; H.C. Browne, who has played for Hampshire county; and C. Gummer and J.B. Morrissey, both Devon county men.*
>
> *Among the backs is J. Egan, a very fine custodian, and who was reserve full-back for Ireland last season, and Trevor King, right wing three-quarter, who only just missed his 'blue' for Oxford University this season. It will be seen therefore that our visitors have a representative side, and they are sure to give us a splendid game, although they will be up against a strong Cardiff combination.*

The match report of a game played that day on muddy turf with a greasy ball stated:

> *At Cardiff yesterday, a company of 8,000 people saw London Irish defeated by two goals and two tries (16 points) to nothing. As in the previous match of their brief tour, the visitors displayed plenty of dash, the forwards making some particularly good rushes, but over-eagerness near the line and lack of finish resulted in a failure to score. Still, as both teams entered into the struggle in a holiday spirit, the football was often bright and generally interesting.*

Astonishingly, Cagney concluded this hectic, physically demanding

The shirts seem hit and miss, the socks are a hotch-potch. But we're assured it's a London Irish side from the mid 1920s. Bill Morgan is seated second from left, next to W.R.F. Collis. I.M.B. Stuart is seated fourth from left.

Christmas tour schedule by returning straight to London and thence to Paris, where Ireland played France at Colombes stadium four days later, on 30 December 1928. To prepare for an international game by playing two matches against tough Welsh opposition within the previous six days and then make the long journey from Wales to Paris via London and the cross-Channel boat was incredible. Ireland won the international, too, 6–0 through two unconverted tries.

Ireland did not win the championship that year, 1929, finishing joint runners-up, with Wales, to Scotland. But they did win for the first time ever at Twickenham, by six points to five, and Cagney, who was in that famous Irish side, was revered as an outstanding player of the era, as a critique of the London Irish forward published that season indicated.

The consistency of Ireland in recent years – for she has been on the verge of championship honours on several occasions – has been attributable as much as anything else to the pack. S.J. Cagney of the London Irish has played a big part indeed. For real genuine work Cagney is comparable with any Irish forward of recent years.

A tall, powerfully built athlete, Cagney, who plays with the characteristic abandon of his countrymen and yet has a steadying influence on the pack, is perhaps more of the English type of forward. He does not spare himself in the least in the interests of his country. He plays a sound, hard-battling game which in a marked degree does much to quell the desperate energies of the rival combination.

Cagney, who commenced his international career in 1925 against Wales, possesses one distinction of which he and the Anglo-Irish are proud. He is the first member of the London Irish club to be directly introduced into the national fifteen. Other members of the club have done so before, but they have in every instance been international players before they arrived in England.

The choice of Cagney for Ireland was a real triumph for the ability of the individual, and the efforts of the officers of the club to obtain official recognition. Good as Cagney is – and he has been worth his place in the Irish fifteen for at least five seasons – it is doubtful if he would have obtained his 'cap' had it not been for the persistency of Martin Doyle, year in and year out, in pointing out to the Irish authorities the justice of giving the London Irish a 'place in the sun' so far as Irish rugger was concerned.

The 'persuasiveness' of Martin eventually prevailed, and it has resulted in Cagney obtaining nine 'caps'. Since he has taken over the leadership of London Irish it has improved tremendously. He has collected around him a young, enthusiastic combination – one of whom, W. Morgan, is a really good forward and worthy of an Irish trial cap – who, inspired by their captain's genuine love of the game, are not easily overcome.

The Rugger Irishmen in London are a happy brotherhood indeed. But with a president such as 'Padre' James, a captain like Cagney and officers of the Martin Doyle, C.R. McGowan and J.B. Quin type, they could not be otherwise.

The 1928–29 season ended with the official London Irish dinner held at the Holborn restaurant. It was, said a report, 'a great rugger gathering'.

The dignitaries who gathered for the club's 30th annual dinner included the High Commissioner of the Irish Free State, along with George Stephenson and S.J. Cagney of Ireland, Dr J.C. Russell-Cargill, A.J. Trollope, Martin Doyle, W. Morgan, A. Lawlor, C.R. McGowan, J.B. Quin, J. MacMahon, Maurice Slattery, J.B. Manning, A. O'Carroll, J. Melville KC, M.B. Browne (captain of the 2nd XV, and prospective Parliamentary candidate for Chertsey) and many others intimately connected with the game.

The great progress of the club in recent years, said Dr Russell-Cargill, was creditable indeed to the officials and players of an organisation that had grown rapidly and consistently. The club was now regarded as one of the most prominent in the country.

S.J. Cagney, who was received with enthusiasm, said the club was making great progress as a result of the pioneer work of the old members. They were particularly delighted at beating during the season the other Exiles – London Scottish and London Welsh.

A happy evening terminated with many eulogistic references to 'Padre' James, whose 'boys' gave him a great ovation when he spoke of the happy days he had spent with them over a long period.

The 1920s might have been closing with tears in many eyes around the world, through the Great Depression of 1929. But at London Irish, eyes were smiling.

Sartorial elegance: Martin Doyle, standing back right, looks ready for golf, not rugby, as the Exiles prepare to meet Constitution FC in Cork, Easter 1928.

CHAPTER FOUR

Popular People

'Training is everything.
The peach was once a bitter almond;
Cauliflower is nothing but cabbage with a college education.'

MARK TWAIN, 1835–1910

London Irish had by now long since established a reputation as welcome guests wherever they went. The brand of fiery Irish rugby they played, and their traditional capabilities in the field of *bonhomie*, had made them popular people. At the start of the 1927–28 season they went to Ireland for a short tour, losing 9–8 to Cork Constitution and then drawing 3–3 with Bohemians, Morgan scoring the London Irish try from a line-out. Whenever a team from outside Ireland visited, there was a clearly discernible sense of importance and anticipation attached to the fixture.

It was reported that a crowd of 2,000 saw the match with Cork Con, and a report of the Bohemians game in the *Cork Examiner*, under the headline 'Limerick's Bank Holiday Fixtures', stated:

It was disappointing to find that the two senior rugby matches at Limerick yesterday afternoon were timed to start practically simultaneously. At the Markets Field, Garryowen were at home to Knock (Belfast) and Bohemians had as guests at the Crescent College Grounds London Irish, who included S.J. Cagney, the international forward. Both games were well patronised, particularly the Bohemians fixture which was more central and the fact that the opponents were from across the channel gave the match an added interest to the average follower of the code.

The 1929–30 season opened for the club with much optimism, along with the hope that the weather would be kinder than the previous winter, when prolonged snow and ice had severely disrupted the club rugby programme. Although Cagney's fine career was almost over, a serious injury ending his reign as captain later in the season, London Irish still had the solid foundations of a fine pack of forwards, the rock on which they had built much of their success in the second half of the 1920s.

W.R.F. 'Bob' Collis, who had won seven caps for Ireland between 1924 and 1926 (following his father, who had played for Ireland in 1884), joined London Irish after spells at King's College Hospital and the Harlequins. Together with I.M.B. Stuart, who had won two caps for Ireland while playing for Dublin University back in 1924, and Bill Morgan, the trio formed the nucleus of a powerful pack, always the bedrock of London Irish sides in those early years. Alas, results were generally erratic, because the excellence of the Irish forwards in that era was seldom matched by the achievements of their three-quarters.

Behind the scenes, the patrician figure of J.B. Quin as honorary team manager was following in the footsteps of long-standing, loyal servants like Martin Doyle in a variety of off-field roles. Quin, tall and elegant, is another figure from that age who exudes the manner of the military man: tall, upstanding, straight-backed, with short, neatly cut hair and a trimmed moustache.

Rugby was becoming an increasingly popular sporting recreation as travel and recreation opportunities opened up in the 1930s. London Underground produced an advertising poster for most Saturdays, giving details of the day's leading matches and how to reach the grounds. For example:

RECTORY FIELD, BLACKHEATH – *Blackheath v. Leicester: by Bus Routes 20, 48, 54, 75d, 108b, 289a.*
RICHMOND – *London Scottish v. Old Millhillians: to Richmond Station; or by Bus Routes 27, 33a, 37, 73a, 65 (group), 127a, direct.*
TEDDINGTON – *Old Merchant Taylors v. Harlequins: by Bus Route 127a, or L.U. Tram Route 69.*
MOTSPUR PARK – *London Irish v. Old Leysians: to Morden Station, then by Bus Route 155.*

Directions were given for these and the other leading clubs of the day: Edgware, Streatham, Old Alleynians, Bart's Hospital, Guy's Hospital, London Welsh and Catford Bridge.

Meanwhile, in county rugby, the county champions Middlesex had only one London Irish representative, hooker Bill Morgan, for their February 1930 championship semi-final meeting with Gloucestershire at Twickenham. They lost 12–6. Perhaps the Middlesex selectors had been influenced by taunts aimed at the 'League of Nations' side when they had won the title the previous year with many non-English players in their ranks. For the 1930 semi-final, they had reduced the number of 'foreigners' in their team to two. With concomitant results.

In January 1930, Irish beat London Scottish 15–6 on the Richmond Athletic Ground. Victories over the Exiles sides, Welsh and Scottish, were always highly

Is it the Eton wall game? No, just London Irish beating London Scottish 15–6, January 1930.

prized, and this year it was again the Irish forwards who excelled. A contemporary account reveals:

The Scottish three-quarters were generally smothered by the quick breaking up of the dashing Irish forwards before they could do anything. The Irish forwards, amongst whom their internationals W.R.F. Collis and I.M.B. Stuart stood out, were always going, and often to good purpose, many of their dashes carrying them a long way, while the handling outside was safe and their backs displayed plenty of enterprise in their efforts to get through, more particularly P. Coote in the centre and P.A. Gummer on the right wing.

For the final Irish trial that year, London Irish contributed three players to the Possibles: Morgan, P. Coote and T.W. King, who won an Oxford blue in December 1929. It was to be Morgan's second and last Irish trial; ahead lay the grand frustration and sad realisation. Morgan, while always a fine, consistent and often outstanding club player forever on the fringe of the ultimate honour, was never regarded as quite good enough for a full Irish cap. For a man who so loved the game, it must have been an enduring disappointment.

That season, a most distinguished Irish international appeared in London Irish colours: W.E. Crawford, who had won 30 caps for Ireland between 1920 and 1927. Crawford, born in 1891 and educated at Methodist College, Belfast, was regarded as one of Ireland's finest full-backs. He captained the Malone Rugby Club in 1913 but when war broke out in 1914 he enlisted in the 6th Inniskilling Dragoons (Ulster Division) and served later in the 3rd–18th London Regiment, the London Irish Rifles and the 1st–4th London Regiment (Royal Fusiliers). All his service was in France and in 1917 he was severely wounded. When he was demobilised in 1919, he returned to Ireland and embarked upon a distinguished legal career.

Crawford played most of his club rugby for Lansdowne but made his final appearance in a London Irish shirt, in the Exiles match against London Welsh. A small cutting, under the heading 'Crawford's Swan Song', records the historic end to a fine career:

> *I was sorry to hear that Ernie Crawford, one of Ireland's very greatest rugby full-backs, probably played his last game in London last Saturday. He turned out for London Irish against the Welsh and played a surprisingly good game, his penalty goal being a fine effort.*

Crawford was a remarkable 28 years old when he had made his debut for Ireland. 'His debut was characterised by a splendid display in the art and craft of full-back play,' said one account. Thereafter, he earned 30 caps, playing at international level until he was 36 and captaining his country. By the time of that appearance for London Irish, he would have been 38.

By the end of the 1920s, London Irish had built up their strength in playing numbers to a level sufficient to put out five teams most weeks. But results continued to be unpredictable for the 1st XV. In 1929, they were overwhelmed 31–3 by London Welsh at Herne Hill, while 12 months later in the same fixture Irish won 8–6.

A year later, in 1931, it was a 5–5 draw between the two clubs in treacherous conditions at Herne Hill. The Irish team for that match included a new recruit, another former international player in full-back J. Stewart, who had won ten caps for Ireland between 1922 and 1929 while playing his club rugby for Queen's University, Belfast, and NIFC. In coming to London on business, Stewart had joined London Irish to bolster their team. A home away from home for another Irishman.

There had been high expectations of a fine season for London Irish among a good deal of observers of the rugby scene, and in season 1930–31 such beliefs began to come to fruition. It was to be arguably the club's most successful season in their 33-year history. They got to within one week of Christmas still unbeaten, but then results came apart over the holiday period, with a 24–3 defeat at Llanelly on Christmas Day followed by a 12–3 defeat at Cardiff the following day. Of the latter match, a report talks of a splendid holiday crowd 'having its wants fully catered for', play moving with a swing from start to finish and bright incidents being plentiful. It went on:

The Irish forward who caught the eye most was Stuart, whose great pace and thorough understanding of wing-forward play made him a constant menace to movements which were initiated in the vicinity of the scrummages. Morgan was a splendid example of the all-round forward.

A review of the club in the *East London Advertiser* at the end of the 1930–31 season stated:

The London Irish Rugby Football Club, although formed 33 years ago, can claim to have had probably its most successful season this year. During the war, its members

The 1930–31 Exiles 1st XV is flanked by two great club servants: C.R. McGowan (standing, back left) and J.B. Quin (back right).

were dissembled in all branches of the service and, to all intents and purposes, the club became extinct. A very lean time existed on its reformation and in the early years afterwards. Today, however, a very different condition exists, as with their first XV in the field they are a match for any team in the metropolis. Amongst many others, they can claim victories over London Welsh, London Scottish (6–3), Dublin University (5–3), Old Leysians (17–0), St Bartholomew's Hospital (10–3) and St Thomas's Hospital.

These successful results are attributable to two specific reasons: firstly, the team is a youthful one, and secondly, in their captain Dr W.R.F. Collis they possess a man of indomitable courage who inspires every confidence and enthusiasm in this team, and as a leader is second to none. Bob, as he is popularly known, is a typical Irish forward, and can claim distinction in the rugby world inasmuch as he is an Old Rugbian, Cambridge blue and Irish international.

That year, among the Irish sides they confronted, London Irish beat Young Munster 19–6, University College, Cork, 6–3 and Dublin University 5–3. Thus, when the Irish trial teams were announced, there was expectation of how selected players might perform, players like the London Irish wing, 22-year-old T.D. 'Rex' King, the Uppingham and Oxford University-educated player ('he is strong and fast and combines with these assets a fine defence'), and, inside him, P.B. 'Paddy' Coote, a 21-year-old who was in the RAF. Sadly for Coote, a knee injury prevented him from taking his place in the Possibles team, and a report concluded, 'It comes as a disappointment. Coote has not yet been seen on trial for his country but from all accounts he must be regarded as a three-quarter of class.'

Of the perennially-in-contention Bill Morgan, one commentator wrote:

I must say I like the look of W. Morgan of Ballinasloe College. Here's a handyman type – the right age, 26, and weight – something over 13 and a half stones – and something over six foot in his socks. A forward who has had experience of three-quarter and full-back play must be very useful if he's any good at all.

On Saturday, 17 October 1931, Morgan and Coote were in the London Division team which met the touring South Africans at Twickenham. The towering new west stand, built at a cost of £65,000, was used for the first time, giving Twickenham a capacity of 72,000 with 27,000 under cover.

The Springboks had been much criticised prior to that game for some unconvincing performances, but they tore London apart, winning 30–3. It was a crushing defeat, but the damage done by the powerful Springboks to the London players' bodies was probably nowhere near as severe as the likely harm inflicted by the list of food and drinks served at the after-match dinner at London's Savoy Hotel, where music was supplied by the Band of HM Royal Marines First (Chatham) Division.

The dinner itself was, well, substantial:

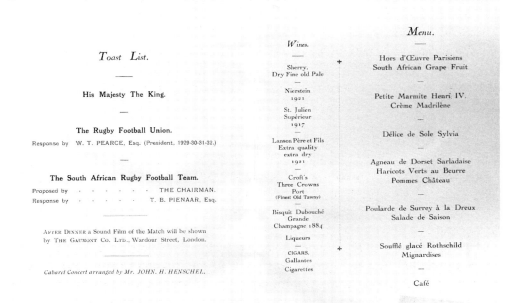

Toast List.

—

His Majesty The King.

—

The Rugby Football Union.
Response by   W. T. PEARCE, Esq. (President, 1929-30-31-32.)

—

The South African Rugby Football Team.
Proposed by . . . . . THE CHAIRMAN.
Response by . . . . . T. B. PIENAAR, Esq.

AFTER DINNER a Sound Film of the Match will be shown
by THE GAUMONT CO. LTD., Wardour Street, London.

Cabaret Concert arranged by Mr. JOHN. H. HENSCHEL.

Wines.
—
Sherry,
Dry Fine old Pale

Nierstein
1921

St. Julien
Supérieur
1917

Lanson Père et Fils
Extra quality
extra dry
1921

Croft's
Three Crowns
Port
(Finest Old Tawny)

Bisquit Dubouché
Grande
Champagne 1884

Liqueurs
—
CIGARS.
Gallantes
Cigarettes

Menu.
—
Hors d'Œuvre Parisiens
South African Grape Fruit

—

Petite Marmite Henri IV.
Crème Madrilène

—

Délice de Sole Sylvia

—

Agneau de Dorset Sarladaise
Haricots Verts au Beurre
Pommes Château

—

Poularde de Surrey à la Dreux
Salade de Saison

—

Soufflé glacé Rothschild
Mignardises

—

Café

Any man still standing at midnight after that lot must have been superhuman.

Only 11 months earlier, London Irish RFC had held their annual dinner, on 15 November 1930, once more under the chairmanship of the Rev. J.R. James MA. The fare offered was, by the standards of the above, humble:

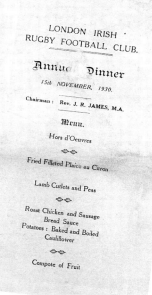

LONDON IRISH ·
RUGBY FOOTBALL CLUB.

Annual Dinner

15th NOVEMBER, 1930.

Chairman : Rev. J. R. JAMES, M.A.

Menu.

Hors d'Oeuvres

Fried Filleted Plaice au Citron

Lamb Cutlets and Peas

Roast Chicken and Sausage
Bread Sauce
Potatoes : Baked and Boiled
Cauliflower

Compote of Fruit

OFFICE COPY
ISSUED BY THE TUNBRIDGE WELLS DISTRICT LAND REGISTRY

Land Registration Act 1925.
Provincial Dealing No.
25094/31

H.M. LAND REGISTRY
23 JUN 1931
RECEIVED.
TRANSFER OF FREEHOLD LAND

H. M. LAND REGISTRY
LAND REGISTRATION ACT 1925.

P85937

District: MIDDLESEX
P: SUNBURY
le No: P.24,432
Property: LAND ADJOINING MANOR LANE AND AVENUE ROAD, SUNBURY

16th of June 1931. IN CONSIDERATION of One thousand two hundred and eighty pounds (£1,280.0.0) paid to GEORGE HENRY WILKINSON the Younger of 8 Stanley Avenue Beckenham in the County of Kent Gentleman (formerly of The Red House 2 Stanley Avenue aforesaid (hereinafter called "the Vendor") the receipt whereof is hereby acknowledged the Vendor as Beneficial Owner hereby transfers to the LONDON IRISH RUGBY FOOTBALL GROUND LIMITED whose registered office is at 6-7, Southampton Street Strand, W.C.2. in the County of London (hereinafter called "the Purchasers") the land shown and coloured red and part hatched green upon the accompanying plan being part of the land comprised in the title above referred to subject to the exceptions easements and other rights specified in the First Schedule hereto. The Purchasers for the benefit of the remainder of the land comprised in the above title hereby covenant with the Vendor to observe and perform the restrictive conditions specified in the Second Schedule hereto. The Purchasers hereby covenant with the Vendor and his successors in title the owner or owners for the time being of the respective pieces of land coloured blue upon the said plan or of any part thereof that the Purchasers and the persons deriving title under them will pay all road and paving charges and all other charges and expenses of whatever description which shall or may become payable if and when the portions of the land hereby

P85937   1

THE MORNING [POST?]

LONDON IRISH NEW GROUND

Rugby Test in Miniature

From Our Special Correspondent

The score of "eight points all" was an equitable reflection in London Irish v. London Welsh—the festival match for the formal opening of the London Irish new ground at Sunbury. And the High Commissioner for the Irish Free State (Mr. J. W. Dulanty), in performing the ceremony, paid a deserved compliment to the enthusiasm and energy of the Club Executive and its friends, not forgetting the lift from the Irish Rugby Union in Dublin and the good fellows of the famous body quartered at Twickenham.

The match itself was splendidly fought under the extreme handicap of heavy going with a greasy ball. Both packs put their traditional rigour into the game; the forwards were always on the ball in the loose —the tackling could not have been surpassed, for everyone made sure of the ball and the man.

EACH SIDE IN THE LEAD

No game could have had such a fascinating course: each side led in turn and the Welshmen only saved the match on the verge of "no side," when they equalised with a penalty goal. London Welsh had opened with a penalty from a try early in the game and then had followed the try and the goal from a try for Ireland. Outside the scrummage the fight for the unfieldable ball was something of a lottery. The only game for the conditions was to get on as far as possible individually.

ECONOMICAL KICKING

There was no end of good kicking and the backs did their best to save the leg-power of their forwards. Naturally London Welsh missed their star performer, Powell, from the base of the scrummage, for on such a day extra genius was wanted to make good the slowness with which the ball came out of the scrum through the morass. In fact, the old-fashioned player would have eschewed any idea of heeling in such conditions.

McCarthy and Collis got tries for the Irish and Hodder placed the goal. Harris scored the London Welsh try and R. Lewis kicked the goal. Gibbons kicking the penalty goal.

London Irish.—I. Marshall; J. J. Buckley, F. S. Hodder, J. W. McCarthy, R. Jyness. M. D. Sheehan; W. H. Collis, H. S. Ruttle, R. J. P. Reidy, J. H. Cullinan, G. S. Barry, W. J. Caffey. J. D. Quinn.

London Welsh.—T. J. Davies; Wyndham Lewis, D. W. Rees, J. R. R. Thomas; R. S. Lewis, J. E. Bowcott; W. A. V. Thomas, Iverwerth Evans, D. Bowen-Jones, Newell, E. W. Evans-Evans. — Garbutt, W. Barnett, P. E. Gibbons.

A SCOTTISH TRIAL

Inter-City —Edinburgh

The original deeds for the Exiles' purchase of land at Sunbury in 1931 and (right) a report of the first match on the ground.

CHAPTER FIVE

A New Home

"Mid pleasures and palaces though we may roam,
Be it ever so humble, there's no place like home.'

J.H. PAYNE, 1791–1852

The 16th of June might not seem a date of much consequence to any northern-hemisphere rugby club. In mid-summer, it is traditionally a time for players to reacquaint themselves with such essential facets of life as lawnmowers, pub beer gardens, cricket bats, wives and children. Usually in that order.

But on that date in 1931, London Irish Rugby Football Club did a rather significant thing. They completed the purchase of approximately 12 acres of land on the north side of Manor Lane and west of Avenue Road, as it was then known, in Sunbury-on-Thames. The vendor, George Henry Wilkinson the Younger, of 8 Stanley Avenue, Beckenham, in the County of Kent – a Gentleman, we are told in the original Land Registry deeds – was paid the princely sum of £1,280. It seems somehow appropriate that the signatures to the deal on behalf of London Irish were two of their most renowned servants since the end of the Great War, J. MacMahon and Major C.R. McGowan.

A report said of the facilities acquired: 'There are three playing pitches, a pavilion with adequate dressing and bathrooms, a tea room and a bar.' Discard from your mind, dear reader, grand notions of a stately Edwardian pavilion, resplendent with the light of the evening sun upon it, and gentlemen with their ladies sipping cocktails on the elegant verandah during a glorious summer. 'Wooden shack' would have been a more fitting description. Not that that mattered a jot. Because, for the first time in its 33-year history, London Irish at last owned its own home.

The ground was not developed and lacked many requirements for senior-grade rugby. Nevertheless, on Saturday, 5 December 1931, the club opened the ground with a match against their traditional rivals, London Welsh, a game which ended in an 8–8 draw. The official opening ceremony was performed by the High Commissioner of the Irish Free State in London, Mr J.W. Dulanty CB, CBE, and to mark the occasion the pipe band of the London Irish Rifles was on hand to play the teams on to the field.

In his address, Mr Dulanty spoke of the bonds between the Celtic races – and then doubtless sat bemused as, according to one report, 'the two sets of forwards went for each other like tigers'. Mr Dulanty had spoken of the great support the Irish had received from the Rugby Unions, and suggested that all Irishmen in London should rally to the support of their own club, financially and otherwise. It was a wet day, but Mr Dulanty shook hands with both sets of players, who were lined up for the presentation before the start.

The match itself was, like all Irish–Welsh Exiles clashes of the time – and ever since, for that matter – fiercely contested. The London Irish team was: I. Marshall, back; R. Lyness, J.J. Buckley, F.S. Hodder and J.W. McCarthy, three-quarter backs; M.D. Sheehan and J.N. Barry, half-backs; W.R. Collis, H.S. Ruttle, W. Morgan, J.P. Reidy, J.H. Cullinan, G.S. Barry, W.J. Coffey and J.D. Quinn, forwards.

John McCarthy, a doctor from Cork, was quick enough to have won the 100-yard and 200-yard sprint championships of Munster five years in succession. J.P. Reidy was one of three Reidy brothers who were to play significant parts in the London Irish story through the 1930s. In season 1933–34, J.P. Reidy won the honours cap for good play by the 1st XV forwards, in 1934–35, C.J. Reidy won it and in 1935–36 W.F. Reidy claimed it, a unique hat-trick of awards for three members of the same family in successive seasons.

C.J. (Charlie) Reidy was qualified for England but elected to try for Ireland and won a cap against Wales in 1937 as a 6ft 5in second-row forward. Ireland won 5–3 in Belfast but Reidy was never chosen again. In the Second World War, Charlie was hit on the head by a piece of shrapnel, lost an eye and his sense of smell and was discharged from the fighting. When the war ended, he went up to Cambridge and won a half-blue for discus throwing. He then went into the Army Education Corps.

J.P. Reidy became London Irish captain later in the 1930s and was a well-known plastic surgeon. All three brothers were big fellows, remembers Con Griffin, who joined the club in 1932 at the age of 22. 'Big fellows, big men,' says Griffin, who now lives in retirement in Manchester, played squash until he was in his 60s and since his retirement has completed a six-year course in computational mathematics at the Open University, as well as undertaking other courses. Well, you need something to fill in the time, don't you?

His nephew, C.S. Griffin, was a fighter pilot in the war and, as a London Irish player, won two caps for Ireland in 1951, against France and England, as a strong, pacy right wing. 'I remember saying to someone before that, he would either be no good or he'd get a cap. Within two years, he had been capped.'

The elder Griffin, the youngest of a family of six, had good reason to thank the Reidys for their presence at London Irish. They invited their cousin Nel over from Ireland to stay with them one weekend, during the course of which they all went off to Sunbury for a match. As the brothers played, Nel watched from the touchline, and after the match she was introduced to Con Griffin.

'We married in 1939 in the first week of the war,' remembers Con, with a smile. 'She came from Tralee and had been studying at University College, Cork.' They had 57 lovely years together, too, before Nel died in 1996.

Griffin, who played on either wing (although he preferred left), made a Leinster trial one year and, following an interception during the match, ran half the length of the field to score. But he ruefully remembers playing outside a centre who, he felt, wouldn't have given a pass even if a member of his own family had been there.

In his first season with London Irish, he broke a leg. But of those days at the club he says, 'It was a very matey club. We didn't have that many big games, not like you see big matches today. London Welsh and London Scottish were exceptions to that rule; they were very strong rivals. One of the great things about the club was that they ran six teams and everybody knew every team's players' names. Of course, the big event of the year was the "B" XV annual dinner; it was quite the best. Strangely, though, it was never held in the same venue two years running. Funny thing, that!

'I remember at one dinner, we were dining upstairs and the staff refused to send any more drink up. We had a small scrum-half around that time, called Wally O'Connell, and we lifted him up, carried him to the opening for the lift shaft for food and held him by the heels, so that his head emerged downstairs in the bar area. Whether we got any more drink sent up after that, I doubt!

'It was a great social club. I remember one St Patrick's night, a dinner-dance was arranged at a smart restaurant just off the Haymarket in central London. It was a white-tie-and-tails job; disastrous place, really, for a lot of rugby players to be let loose.

'After one match with London Welsh, the ladies made the usual tea, with sausage and mash supper, and then in the evening there was a quartet arranged to provide music, with step dancers and guys playing the fiddle. There was a railway porter at Sunbury station, a man named Pat Kennedy, who used to come along for the evening and play his flute. He got free drinks for his trouble.

'It was a club filled with great characters. The rector of nearby Staines, the Rev. J.R. James, a Protestant clergyman, was chairman at that time. He was quite an old man, in his 70s, when I knew him, but he was most affable. Martin Doyle, the team secretary, followed us around and sent reports of our matches to the newspapers. Doyle was also getting on by that stage but he was a very tough fellow, and swam in Highgate Ponds during the winter.

'I won an honours cap, a most prized possession, in the 1937–38 season, but they sent me the wrong size, six and seven-eighths, rather than the seven and three-eighths I needed, so it never fitted. But I was still proud to have it.

'I played in one London Irish three-quarter line towards the end of the 1930s with Peter De Mestre (brother of J.W.), Owen Horrigan and John Woods, and all three of them were to be killed in the Second World War. Woods was killed in a flying accident; the other two were bomber pilots who lost their lives on missions.

'We all lost friends at that time. But as for the club, I have lovely memories of London Irish.'

The club had its own ground from 1931 but results were erratic. London Welsh returned early the next season, 1932–33, after their appearance in the inaugural match the year before, and won 19–11. Guy's Hospital beat them there too, 26–13, and the same season St Bartholomew's Hospital won at Sunbury, 11–8.

Bill Morgan was captain at this time but did not play in the 1932 Irish trial, when London Irish had three representatives. Starting the match were P.B. Coote, at centre for the Blues, and M.D. Sheehan, at scrum-half for the Whites. Another London Irish man, J.L. Reid, was introduced at half-time as outside-half for E.O'D. Davy.

At the end of January 1932, London Irish went to Dublin to meet Trinity College and won a close encounter 10–9. A report in the *Irish Times* the following Monday, 1 February, concluded that from the selectors' viewpoint the game had served a purpose by eliminating altogether one or two of the 'cross-channel men' who had shown promise in previous games but were now deemed to be not quite good enough for international rugby. 'The game proved that E. de V. Hunt is a very useful type of centre, and that M.D. Sheehan is not yet quite good enough to oust P. Murray from the scrum-half position,' it said. The best of the London Irish forwards that day, it added, were 'Collis, who retains his form remarkably well, J.P. Reidy, Hogan and Ruttle'.

Barely had that report been published than Hunt and Sheehan were promptly chosen for the Irish side to meet England at Lansdowne Road, Dublin, that year. But Ireland lost 11–8 and Sheehan was never again to experience international rugby. Hunt, the army officer who could play full-back or centre, lasted a little longer, winning five caps in all, the first as a full-back in 1930 against France, the rest at centre.

There occurred in that match against England an extraordinary incident which would have been ripe for exploitation by the modern-day tabloid press. But in those days such institutions were unheard of, and the antics of the Limerick man Danaher Sheehan were commented upon in a relatively sober fashion.

Sheehan astonished the Lansdowne Road audience at one set scrum by running over the top of the England scrum and jumping on his English opposite number, Leicester's Bernard Gadney. The Scottish referee, W. Burnett, was as non-plussed as the crowd at an incident no one could ever remember witnessing before.

There was an enviable combination of strength, power and pace in the London Irish side of that time. Great experience up front was epitomised by players like Collis, Morgan, G.S. Barry, H.E.P. Anderson and W.J. Coffey, while J.P. Reidy and H.S. Ruttle were also strong players. Behind them there was a backline of real pace and ability: Marshall's skills at full-back, the speed of King and McCarthy on the wings, Coote's craftmanship at centre beside Hunt, with J.L. Reid and Sheehan two very capable half-backs. G. MacMahon, also at the club around that time, was a highly talented full-back with tremendous kicking skills.

In October 1932, the season opened with a combative 3–3 draw against the Old Paulines club at Thames Ditton, Reid making the break for a first-half try by Lyness, which J.P. Reidy could not convert. Also that season, Irish met Rosslyn Park, the game being played at Park's then home ground of Old Deer Park. Irish won it, surprising the critics, 6–3, a rousing performance by their pack and a supreme exhibition by full-back MacMahon being chief factors.

Park had recently conquered Richmond and were regarded as arguably London's top side at the time. But 'Half-back', writing a Monday-morning match report, said, 'It is a long time since I have seen a pack of forwards show such life and "devil" as the London Irish did. They scrummaged moderately enough and got just about their share of the ball from the tight, but in the open, line-outs and loose mauls they outplayed the Park completely.'

Irish won the match with second-half tries by McCarthy and C. Beamish, against Park's first-half penalty goal. But there was an oddity. A correspondent wrote, 'C. Beamish – the only man on the Irish side, incidentally, to wear a number – scored a splendid try which Collis failed to improve. The question of numbers, by the way, is one I would commend to the attention of the London Irish committee.'

In their review of the season in which London Irish won 16 of 28 games with 11 defeats, one English national newspaper report was charmingly evocative of the times.

Club supremacy in London has not been fought to a very definite issue. Blackheath have had, on the whole, a disappointing season considering their resources, but the Harlequins are still an attractive force. The London Scottish have gone ahead surprisingly, while the London Welsh and London Irish, without setting the Thames on fire, have managed to get their usual enjoyment out of the game.

After all, it is the game and not the result that counts and, so long as that spirit prevails amongst our players, we need not worry about 'Played, won and lost' or the aggregates for and against. When that spirit arises in France, too, there will be no need for ultimatums, and the best we can wish our much-troubled friends across the Channel is that they will come into line with the British point of view as soon as possible.

Doubtless the writer felt better after that. A good old dose of telling rotten Johnny foreigner where to go was always considered therapeutic for the English soul. Subsequently, France were banished from the Five Nations competition from 1932 to 1947 because of the problem of alleged payment to players and the French authorities' failure to convince the Home Unions that they were running their affairs properly. Tut, tut.

By and large, the 1930s at London Irish mirrored the unpredictable swings and fortunes of the world political scene in that era, full of ups and downs. One minute the outlook was bright, the next it was grey. London Irish were fielding six teams regularly each Saturday, bringing together complete strangers from all over Ireland, north and south, into a rugby side in the leafy outskirts of south-west London. Often, players ran on to the field as complete strangers to team-mates of the day, yet years later had formed lasting friendships which endured long after the respective players' association with the playing side of the club had ended. If London Irish cannot lay claim to another single achievement, then this factor surely justifies its very existence and rewards all those loyal servants who worked so mightily down the years to make the club what it was and remains to this day.

That original qualification – 'that a player be an Irishman and a good sportsman' – continued to hold good. And they continued to come from the four provinces: from the great educational establishments of the south, such as University College, Cork; Trinity, Dublin; and UCD; so many of the great schools of the south, like Blackrock and Rockwell Colleges; those two fine Cork colleges, Presentation Brothers and Christian Brothers; and, from the north, the likes of Campbell College, Royal Belfast AI and Belfast Methodists. Players were drawn from diverse backgrounds to an exiles' club in England which provided a welcoming home for all Irishmen, regardless of class, religion or fortune. It was a mighty achievement.

One of those who joined around that time was Albert Hill. He first went to the club in 1932, played 1st XV rugby from 1937 until 1954, interrupted only by the war years, and was then only denied a long and productive career with the Wild Geese and other junior teams at the club when his wife Betty put her foot down! Alas for Betty, Albert then became a committeeman instead. Today, at the age of 82, he lives on the Kent coast and remains a London Irish member, still fit and sprightly enough to get down to his favourite local hostelry to sample a glass of the black stuff and chew over old memories.

The 1935–36 1st XV pose beside Sunbury's famous old tin shack. 'Padre' James is standing, back left.

'We used to wash all the 1st XV clothes at one time. We did that for some years and often had to carry them home in a bag on our backs because we didn't have a car. John Brown was the only man who owned a car at the club for years, a Ford, and you had to be kind to him to get a lift!

'There have always been so many characters at the club. I remember Martin Doyle, who had been in the club's first ever team in 1898 and then served London Irish right through until the Second World War. He was a grand little Irishman, very keen, and the serious man of the club. If you wanted to get anything done, he was the guy to see. He died just after the war.

'In those days before the war, after the club had bought Sunbury and was playing there, we only really had a changing-room and tea room. After the match, there was one barrel of beer and one bottle of whiskey, and when that was finished we went to the pub. We had to give the opposition half the beer out of the barrel, of course, so it didn't last that long. But Fitzy, who was a loyal servant of the club for years and came to run the most famous rugby bar in the world at the ground, then arranged for us to have two barrels of beer and two bottles of whiskey, and then it went up to three of each. Quite soon, he was showing £250 a year profit.'

What was also fascinating about that era was the make-up of teams. Published team lists on programmes ('1d. each,' remembers Albert Hill) show players appearing in a variety of positions, something unheard of today. He explains, 'We played first up, first down very often. In other words, if you were too slow keeping up with the play and ended up late at a scrum, you'd bind in somewhere in the back row. We didn't specialise, really.'

In terms of bald statistics for international honours, the 1930s were not the zenith of London Irish's achievements as a club. George Beamish continued to play international rugby until 1933 but was by then with Leicester. Meanwhile, a year later, the Irish selectors awarded a first cap to the Oxford University loose-head prop N.F. McGrath, who later played for the losing Oxford side (or rather the humiliated Oxford side, given that a Cambridge team containing Cliff Jones and Wilf Wooller thrashed them 29–4) in the 1934 Varsity match. McGrath had joined London Irish and was capped by Ireland against Wales earlier that year. But the Welsh won 13–0 at Swansea, and McGrath never received another cap. Also in the Irish international side that day was J.L. Reid, who had by that time moved to Richmond, from where he earned two caps in 1934, against Scotland and Wales. Alas, Ireland lost to the Scots, too (they also lost to England that season), and Reid, likewise, disappeared for ever after the defeat at St Helen's, Swansea.

At Easter time 1937, London Irish played in the Lowestoft Festival, and later in the year, at Christmas, they set off for their annual holiday match at Cardiff, agreeing that the team should meet up at Paddington Station and travel down together. Alas, one J.C. Daly, of whom we shall hear more, missed the train, together with another player. Irish officials like Brendan Quin and Bill Morgan were beside themselves with fury.

Upon arrival at Cardiff, the Irishmen explained their predicament to Cardiff club officials. 'No problem, mun,' they were told. 'We have two players you can borrow, see? We'll send 'em round to your dressing-room.' One duly arrived, was asked his name and was accepted. The next shuffled into the room with an air of hesitancy. 'What's yer name?' he was asked. There was a little more shuffling of feet, and an embarrassed look at his shoes. 'Well, see,' stammered the poor man. 'It's John Thomas, like.' To which an Irish voice at the back of the dressing-room promptly replied, 'Jaysus, we can't have a John Thomas in our side. Yer Seamus O'Toole for the day!' And thus the poor fellow was rechristened.

Sadly, such moments of delightful humour were becoming increasingly rare in the world of the late 1930s. Another London Irishman, Charles Reidy, who was club captain in 1937, did earn a solitary cap in a winning Irish side against Wales that year. Reidy was followed as captain in 1938 by Harry St J. Gallagher,

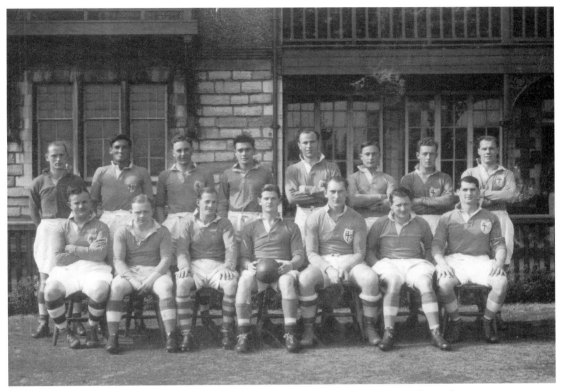

Harry St J. Gallagher's 1938–39 Exiles team. Nine first-team players from this side were to lose their lives in the Second World War. Charles Reidy is seated third from right.

who had been a schoolfriend of Albert Hill at Bangor G.S. some years earlier. Gallagher was to have a distinguished war, joining the army as a private in the Irish Guards and ending up as a Lieutenant-Colonel in the London Irish Rifles. He fought in Tripoli and also in the Italian campaign.

Another London Irish man of the period was also capped for Ireland. Tommy Headon, prop forward *par excellence* and a man of great repute from UCD, won caps against Scotland and Wales in 1939. But that Welsh match brought only more frustration to Ireland – for the seventh time, they failed to beat Wales and win the Triple Crown, a feat they had not achieved since 1899 when captained by Louis Magee.

Inevitably, the volatile political situation worsened. Germany was challenging the world to the worst kind of match, and Britain and the Commonwealth eventually took up the challenge. Following Neville Chamberlain's declaration of war in 1939, the so-called phoney war lasted six months, during which time the rugger buggers down at London Irish, irrational lot, managed to combine with London Welsh men to form a team known as 'The Shamleeks', a name doubtless dreamt up by some nine-year-old paper boy on the street corner.

No matter, The Shamleeks were destined to go into a prematurely shambolic liquidation when war broke out for real. For the second time in a quarter of a century, the London Irish Rugby Football Club virtually closed down as the world went once more to war.

CHAPTER SIX

The Canonisation and Sacking of J.C. Daly

'There are many canonised on earth,
that shall never be Saints in Heaven.'

SIR THOMAS BROWNE, 1605–82

When Adolf Hitler marched into the Low Countries in 1940, decided a spot of sightseeing was just the thing for Paris in summertime, and sent packs of young zealots off into the waters of the North Atlantic Ocean to hunt down enemy shipping, it is doubtful whether he had considered the steely resolve, guile and cunning of certain London Irish rugby club players and members.

Idiot! Underestimating anyone associated with London Irish is unwise. Although the names M.V. Delap and G.R. Beamish might not have been as familiar to Hitler and his generals as W. Churchill and J. Stalin, they will doubtless have been greeted with much angst in Berlin when news of the London Irish rugby men's feats emerged.

Delap, good enough to have played in the 1st XV under the captaincy of S.J. Cagney in the late 1920s, was to claim rather greater fame as captain of the first Allied aircraft to sink a U-boat in the Second World War. Beamish, meanwhile, achieved promotion to high rank in the RAF and is reputed to have been the first man to sight the great German battleship *Bismarck* as she made a run for home from Germany's commandeered French Atlantic ports to her base in the Baltic. High above the English Channel, Beamish is said to have been flying the plane which first spotted her. Another distinguished flyer was Brian Curtis, who was to win an Oxford blue in 1949 and then three Irish caps the following year, after earning the DFC during the war years.

Another London Irish player, Albert Hill, joined the Royal Navy, starting on corvettes and serving in India before getting his commission and joining HMS *Bulham* on the North Atlantic run. He began as navigator, became No. 1 and then captain. 'We used to leave with 40 ships and arrive with 11,' he remembers, matter-of-factly. Bill Pedlow was in the Navy, too, getting sunk in Olsen Fjord,

Norway. Pedlow's eldest sister, Doreen, was on a ship shelled by the Japanese in the Far East. She was wounded, taken ashore but died.

If Delap, Beamish, Hill and Pedlow among others ever had time to wonder what had happened to the Exiles' ground back at Sunbury during their wartime service, they might have been interested to know it had been taken over by the Ministry of Agriculture and was being used partly for growing food, including potatoes. But one area of the land was used as a rifle range, and those playing rugby in the first seasons after the conflict had ended in 1945 often reported finding small pieces of metal lying around on the grass. Part of the Sunbury ground familiar to today's London Irish followers was heavily wooded at one time, and when the club returned to their premises in 1945, they also found that certain residents whose homes backed on to the ground had taken the opportunity of the war to extend their gardens. A little local case of *Lebensraum*. In some cases, it took a couple of years of argument to get them to return to their original boundaries.

There was, too, in early times at Sunbury a proper stream running along at the back of what is today the main stand. It had fish and bullrushes in it, and when the ball went in there, the small boys scampering to retrieve it could expect a handful of stinging nettles with the ball as they hauled it out. Whenever the Thames flooded, the land at the back of that area would be filled with water. It was a severe problem for a long time, because wartime activities had somehow damaged the drainage system. For which, doubtless, the blundering Captain Mainwarings of the time should be blamed.

During the war there had been a few matches played. Just before the conflict really flared, Albert Hill was sent to Wales and played in the same Cardiff team as the great Wilf Wooller, of Rydal school, Cambridge University, Welsh rugby and Glamorgan cricket teams fame. At Ravenhill, Belfast, an Irish XV played five matches at various intervals against British Army teams, one each in 1942, 1943 and 1944 and two in 1945. The British Army won four of them and J.C. Corcoran, a prop forward who was to join London Irish in 1947–48 and win two full Irish caps, against Australia in 1947 and France in 1948, appeared in the 1944 and 1945 games. Professional rugby league men were given special dispensation to appear in the same team as union men during those war games. Hence, Air Commodore R.H.G. Weighill, pillar of the establishment who won the DFC during the war, was to be seen, memorably, playing alongside men regarded as pariahs of their sport for having gone north to rugby league. Once the war finished, of course, their pariah status was resumed. It was as dottily and deludedly daft as the German and British soldiers climbing from their First World War trenches at Christmas, embracing each other with the Yuletide spirit, and then a while later clambering back and quickly resuming the machine-gunning of one another.

The Wasps and Rosslyn Park clubs did struggle on during the war years, Harlequins played a few games too, and there was an enormous number of Services XVs in action. In one of the war years, over 80 people played in the Wasps 1st XV, many of them overseas servicemen posted to England or just passing through. Des O'Brien, who played for Wasps at that time, remembers, 'I had a lot of good rugby during the war, getting a lot of experience playing against good internationals every second Saturday.' O'Brien spent two years based in London and asked if he could join up. 'Sorry, son,' he was told. 'You are in a reserve occupation.' O'Brien worked for the Guinness brewery in Park Royal, north-west London.

The ending of the conflict did not mean, of course, such things as an overnight return of commandeered land to its original owners. Thus the club played its home matches in the first season after the war back at the BBC ground at Motspur Park, familiar territory for those who had been with Irish in the late 1920s. For the next season, 1946–47, one pitch was available back at Sunbury (changing-rooms were still in the famous old wooden shack at one end of the ground) and the 1st XV returned at that time. But for the lower sides, from the 1946–47 season to the 1948–49 season, temporary accommodation was arranged at the nearby General Accident Fire Life Association company ground in Sunbury.

For those whose knowledge of the mood of the nation in summer 1945 is limited to brief film clips from Pathe Newsreels, most of them showing London in delirious celebration with any man in military uniform fair game for the female population of the land, then the reality of the situation might come as a shock. But Bill Morgan, who followed P. Ashe as honorary team secretary midway through that first season after the war, wrote a sobering comment on the spirit and prospects for his beloved club in the autumn of 1945:

The prospects for London Irish were meagre. To begin with, nine of their first-team players who played for the club in the season 1938–39 lost their lives in that struggle. Some of the other players, notably Harry Gallagher, the captain, had not returned from abroad and W. Igoe, the vice-captain, led the side for the season.

Nevertheless, a start was made on 29 September 1945 at Richmond Athletic Ground against London Scottish. Pipers from the London Irish Rifles played the teams out on to the field and the match was attended by dignitaries from the American Embassy. There was a large crowd at the ground to see Scottish win 27–0. London Irish, according to reports, were hard-pushed to field a team of any substance at all, although David Orr, a fine centre three-quarter who would later become club captain and then president in the 1980s, did play. 'I had been in the

Action from the 1949 Exiles clash with the Scottish at Richmond
Athletic Ground. Bill Pedlow (left) and C.S. Griffin (centre)
hunt the ball.

Army and just got back to London. We were soundly beaten in the match,' he recalls. It was a particularly difficult start for Irish, for they lost their first four games by a combined points aggregate of 65 points to just eight scored.

There was another bad run, of five consecutive defeats, around Christmas that year, but gradually better players became available. Albert Hill got back from the Navy late that season and his presence was important. 'Albert was the soul of London Irish – he typified the spirit we had in those times,' was Orr's generous testimony. There were some notable victories, and two teams were run for most of the season. Old Millhillians and Old Merchant Taylors were both beaten, so too were the Royal Australian Air Force in a memorable encounter shaded 10–8 by Irish. Two of the Australian players, Campbell and McHugh, were to turn out for Irish on several subsequent occasions during the season. Both were presented with London Irish ties when they finally left for home.

The matches with London Welsh that season were, however, as close and hard fought as ever. A 13–9 win for Welsh in December on their ground was followed by an Irish victory, by 15 points to 11, at Motspur Park after Christmas. In all, more than 100 players appeared in the 1st XV that season, and out of 25 games played, ten were won and 14 were lost, with one drawn. It was an acceptable record, given the tremendous difficulties under which the club had been operating.

If the clouds of war had still seemed to be hovering above London Irish that season, then clouds of a different nature, the climatic variety, retarded their progress the following year, season 1946–47. As war-torn Europe was still trying to throw off assorted hangovers from the war such as rationing, a ferocious winter descended, adding to hungry people's misery by ensuring they were also freezing cold. For eight weeks during January, February and March, hardly a match was played by any of the first-class clubs in London. Sunbury must have been a dismally depressing sight: two pitches still under the plough, and the only one available frost-bound for long weeks of the season. By the time the Arctic freeze-up relented, the winter was almost over, trimming the London Irish season to only 20 games, of which nine were won, seven lost and four drawn. The strong London clubs – Rosslyn Park, Harlequins, London Scottish and Met. Police – all beat Irish, although Richmond's scalp was taken and there was a 3–3 draw with London Welsh.

However, there were silver linings to the clouds. A scrum-half of much promise from Ireland's Clongowes Wood College, J.B. 'John' Holland, arrived to study medicine in London, and a centre, J.S. Lowry, also emerged. Relations with the IRFU were also strengthened by a financial grant made to the club by officials of the Union in Dublin. And when London Irish went to Dublin to play UCD, the Irish selectors attended the game and the president, W.A. Douglas, visited the players in the pavilion before the kick-off. Furthermore, there was the distinct pleasure of seeing another London Irish player, J.C. (John Christopher) Daly, earn international recognition in the 1946–47 International Championship, holding his place all season to end the year with four caps.

But if that had been largely a season to forget for Irishmen and London Irish, then the 1947–48 season that followed was to be one of glorious triumph. London Irish had a new president in Brendan Quin and a new captain in Des O'Brien – the latter had been persuaded to join the club by the 'very persuasive' Billy Igoe, he reported years later – while Ireland were to achieve a triumph at international level which would be the talk of Five

J.C. Daly, who was to play a vital role in Ireland's 1948 Grand Slam triumph.

Nations rugby for years to come. Bill Morgan was beavering away in his usual gruff, no-nonsense sort of way, and Major John Donnelly, secretary of the ex-Services welfare committee in London, was his loyal, long-suffering assistant. The fare to Sunbury from Waterloo in those days, remembers Bill Pedlow, was 4s. 8d. – 'but no one ever claimed travelling expenses. Morgan would not have allowed it. The only ones who got expenses were those coming down from Lancashire or the Midlands, or some of the University chaps.'

For London Irish, 1948 represented their 50th anniversary, and a Jubilee Ball was held at London's Hyde Park Hotel on the night of Saturday, 5 February 1949 from 8 p.m. to 1 a.m., dancing to Howard Aynstey and his Orchestra. Tickets were 30s. each, inclusive of a buffet supper.

It was a fine moment for the 1st XV to produce the most successful season in the club's history. Of 30 games played, just nine were lost, with 19 wins and two draws. There was a points difference of 305 scored against 163 conceded. Four teams were fielded during the season, but at 1st XV level a squad of players came together with quality in every department.

Bill Pedlow, who would prove to be a thoroughly valuable points-scoring full-back, had originally joined the club in 1938 but had by now reappeared after wartime service. Kevin Quinn, the Old Belvedere centre who had won two Irish caps in the 1947 championship, had also arrived. One of Quinn's new team-mates at London Irish was wing three-quarter Kevin O'Flanagan, who, like Quinn, was capped against Australia in Dublin on 6 December 1947.

O'Flanagan was a remarkably talented all-round sportsman. He was also a soccer international and a champion athlete, and he was to become a most proficient and successful golfer as well. His brother Michael, similarly a soccer international, mirrored Kevin's international rugby experience by winning a single cap for Ireland 12 months later. Although you could dub them both members of that unfortunate brigade the 'one-cap wonders', the fact that both brothers had won caps for Ireland at both rugby and soccer marked them out as holders of a unique record.

Father Tom Gavin, who was also with the club at that time, remembers, 'Sometimes O'Flanagan would play for us on a Saturday, sometimes he would play for Arsenal. He had an incredible boot. We used to give him long kicks for goal with one of those old heavy wet balls. We marvelled at the fact that he got it so far.'

London Irish, meanwhile, had plenty more reasons to anticipate the fine season they were about to enjoy. One of the chief factors was the arrival at the club of Des O'Brien, one of the grand back-row forwards of his time and a man whose rugby pedigree became such as to earn him the privilege of managing a British Isles tour, Mike Campbell-Lamerton's 1966 Lions to Australia and New

Zealand. But there was talent to be seen throughout this London Irish squad. Tommy Headon had won two caps for Ireland back in 1939 and was still around up front. A.B. Curtis, a back-row forward, was good enough to progress into the Irish international side in 1950, where he would win three caps. Holland was the scrum-half of whom the club's high hopes were already proving justified, and C.S. Griffin, who had come into the 1st XV on the wing, was destined to win two Irish caps in 1951.

Other three-quarters who were to become stalwarts of the club in the years ahead had also come together: G.M.D. Archer and the Australian centre C.J. Windsor, and, at outside-half, P.J. Isola. Then came the rugby-playing priest, Father Gavin, a player of fine skills who would become the first ever priest to play international rugby for Ireland.

If those were some of the star names, others, less well known internationally, were very fine club players. It added up to a supreme group of players who gave London Irish the most memorable season in their 50-year history.

Bill Morgan, a good, upright, honest citizen, bank employee and a man whose whole life revolved around London Irish and rugby, wrote with a quiet yet discernible pride in his review of that season:

> *The past season has been a most successful one. Admittedly, the team failed to hold the brilliant form they showed in the earlier part of the season, but some of their lapses towards the end can be ascribed to the fact that star players had to be released for international matches and other representative matches. Four players from London Irish – K.P. O'Flanagan, J.M. Corcoran, J.C. Daly and D.J. O'Brien – played for Ireland during the season. In addition, G.M.D. Archer played in the final Irish trial, Harry Gallagher played for Ulster and D.P. Kelly played for Co. Dublin. O'Brien and Daly were also honoured by the Barbarians.*
>
> *The team visited Ireland on two occasions and played Lansdowne at Lansdowne Road in October. The other occasion was an Easter tour when UCC and Garryowen were the opponents. The tour was a grand success and on their return everybody was full of praise for the warmth and kindness with which they were received wherever they went.*

London Irish's start to that season, 12 wins from the opening 13 games, was tremendous. They did lose 7–0 to London Welsh but walloped Harlequins 22–0 and also toppled Richmond 3–0, London Scottish 6–0 and Lansdowne 9–0. Rosslyn Park, UCD and UCC were other victims. But London Welsh beat them again, 3–0, at the end of the season, and they lost, too, to Garryowen. In all, 63 players had represented the club's 1st XV that season in the 30 matches.

In one of them, at Bedford, Father Tom Gavin found himself knocked cold in

THE FATTED CALF WAS KILLED AT LANSDOWNE RD LAST SATURDAY TO CELEBRATE THE RETURN OF THE PRODIGALS

AND A POSSIBLE DOMESTIC DISTURBANCE WAS PREVENTED BY PUTTING THE O'FLANAGAN KIDS ON DIFFERENT WINGS.

INCIDENTALLY DR KEVIN O'FLANAGAN SHOULD HAVE BROUGHT HIS LITTLE BLACK BAG WITH HIM AS HIS MINISTRATIONS WERE FREQUENTLY NEEDED BY THE OPPOSITION

TOMMY HEADON, - STRONGLY RESEMBLING THE NEIGHBOURING GAS-WORKS, PUT IN SOME STOUT WORK IN THE FIELD

WHILE OTHER IRISH FORWARDS, INCLUDING J. DALY, KEPT GETTING INTO P. HORAN'S HAIR

DES O'BRIEN (EX-OLD BELVEDERE) AND REV. BILL MOYNAN WERE THE OPPOSING CAPTAINS.

WIN 9pts-0

The london Irish may be exiles, but they certainly cannot be regarded as DISPLEASED PERSONS!

MR MARTIN DOYLE IS A SORT OF CABINET MEMBER OF THE 'EXILED GOVT' IN ENGLAND

A cartoon from the Irish Field *in 1947 showing the leading characters of the London Irish club.*

an incident. The sight of a good man of the cloth laid out on a rugby ground was too much for a tough, bruising forward – yet respectful man – like Tommy Headon.

'I woke up to find this friendly face peering down and looking concerned about me,' said Gavin. 'Now, Father,' Gavin heard a voice say gently, as he opened his eyes and sat up, trying to recover. 'Just tell us, who did it?'

The game then continued in perfect peace for some ten minutes without a whiff of cordite in the air. But, a little time later, a large forward of the opposing side was seen lying motionless, face down, on the ground. Headon's revenge!

Tommy Headon was one of the great London Irish characters. Only 5ft 11in tall but about ten foot wide, he had been a very tidy shot-putter and could play anywhere in a pack of rugby forwards. He was to die virtually a millionaire after starting with Pascall's, the confectionery company, as works manager and climbing the ladder all the way up to become one of the top directors. He was out for a run with his dog one day when he suddenly collapsed from a heart attack and died. If Headon had need to hit anyone on the rugby field, they felt it.

And then there was Paddy Horne, a former welterweight boxer well used to landing a timely blow, whatever the sporting shirt he was wearing!

But perhaps the greatest character of that era was J.C. Daly, a native of Cobh in Co. Cork, the last port of call for the ill-fated *Titanic* in 1912. Daly was to be immortalised in Irish rugby for his feats on the afternoon of 13 March 1948 at Ravenhill, Belfast. It was a day for Irish rugby always to recall, and the stories that followed, through the years and the decades, have become legendary. Strange thing, that, about Irish stories – they seem to get better and funnier as the years go by . . .

It remains Ireland's only Grand Slam in their entire history, and it was their first Triple Crown since 1899. The possibility of such an achievement had been created by a 13–6 win over France at Stade Colombes on New Year's Day, a famous 11–10 victory over England at Twickenham and a 6–0 defeat of Scotland in Dublin. The grand denouement was played out before a wildly excited capacity crowd at Ravenhill, and the great Bleddyn Williams, one of the Welsh centres that afternoon, remembers it vividly to this day.

'It was an incredible atmosphere. Ravenhill didn't hold many more than 30,000, for there was only the one stand down one side of the ground. Ireland were always a difficult side to play against but on that day, with such a tremendous atmosphere, it was even harder. They went berserk. There was real class in that Irish side, and we wished we'd had Des O'Brien on the 1950 Lions tour in New Zealand. He was one of the great No. 8s: he read the game so well and was a good ball player, such an athlete and a very, very fit man. He wasn't tremendously physical but made up for that with his knowledge of the game and his rugby brain. He used to swing the scrummage and dribble away off the back of it, for he was a great controller of the ball in the dribble.

'There were plenty of other fine players in that side. J.C. Daly was a very good forward, an aggressive player and a hell of a good scrummager. He put himself about the field and was one of the first running prop forwards.'

Barney Mullan's try gave Ireland the lead but the brilliant Williams brought Wales level with a superb try of his own. There was just a single score in the second half, and it came when Daly and O'Brien burst through from a line-out on to the loose ball and dribbled upfield some 30 or 40 yards for Daly to score the famous try. At the final whistle, thousands invaded the pitch and Daly was carried off shoulder high, his shirt torn to shreds and snatched away by souvenir hunters. O'Brien, looking back in 1998 on that moment 50 years earlier, remembered, 'As

J.C. Daly, flanked by Des O'Brien (left) and Jackie Kyle, meets Lord Craigavon before Ireland's 1948 Grand Slam victory over Wales in Belfast. The match ended Ireland 6, Wales 3.

we were trotting back from the try, Daly said to me, "Jaysus, Brien, if Wales don't score again I'll be canonised!" Daly was a marvellous character. I remembered him before the war, and he had just joined the London Irish Rifles. He pinched a ball from wherever we were, and said, "I'm coming back after the war and playing for Ireland." He did, too, after serving in North Africa and Italy. In the Italian campaign, he was involved in the famous siege at Monte Cassino. He was attached to a radio unit and spent the time carrying one and a half hundredweight of equipment around on his back. He and his wireless operator were put into a location in no man's land, and told to hold a little bridge over a culvert. But, apparently, they couldn't then get back to them during the day and could only supply them at night. They were up there for the best part of six weeks.

'When it was all over and they had got the pair of them out, someone asked Daly what it had been like. He looked unfussed by it all and said, "It was like living at home; we were very comfortable."

'He was a lovely man and a remarkable character.'

J.C. Daly prepares to kick through, supported by Des O'Brien (right). 'Jaysus, Brien, if Wales don't score again, I'll be canonised!' said Daly after his try.

For the Welsh at the end of that match, there was the official dinner and then all aboard the boat for the night sailing back to the Welsh coast. But in Ireland the celebrations raged all weekend. On Monday morning, Daly was spied walking down a street in the centre of Dublin by a young lady who was driving a car. She pulled up, got out and rushed up to him, saying, 'Are you J.C. Daly?' He conceded as much, at which point the attractive woman replied, 'Well, I'm wearing half of your shirt beneath this blouse.'

Daly and the lady disappeared together, and apparently did not surface for five days. Des O'Brien said, 'That was very unusual for Ireland in those days, believe me.'

When he got back to his job, he found he had lost it, which gave him a serious problem. His mother was ill in Ireland and he was told he might need as much as £2,000 for an operation she required and subsequent care for her. Thus, not long after, Daly accepted a £1,000 offer to turn professional with Huddersfield rugby league club, with a match appearance fee of £8, £9 for a draw and £12 for each win. Of course, he never played for Ireland again.

Jim Corcoran remembered playing with Daly for Munster. When they were both at London Irish, Corcoran played tight-head, but each could perform on the other head. 'We would change heads during a game sometimes; that used to confuse the opposition,' he chuckles. 'J.C. Daly was a very outgoing character, more mature and more a man of the world. But he was three or four years older than most of us at that time. He was good looking, had lovely wavy black hair and wore it longer than the average prop forward of today. He would get up and sing a song wherever he was, at Victoria station, on a hotel dining table – it didn't matter. He would also walk on his hands at times, and I remember him going round the foyer of the Russel Hotel in London like that one night. He was a very unusual character.'

During that remarkable season, London Irish took a significant decision which was to change the course of their fortunes for the coming years. With Sunbury still very much out in the sticks and virtually undeveloped, the idea had been raised of sharing the Blackheath ground at the Rectory Field in south-east London, still a fashionable rugby venue although, as the years went by, one that became far less in vogue.

However, it was felt that by combining with Blackheath, a club that boasted the best fixture list in London, the Irish would form a rugby centre of excellence where top-class matches would be seen every week of the season. Larger crowds might attend, thereby raising revenues for the Irish. The members duly approved the scheme and Bill Morgan wrote in his review of the season:

This was a very important step . . . and the first match was played there against University College, Dublin, on 15 November 1947 [Irish winning 17–8 with two tries by Tommy Headon and one by J.B. Holland]. This partnership should prove of immense advantage to both clubs in the future and will provide London Irish with a home in London which has been the ambition of many for years. There is no reason left now why London Irish should not prosper.

CHAPTER SEVEN

'The Best in London'

'Nothing great will ever be achieved without great men,
and men are great only if they are determined to be so.'

CHARLES DE GAULLE, 1890–1970

Ironically, the next season, the club's full jubilee year, started with a defeat, 20–17 to United Services at Portsmouth. But the fact that Headon, Pedlow and Quinn missed six penalty goals between them from fairly easy positions may have had something to do with it! There then followed seven straight wins, including a 14–3 success over Bedford, a 12–8 win over UCD in Dublin and 29–3 and 24–5 wins over St Bart's and Aldershot Services, followed by a 16–9 success over London Scottish and a 15–6 win over Rosslyn Park. A hiccup in the middle of the season was negotiated, and Irish finished strongly, with seven wins and a draw from their last nine matches.

It was a club in fine fettle, with just six of its 28 matches lost that season. Seven full internationals were in residence: K. Quinn, T. Gavin, C.J. Windsor and K.P. O'Flanagan behind the scrum, and T.A. Headon, J.M. Corcoran and D.J. O'Brien up front. O'Brien was to captain the club in two of his three seasons with them. Two other players, T.S. McRoberts and C.T.M. Wilson, were the tight-head props in the Varsity match that year, for Cambridge and Oxford respectively. London Irish players were off and performing for all manner of English counties, the Irish provincial side Leinster, the Services and the Irish trial teams, not to mention invitation sides like Mickey Steele-Bodger's annual encounter with Cambridge University.

At lower levels, too, there was a thoroughly healthy situation to report. Although the 'A' XV lost 14 of its 25 matches, the Extra 'A's lost only eight of 26 matches, the indefatigable 'B's won 17 of their 25 games and the Extra 'B's lost 11 of 23 played. A review of that season stated:

London Irish have every reason to look back on their Jubilee year with satisfaction. They have maintained their record as champions of London . . . were Surrey Sevens holders . . . and but for injuries and calls upon their best players elsewhere, they might well

75

have come through with an even smaller number of defeats. Once again, Des O'Brien played for Ireland in all internationals [Ireland won the Triple Crown for the second successive season], and left centre three-quarter T.J. Gavin received two caps. Two other backs, G.M.D. Archer and D. Orr, appeared in trials, and Con Griffin, an outstanding right wing, was unlucky to receive an injury while playing for Middlesex against Eastern Counties in November which kept him out of the game and ruined hopes of a trial.

In his first full season for London Irish, Kevin Quinn quickly made his mark and was the outstanding half in London rugby circles. His understanding with scrum-half J.B. Holland and his ability to cut out openings with spectacular dashes through the centre was the inspiration behind London Irish, while intelligent anticipation and lengthy touch-finding repeatedly turned defence into attack. The backs, too, had the pace to take advantage of his cross-kicks and punts ahead.

Des O'Brien dominated a lively pack in which Tommy Headon, J. Corcoran, A.B. Curtis, Brian McGuirk and T. Wilson were always prominent, and in D.P.W. Kelly they had a wing forward who tackled fearlessly and was always well up with his backs.

Just ten matches had been played at the Rectory Field, Blackheath, that season, as a preliminary to the new ground-sharing agreement, but from the following season, 1949–50, all 1st XV games were played there, with the junior teams' players sitting in those lovely elegant, green-liveried railway carriages for the cheerful, clattering ride out to Sunbury in the suburbs for their games. The intensive housing developments which were to blight so badly the outer London suburbs had yet to materialise; it was still largely a green and pleasant land once out beyond the inner fringes of the great city.

It was a happy time, too, memories of the war being replaced by simple pleasures like picnics in the park and day trips to the seaside. There was a generally upbeat mood abroad. London Irish had strength and class in their playing squad, Bill Morgan was a workaholic figurehead behind the scenes, running the club with a rod of iron but making it most effective and efficient, and then came the move to Blackheath. The club was humming, and not just because results were generally good. The place was littered with characters, and where they reside, you tend to find the best stories.

Father (now Monsignor) Gavin remembers, 'We were easily the best team in London at that time and probably the best around, with all those internationals in the side. People had always thought that if London Irish ever started trying seriously, that would be the end of it for other sides. Kevin Quinn was an excellent player who could kick the ball from one end of the field to the other. I thought he should have had my place in the Irish side in 1949. And I might not have been included anyway. That Sunday night when I knew I had been picked for the French international, I telephoned my mother. She told me I would have to ask the Archbishop for permission to play, but I said, "Don't be daft." She kept on at me to do it, and so I did – and was told I should not play. Archbishop McQuaid of Dublin did not want his priests playing Gaelic football or rugby union.

'I think the word got out, though, and Cardinal Griffin from Westminster phoned Archbishop Masterton of Birmingham and said to him, "Tell McQuaid to regard Gavin as a foreign student and not one of his own." So only after that was I able to accept the invitation to represent Ireland.'

Gavin suspected the media had got wind of the story 'on the grapevine', for they contacted him and asked if it was true. Referring to one aspect of the tale they had related to him which he knew to be

Father Tom Gavin, in rugby garb . . .

factually incorrect (albeit pretty close to being accurate), Father Gavin replied with charming honesty and openness, 'Oh, no, that just isn't true at all.' Which it wasn't, of course. And so they went away and the story was never written. Until now.

All but 50 years later, Monsignor Gavin, still based in Coventry, smiles and says, 'Perhaps we should say it was a little white fib. But I didn't want all the fuss that would have been made, and there would have been a lot going around Dublin. There was a sense of adventure about those early years after the war; all sorts of things took place.

'And, of course, you never knew what was going to happen next at London Irish. They had an old soldier who was put in charge of the jerseys for cleaning. One night, he left them draped over pipes down in the furnace to dry. The following Saturday, every first-team player took the field wearing jerseys with burnt holes all over them. People used to turn up minus a jersey sometimes; it was all a bit hand-to-mouth. Except that when we were out on the pitch, there was nothing hand-to-mouth about the performances. Bill Morgan used to grumble about things, such as players travelling further than before, and complaining that they all got colds.'

. . . and working clothes

Gavin's skills were obvious, but they were denied to Irish for most of his second season after he tore knee ligaments at Moseley in September, ruling him out for the rest of the season. He was at Cambridge University by then and appeared in 13 matches in the build-up to the Varsity match. But the regular fly-half, who had been injured, was brought back to play at Twickenham and Gavin never won a blue. 'But I got an Irish cap instead in 1949, which was certainly consolation for that.'

But Gavin's cap against France only came after an extraordinary incident before the match in Dublin's Shelbourne Hotel, where both teams were staying. The Irish boys went in for lunch and saw the French team eating, ordering their sweets off the trolley. When the Irish lads sat down, they were presented with a set menu, but after the main course they said, 'Oh, well, we'll have our sweets off the trolley like the French boys.' So they ordered the best, consumed it with the satisfied manner of cats who had discovered a way into the cream pot, and left the dining-room. A little while later, as they were preparing to set off for the ground, the secretary of the IRFU called them together and coldly informed them that unless each player paid, there and then, three shillings and four pence for his 'extras' at luncheon, the player would not appear in the international that afternoon. They all paid up.

A few years later, Father Gavin bumped into another former London Irish luminary outside Twickenham. 'I saw J.C. Daly standing around and called him over. "I dare not go in," Daly told me, but I replied that was nonsense and to come along with me.'

So the pair entered the sacred territory of RFU headquarters. It would have been viewed as sacrilege in the eyes of some for a rugby league man to be walking such holy ground. Father Gavin, a man who knew more about holy things than ordinary mortals, took a different, more Christian view. 'Of course, it was seen as a slur on the person if he went to rugby league in those days; you were a semi-traitor if you signed professional. But I didn't take that view. I felt it was all right for us. I was a priest and although I didn't have much money, at least I had a job. Subscriptions for London Irish were around two or three guineas at that time, I recall, but they didn't charge me subs, although I had to pay my own fare down from Cambridge when I played for them. But you just got on with it . . .'

And Father Gavin always had a twinkle in his eye, a ready smile and a joke. Shortly before he was due to go to Ampleforth College, that fine Catholic school in the north of England, he played a match for London Irish against United Services, Portsmouth. He damaged his wrist, but . . . well, just got on with it. 'Next day I was saying Mass and found I couldn't use my hand. My mother told me to go down to the hospital, and I came back with a great big plaster over my

No Ryanair flights, no taxis home from Heathrow. An early London Irish team prepares to cross the Irish Sea by steamer.

wrist and lower arm. I had broken the wrist and first finger on the hand. I had to go ahead with my move to Ampleforth, so when I got there and was introduced to the school, I said, "I would like to deny the rumour that I broke this on the head of a boy at my previous school."'

Funny thing, but he never had any trouble with pupils after that. At Ampleforth, he met Cardinal Basil Hume, who used to coach the school's 1st XV forwards while Father Gavin took the backs. Fortunate young fellows.

London Irish, meanwhile, were embarking upon a short tour to France around that time, playing the famous Racing Club in Paris, and then Brive in the Corrèze region of the south. They travelled south by train, overnight from the famous Austerlitz station in Paris, and stayed at some of those delightful Michelin abodes.

But for Father Gavin, there was another venue to visit in France. He went to Lourdes, not to see the great rugby team that famous club had at the time but to pray for his sick brother Kevin, who had been ill, confined in a plaster cast in bed for 18 months. He was suffering from ankylosing spondylitis, arthritis of the spine affecting the vertebral and sacroiliac joints, leading to stiffness or fixation of the joints. It was a disease which usually affected young men. The cure, when it was found, came from an unusual source. 'They found a German doctor who

was in a prison camp in England at that time and he gave him new treatment for it.'

It worked, although it is unknown whether the actual illness or the experience of dropping a cigarette down the plaster cast one day and having to endure a bucket of cold water being poured down it was worse.

In season 1949–50, George Beamish was posted to RAF Cranwell and knew he would not have the time to continue as president, so Major-General W. Brooke Purdon CB, OBE, MC was invited to be his replacement. Swapping an Air Commodore for a Major-General suggested London Irish had pretty good contacts in the military business. Des O'Brien replaced Brian McGuirk as captain (Kevin Quinn became vice-captain) and found a rather unusual quality to his men. 'We had one of the best singing teams in Britain. There was a good social side, but only on Saturday nights. Then, they were always singing songs, a delightful side of the game at that time.'

O'Brien's ability as a leader, motivator and footballer was obvious. Years later, Sir David Orr, who led London Irish in 1953–54, said of him, 'He was an outstanding man in his sport and his personal life.' O'Brien was 79 in 1998 and continues to play tennis and golf in Scotland near his Edinburgh home.

A fascination of that era (and most others) was the influence of Bill Morgan, or 'Der Führer' as he was charmingly known around the club. He ran London Irish single-handedly, O'Brien remembered, and when it came to selection of the team, strange things tended to happen. 'We used to have a selection meeting in a bar somewhere near the City. I had to travel one hour on the tube, and we would spend some considerable time discussing names.'

But O'Brien found there was much difference between a London Irish team selected on a Monday or Tuesday night and the one which would take the field the following Saturday. By Saturday afternoon, when the players had made their way to Blackheath individually, O'Brien would walk into the dressing-room and find three or four different faces, changing for the match. 'You would walk in and say "Hello, what are you doing here?" to a player, or "Where's so-and-so?" to Bill Morgan. He would tell you that "so-and-so" couldn't travel at the last minute or wasn't fit! Very often the team that went out on Saturday bore no resemblance to the one we had selected. Bill would pick his own team and invite any players he fancied from anywhere in the country. If Bill could find a good player in Britain, he would bring him down.'

Without much doubt, London Irish benefited from the very generous unofficial 'gifts' of a club supporter, Pat Kelly, in those years. A small man but a wealthy bookmaker, Kelly gave the club money on a pretty regular basis, assisting to build up the coffers and strengthen the club off the field.

O'Brien recalls clearly one particular visitor to the club in those days: Louis MacNeice, the poet who had been born in Northern Ireland in 1907. His works included the poetic works *Autumn Sequel* (written in 1954) and *Solstices* (1961), as well as a translation of the *Agamemnon of Aeschylus* (1936). He died in 1963.

But for the club, 1949–50 would always be remembered as the season when two of its greatest stalwarts, Martin Doyle and Captain R.S.V. Dyas, who had been associated with London Irish from its inception, passed away. The club was fully conscious, wrote Bill Morgan, of the great loss undergone. Yet both men lived long enough to see the tiny, frail sapling they had helped plant blossom into a healthy, vibrant tree. For, by 1950 – and, indeed, long since – London Irish rugby club had become not only a renowned club in terms of its appeal off the field but also a strong, successful organisation on the pitch. They were respected throughout Britain and Ireland and had created an enviable reputation. They were soon to become the first club in Britain to host a touring Italian team, Roma, who visited them in 1951.

In a sense, they had also become victims of their own success, for in one of the seasons when O'Brien led them, they returned a playing record of 19 wins and ten defeats from 29 matches – a decent achievement, for sure, but hardly what it might have been had they not been supplying half the teams in the British Isles and Ireland with representative players. The list makes formidable reading:

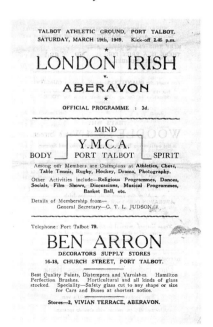

- Among the 65-man first-team squad, there were six internationals.
- D.J. O'Brien played for Ireland in all four Home Championship matches that season.
- A.B. Curtis appeared in three internationals.
- Five players played in the final Irish trial: O'Brien, Curtis, J.D. Clancy, M.T. Maloney and C.S. Griffin.
- Clancy played for Connacht; T.S. McRoberts represented Ulster; D.P.W. Kelly and O'Brien played for Leinster.
- Griffin and O'Brien represented Middlesex in the English County Championship.

- W. Pedlow played for Kent; N. Bailey played for the East Midlands.
- D.P.W. Kelly played for the Royal Navy.
- Curtis was an Oxford University blue and he also represented the Barbarians.

Little wonder that the wily Morgan needed a squad of 65 names from which to select a team! That season, the 1st XV honours caps went to C.S. Griffin from the three-quarters and Albert Hill of the forwards. And the club put out six sides most weeks, making it a thriving hub of London rugby as the 1950s dawned. The victories over what Morgan called 'three of Ireland's leading clubs' – Dublin University, Lansdowne and University College, Dublin – were much prized. For those matches, London Irish were at full strength.

By this time, Morgan was revealing that the club had in total around 170 players on its books and that an extra side, led by Dick Harris, had had to be started up during the season to give everyone some rugby. This explosion of interest in London Irish had also been matched at schoolboy level, for three matches were played during the Christmas holidays, a trend that had begun prior to the Second World War. Morgan rightly called the schoolboys 'our stars of the future'.

One future young recruit, a certain A.A. Mulligan, would develop into one of the great players of world rugby in the years ahead.

CHAPTER EIGHT

Nature's Call, the Missing Turkey and a Strange Recruit

'Mate, it's all about enjoying life!
There are very few people who get to their death-bed and say,
"Gee, I wish I'd spent more time at the office."'

BOB DWYER, 1997

Tom Gallagher had a problem. It was the middle of the night, pitch black in the small room, and the bodies of large men were spread around in the most intriguing shapes and patterns. But nature was banging on poor old Tom's door, with ever-increasing urgency.

T.A. Gallagher – 'the Bish' to everyone, because his father was known as the Pope – was awake in the unlikely environs of a Bath doctor's house at four o'clock on a Sunday morning in March 1951. The big London Irish second-row forward had managed to commandeer the only bed available for four London Irish rugby men that night, the result of 'just one more for the road' after an evening with the Bath boys following the West Country club's 5–0 win over Irish that day.

'St Patrick's Men Bogged Down' ran the headline in the Bath Saturday-evening newspaper the *Pink 'Un*, known as the *Football Herald and Chronicle*. 'Being St Patrick's Day, the London Irish players travelled down wearing sprigs of shamrock and a number of London Irish spectators were similarly adorned,' it reported.

A dash for the last train to London had proved fruitless; there wasn't even any evidence of the clouds of smoke and soot, so long before had the train chugged away into the night. Luckily, one of the Bath men, Dr Allan Todd, who had played for

PASSION IN EXILE

his club in the second row that day, offered to put the quartet up for the night at his home. 'Bish' got the bed, J.D. Clancy slept in the lounge, Albert Hill dozed fitfully in a chair and J.L. Brown was sprawled out on a mattress on the bedroom floor. A typical rugby scene.

The irony of the newspaper headline about being bogged down might just have crossed Gallagher's mind at that moment, for he certainly needed a bog. Whether it was up or down, he knew not. Which was his problem. Thus, spying a tankard on a shelf in the bedroom, Gallagher found the answer to the problem, put nature back in her place and poured her residue out of the window before retiring back to bed.

Next morning at a late breakfast, Dr Todd witnessed four bleary-eyed victims appearing downstairs and enquired, with doctorly concern, as to their well-being in the night. 'We had a grand night, doctor,' said Gallagher.

Nevertheless, the good doctor promptly prescribed the ideal antidote to any lingering effects from an evening's excesses. Disappearing briefly from the room, he reappeared clutching the tankard that had known sterling service during the night and reached for the milk jug. Four men cried in unison, 'Don't pour it into that!' Alas, too late. Gallagher found the tankard in his hands for the second time in a matter of hours and was ordered to down the milk as a restorative. Gallagher, sporting a queasy expression, duly acquiesced.

Visits to the West Country clubs and Wales were often notorious. After one Saturday afternoon match at Bristol, who had come back on to the London Irish fixture card in 1949 after an absence of 21 years, some of the players made a retreat to London every bit as slow, painful and disorganised as Napoleon's men returning from Moscow. They finally shuffled into the capital at seven o'clock on the Sunday night! Albert Hill reported dolefully, 'The wife told me she didn't mind me coming home at one o'clock on Sunday morning, but seven on Sunday evening was too much.' A warning shot across the bows, in other words.

But Bill Pedlow remembered staggering back to Paddington in the early hours of Monday morning after one Saturday match at Aberavon. 'We spent the whole Saturday evening drinking with them, resumed on Sunday morning and went through all Sunday before sleeping it off down there Sunday night and catching the early milk train up to London.' And returning in fine fettle for a day's work, no doubt.

Even normal fixtures in London very often meant an extremely late night, or, rather, early morning. Bill Pedlow would frequently catch the 0300 milk train out of Cannon Street on the Sunday morning back to Westgate-on-Sea on the Kent coast, where he lived. Pat Murphy, who was editor of the *Sunday Times* around that period and lived next door to him, would often be on it too, and they'd read the early editions of the Sunday paper, if they weren't too tired!

84

'We used to get home at about 6 a.m. and keep each other awake so we didn't go through to Ramsgate,' laughed Pedlow. 'I'd ring up the missus and say, "Come and pick us up, love." We'd be very popular!'

Shocking, incorrigible lot they were, really. A trip to the Lancashire coast one year to play New Brighton and Fylde proved it. 'Wasps were up there too, playing a couple of matches in the area and staying at the same hotel,' said Hill. On the Saturday night, in the small hours, someone got down into the hotel kitchens and pinched the nice plump turkey which was ready for the Sunday roast the next day. The proprietor knew exactly who was to blame.

'You London Irish boys are so well behaved,' she said, smiling sweetly. 'I knew it wouldn't be you.' Suspicion fell heavily on the Wasps men, yet the missing turkey was not to be found. Not at the hotel, anyway. Albert Hill, who had been sharing a room with Der Führer, Bill Morgan, picked up his bag later that morning and headed for home. When he got there, he opened it up for the

Bill Morgan, the administrator, with the London Irish VII which won the Ealing Sevens, Easter 1950.

dirty washing and out tumbled the bruised, battered and smelly remains of a turkey. 'The boys had thought they were putting it into Bill Morgan's case,' he explained cheerfully.

The trips and the stories generated from them were legendary. On the weekend of 28/29 October 1950, London Irish set off across the Irish Sea for a fixture against University College, Dublin, at Donnybrook, and another against a Connacht/Ballinasloe Select XV the next day. The UCD link was obvious, the Ballinasloe one less so, except that Bill Morgan hailed from Mullagh, Ballinasloe. And London Irish had a tradition for playing a 'country' side in tandem with a Dublin fixture on one day of the trip. The visitors achieved two good victories, 11–3 over UCD and 17–6 at Ballinasloe, after which a small reception was held in the club which was attended by, among others, W.E. 'Ernie' Crawford, that fine old Irish international full-back who was by then an Irish national selector.

A local man stood up and enquired bluntly, 'Now that we have got the Irish selector Ernie Crawford here, perhaps he can tell us when is a Connacht man going to be picked for Ireland?'

Crawford was a man who liked to speak his mind, and he also possessed a devilish sense of humour. He needed the latter, given his reply. Standing up slowly and surveying his audience, he replied, firm of voice, 'As soon as Connacht gets a man good enough, we will pick him. But I am an Ulsterman, I am an Orangeman and a Mason, and to hell with the Pope.'

The predictable shower of beer glasses flew across the room like bullets in a firing gallery. The London Irish players, hustling out after Crawford, had to wade through a carpet of glass to reach the door. Things calmed down enough for the teams to attend a dance that evening in the local town hall, but Crawford was long since on his way back to Dublin by taxi. It was said it cost him £40 to find any local taxi driver prepared to take him!

A little later, Des O'Brien and Albert Hill followed in another cab, with more dramatic consequences. Hill remembers, 'It was so cold and the driver put the heater on. The next thing was, he started yelling and shouting. The idiot had fallen asleep and was having a nightmare! Des pulled the wheel, saved us from flying off the road and stopped the car. He kicked the idiot out and drove the two of us back to Dublin. We could easily have been killed. Des was that sort of man, yet when I met his mother once, she said to me, "I never thought I would rear that boy – he was such a weakling!"'

You couldn't take some folk anywhere in those days! On another occasion, on a visit to Williamson's whiskey plant at Tullamore one cold, wet day, the players were shown around and offered a warming glass or two of the house's finest. This was duly dispensed and the old butler, a genteel fellow indeed, then reappeared after a suitable time and asked one of the players if he would care to

Action from an early Exiles match at the Rectory Field, Blackheath. 'Bish' Gallagher is behind the United Services player kicking ahead.

have his glass refilled. Jimmy Dillon, an occasional full-back with the 1st XV, shot back, 'I'd certainly like another. That was a lovely gin.'

Players were coming to London Irish from all parts by that time. But discovering one in a Surrey electrical goods shop one Saturday afternoon was extraordinary. John Brown was a solidly built sort of fellow, amiable enough, and out for an afternoon's shopping with his wife, who wanted a new vacuum cleaner. They strolled into a Kingston store and a rugby match on TV caught Brown's eye, even though he'd never played the game in his life. But London Irish had their recruiting agents in the most unlikely places, deployed to be alert to new men wherever possible. So the vacuum-cleaner salesman, who just happened to be a club member, noticed his interest and suggested Brown sit down and watch the rugby in the showroom while his wife was sorted out with a new cleaner. He pulled up a chair and the greatest conversion since that of St Paul was made. They both left the store an hour or so later clutching something – Brown a telephone number for a contact at the Irish, and his wife a new cleaner.

Bill Morgan's handwritten ledger with every team and result from the post-war years.

Brown was the most English of Englishmen ('as English as roast beef,' said Terry O'Connor) and initially caused raised eyebrows at the club. But he was started off in the 'B' team and proved to be so good that he quickly progressed through the ranks to play first-team rugby season after season. He also went on to represent Surrey. Ireland even inquired about his availability, but he could not find a convincing Irish qualification. That was no wonder; a former public schoolboy, he had an impeccable English accent and enjoyed the benefit of an inheritance. His background was about as Irish as the Dalai Lama's. He went on to appear in two England trials and played about 360 first-team games for London Irish as a tough-scrummaging prop, making him one of the most loyal servants in their history. The England selectors eyed him up all right, and told him he might get a cap if he left the Irish and joined an English club. Brown told them where to go.

They were days of great yore, and a capacity to drink more. An intake of ten or 12 pints a night wasn't anything out of the ordinary, but there was a proviso. 'A pint of beer then cost 6d., but if you drank bitter it affected your liver, so we all drank mild at 5d. a pint,' explained Albert Hill, with medicinal concern. And if they felt like really splashing out, they might fit in dinner somewhere between the pints. Sausages at 2d. each were the usual fare. But on some Saturday nights they might make Stone's chop house at Leicester Square by 9 p.m. or 9.30 p.m. for supper, which meant it was a place to avoid at all costs for ordinary citizens of the realm. One poor waif lived to regret ever going near the place. On that occasion the rugger buggers ordered supper, but their restless eyes searched the restaurant for mischief; the lads in their pomp. Most eyes descended upon a poor scraggy-looking individual sitting beside his girlfriend at a nearby table. Three of the Irish boys went off in search of a large pair of scissors, returned and calmly took possession of the youth's arms and legs. A little while later, half his beard removed from his face, they returned to their table for their chops.

Ordinary folk couldn't expect much better down at London Irish either. Neighbours, hearing a shocking noise at the club late one night during a raucous party, telephoned the local police to complain. One householder whose property backed on to the ground turned out into his garden, saw a police car parked in the Sunbury club ground and confidently went to have words with its occupants, assuming the complaints were being dealt with. The sight he came upon of two policemen sitting in their car quietly supping pints of Guinness did not altogether convince him that the residents were in for a quiet night.

But they were the salad days of their lives, no question of that. 'Even if it was the most boring match, you enjoyed every minute of it. It was a game for players. The pitches were muddy, the balls heavier. But no one ever minded,' Albert Hill remembered, a shade wistfully.

J.D. Clancy in possession for the Exiles against United Services at Blackheath, September 1951.

CHAPTER NINE

A Seat at the Top Table

'The Irish are a fair people;
they never speak well of one another.'

SAMUEL JOHNSON, 1709–84

The 1950–51 season had not been wondrous for the club, with 13 defeats, one more than their number of wins. But there again, 12 players were called up by the Irish provinces and national team and six made the final Irish trial, while G.M.D. Archer, originally a wing three-quarter but by then a wing forward, won a Cambridge blue that season. London Irish had become the home of rugby's rent-a-player business.

Nor had it been a wonderfully happy season off the field, for events were overshadowed briefly by the sudden death midway through the year of the club president, Major-General Brooke Purdon, who was in his second year of office. The man known everywhere simply as 'Brooks' died at the age of 68. He had won three caps for Ireland in 1906 and was a product of the old Queen's College, Belfast. A minute's silence was observed before London Irish's match against Richmond at Blackheath on Saturday, 2 December 1950, a game Irish lost 8–3. Another London Irish official, vice-president Lieutenant-Colonel F.A. Lacey, also passed away during the season.

Ireland had won the International Championship that year, only a 3–3 draw with Wales in Cardiff denying them a Grand Slam. C.S. Griffin, J.H. Smith and D.J. O'Brien from London Irish all represented Ireland. It was the era of Jack Kyle, in which the famous outside-half forged his reputation as one of the greatest players ever seen in his role.

At the club, Stan McRoberts, originally from Banbridge Academy, had begun the season as 1st XV captain following his departure from Cambridge University, where he had won blues in 1946, '47 and '48 while studying physics and chemistry. But the captain could play only seven matches all season because of injury. In fact, injuries and unavailabilities were a theme of the year: against Rosslyn Park in November, Irish had to field eight substitutes. The weakened team did well until scrum-half J.P. Aldron had to leave the field after half-time, also through injury. They lost 14–3.

On 1 January 1951, the teams were announced for the final Irish trial, and an uncapped forward, R.H. Thompson of Queen's University, was chosen at lock in the Whites, or Probables team. Within four years, Robin Thompson would be heading off to South Africa as captain of the 1955 Lions. With him would be two other men who would have London Irish connections during their careers, lock forward Tom Reid and hooker Robin Roe. Reid, a marvellous man, once confided to a playing colleague, with a perfectly serious expression, 'I had a nightmare last night. I was all alone, out in the open field at Twickenham, with the ball in my hands, and I didn't have a clue what to do with it.'

Years later, Tony O'Reilly would tell a delightful tale about Reid. 'He was playing against England one year and went wandering off outside the Irish dressing-room. In the next room, the English captain was exhorting his players to stirring deeds by invoking images of Agincourt and God knows what else. Reid poked his head around the English dressing-room door and said, "Would yer excuse me, lads, but have any of you fellows got any hairy twine? Me laces are broken."'

The Blues, or Possibles team, in that 1951 Irish trial contained four players with London Irish connections, past, present or future: G. Archer, R. Roe, T. Reid and A.B. Curtis.

McRoberts had followed Des O'Brien as Exiles captain, for by now O'Brien had left, posted to Wales by his employers Guinness. He promptly joined the Cardiff club. McRoberts recalled O'Brien coming back to London Irish from one Irish trial before he had won a cap and scratching his head. 'I don't know what's wrong with the Irish selectors,' O'Brien told him. 'I know I played well, I even dropped a goal, and yet still I didn't get capped.'

'That's what's wrong,' McRoberts told him. 'Forwards are not supposed to drop goals!'

McRoberts, a loose-head prop although he was six foot tall, reflected on a period of ordinary results but extraordinary characters. 'Maurice Fitzgerald, an ex-Irish Guardsman, helped us with fixtures in those days. He was quite pukka. Brendan Quin was another great man; he did so much for the club.'

McRoberts had known Tommy Headon in the late 1940s, and he remembers breaking his nose in one match which Headon was watching. 'Headon came up, saw my injury and told me this friend of his standing beside us was a medical student and would put the nose back in place there and then. It hurt like hell to do it and it's been bent ever since!'

The Exiles pack in those times was strong, hard and fiery. And such qualities fitted neatly the character of full-back Bill Pedlow, who was no stranger to brushes with referees. McRoberts remembers, 'Bill was a controversial character in those days; he always thought the referees were biased against the Irish. He would try and teach the referee a few things. One day, Arthur Rees, the well-known Welsh rugby chap who became a major figure in the police force, was refereeing our match, and when the opposition scored, he came behind the posts searching for Pedlow. 'He said to him, "I'd sort you out pretty quickly if I could play now." I think Bill got the message that day.'

But there was always the bar that night to smooth over minor disagreements. McRoberts says, 'Clubs used to come almost with the sole intention of trying to drink us under the table. Unsuccessfully, I might say. We had usually drunk the place dry by 10 p.m. so we would head off at that time for a pub, somewhere near or in central London.'

McRoberts played on for another season after his captaincy year, but was dropped when David Orr became captain the following season. 'Five of us were left out, and the team due to play the London Irish Wild Geese paid the price the following Saturday,' he said. 'We nearly killed them.'

Eamon 'Bull' Lanaghan was captain of the Wild Geese at that time, an unusual man with the even more unusual habit of leading his pack from about 20 yards back, and bellowing all the while, 'Come on, you hewers!' Stan McRoberts remembers, 'Old Bull would still be back on the halfway line when we were on the 25! He finished up as governor of a prison somewhere, probably still married to the terribly attractive wife he had, Joan, who was trying to civilise him!'

The appeal of London Irish? 'Oh, I think it was a great club as much for its social life as for the rugby it played. Wherever we went, we were very welcome. There was an aura about the Irish: whatever sort of rugby we played, it left a good feeling. Which other club in the world would make visitors so welcome?'

AN IRISHMAN'S TALE

Stan McRoberts, the London Irish captain in 1950–51, met the Argentine President Juan Perón during the Combined Oxford/Cambridge Universities tour of Argentina in 1948.

'The Oxbridge side had been invited to go, and our hosts paid for everything, including the £1,400 air tickets. We met Perón, a man of good build and over six foot tall, seemingly an affable sort of chap who made a neat little speech, although he didn't want to speak any English. He was surrounded by a lot of flunkeys from the officer class. But we were terribly disappointed because we had been told we would meet Eva too. But she did not turn up. She was out preaching to the disadvantaged, it was said. Of course, the working classes worshipped her, while the middle classes feared her. They were terrified the "shirtless ones", as the poor were known, would be given some of their estates. Perón came over as a confident character, a man who knew where he was going.

'I remember we travelled by train into the country. The government had nationalised the railways, which used to be owned by the British. The shirtless ones thought they were "their" railways after that, and that they could travel free. But the government brought in fines for those without tickets and several of our chaps on the tour got caught and had to pay fines of £20, which made quite a hole in their pockets in those days. It was a huge sum of money. It was made clear they had to pay up; the alternative was to be taken to jail.'

The 1st XV were by now well ensconced at Blackheath, and the locals in that area were spoilt rotten for choice of matches. A typical season's fixture card for the Rectory Field in those years of the 1950s might contain such distinguished visiting teams as the following, playing either Blackheath or London Irish in successive weeks: Bristol, Llanelly, Coventry, Oxford University, Wasps, Richmond, Harlequins, Racing Club de France, Cardiff, Newport, London Scottish, London Welsh, University College, Dublin, Lansdowne, Leicester, Bedford, Rosslyn Park, Swansea, Cambridge University, Bath, Northampton, Royal Navy, Aldershot Services and the leading hospital sides. There were few of the leading teams in England, Wales and Ireland who did not grace the ground.

Bill Pedlow remembers those times, and the big matches which drew increasing coverage by the national press. 'There was some logic to the decision to go to Blackheath; you could see their argument. And we had a lot of dual members because people were keen to see so many big games on the ground. So the crowds came in and there was a good financial return. The only problem was, our club was split in two with the junior teams playing all their rugby back at Sunbury. So the 1st XV and the lower sides never met. It was odd.

'Sundays became great days at Sunbury because there were lots of fixtures against mixed teams at the ground on that day. And it was a day when you never knew who might turn up at the club. Many who came with no soles on their shoes, just arrived from Ireland, ended up millionaires. And many of them have never forgotten the club. They have given generous amounts of money to help, during the years.'

Pedlow held the club's 1st XV points-scoring record for 15 years, with 128 in a single season. Players from more modern times like Dusty Hare and Neil Jenkins might scoff at such figures, but in those days they were intimidatingly impressive. Like any successful kicker, Pedlow practised assiduously to perfect his skills. 'I used to take a ball or two over to the school playing fields opposite our home at Westgate and spend hours over there working on goal-kicking.'

It was easier than trying to perfect his kicking during official club training at the Duke of York's HQ at Chelsea Barracks on Tuesday and Thursday evenings. There were only one or two lights available to offer anything other than the gloom through which the keen young London Irishmen completed their rudimentary paces. And when they got to the northern end of the ground, they had to rely on the old gas streetlights outside to see anything. There was hardly any ball work, just physical training – followed by specialist physical arm-strengthening exercises in the nearest pub. 'Rugby was a different game in those days,' Pedlow smiled.

He was a prickly customer in his playing days, not averse to bringing down someone by fair means or foul if they tried to pass him. Whether or not they had the ball at the time was merely incidental. Rosslyn Park once suggested that if Pedlow appeared against them again, they would cancel the fixture!

He had his disagreements with club officials, too, and was banned by the committee at one stage, which led to Pedlow walking out of the club and joining Richmond. But he was back at the Irish within half a season. Bill Pedlow knew when he was among his own. But his grouse was simple. 'I was objecting to late tackling, and I used to say to the referee, "Either you do something about it or I will." When he didn't, I gave a couple of players uppercuts, and they didn't like it.'

Pedlow also objected to the club selecting someone who had just turned up from Ireland or one of the universities, which meant dropping a player who had been in good enough form in the 1st XV. 'You would play in the 1st XV one week and the "A" team the next, for no good reason. I told them that and had a bit of a row.' But he loved the club and still does. People don't stay members for 54 years if they don't.

Season 1951–52 was a crushing disappointment results-wise, the 1st XV winning only seven of their 27 matches under the captaincy of David Orr. From just before Christmas, they lost 12 of their last 14 matches, including a fixture against Rugby Roma, the first Italian team to tour Britain, who came to the Rectory Field and demonstrated some classy three-quarter play to win 11–3. Yet the club had plenty of ability on paper – alas, the surface on which matches are so rarely won.

Two players represented Ireland during that season: R.H. Thompson and N. Bailey. There were a few notable wins, too, over Northampton, London Scottish, Richmond and Bath. But by recent Irish standards it was poor, with a points aggregate of 143–241. The next season, 1952–53, under the captaincy of Robin Thompson, was a slight improvement, with 13 wins, 13 defeats and three draws from 29 matches, although Thompson missed much of it through illness, which meant that David Orr continued as captain.

What was essentially the most cheering news from this season was the decision of the Irish Rugby Football Union to offer the club a seat annually on their council. Bill Morgan called it 'one of the outstanding events in the long history of London Irish'. Morgan was appointed by the club to be their first delegate to a council meeting and he regarded such an honour with obvious pride. He was able to include in his handwritten log among the list of club officers for the year completed: 'Representative to the Irish Rugby Union – W. Morgan.'

At Lansdowne Road, Dublin, on 24 October 1953, there occurred a most extraordinary incident which enabled London Irish to preserve their record of not having lost to any club in Dublin since the end of the war. Paul MacWeeney, reporting on the 9–9 draw with Lansdowne, wrote:

Among Lansdowne's assets are an intensive club spirit and this, as much as anything else, enabled them to beat the clock by a matter of seconds and snatch a draw with London Irish on Saturday. The equalising try was scored near the posts and the Lansdowne halves, R. Carroll and S. Kelly, were performing a somewhat elaborate ritual of placing the ball for Kelly's vital goal kick when the referee, the Rev. Austin Carry, decided that time was being wasted and blew his whistle for full time. His decision, I thought, was a trifle harsh, for the kick, after all, was of considerable importance. To come so close to victory over what is probably Ireland's strongest club side represents an excellent performance by London Irish.

In truth, said Colin Gibson, who was on the London Irish left wing that day, the Exiles had been under heavy pressure for much of the second half. 'Maintaining that record of not having lost in Dublin for some years was terribly important to us. But we thought it was gone when Lansdowne scored so close to the posts. There was no way the conversion could miss. We knew Bill Morgan would have us for meat! But the kicker asked permission to readjust the position of the ball three times, and at the third attempt he was told he was wasting time and the match was over. Only a man of Carry's impeccable record would have got away with it.'

Ironically, two days later, having lost to a Tullamore Select XV the day after the Lansdowne game on their short tour consisting of three matches in three days, London Irish did finally lose in Dublin, to Dublin University at College Park, by six points to three. Colin Gibson was one of several players who turned out in all three games in the 72-hour period.

One of the Exiles' try-scorers against Lansdowne was a Canadian inter-

ABOVE: A much-prized honours cap, won by Con Griffin for 1st XV back play in 1937–38 (© Jack Kay)

LEFT: Another quiet night in prospect: dinner at Trinity College for the visiting London Irishmen in 1932

Niall Woods, the prolific Irish points-scoring wing who amassed a total of 330 points for the club between 1996 and 1998 (© Michael Peel)

Irish captain Conor O'Shea, whose inspirational play and determination in joining the line have been features of the Exiles' performances in recent years (© Michael Peel)

Kent-born prop Peter Rogers, who established his reputation with the Gauteng Lions, shows the form for Irish early in the 1998–99 season which attracted the attention of Welsh coach Graham Henry. Unfortunately, a serious knee injury suffered in the match against Richmond set back the influential forward (© Michael Peel)

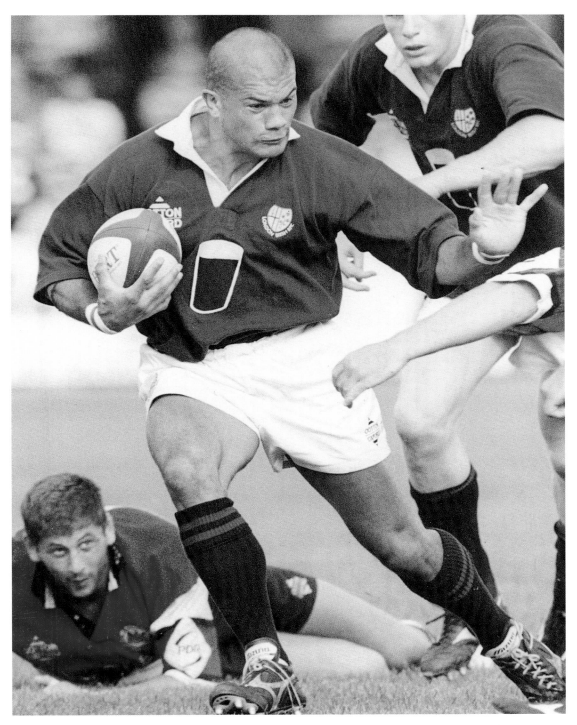

The New Zealand attitude creeps into Sunbury. Auckland-born centre Robert Todd wards off all comers during the Exiles' opening match of the 1998–99 season at Gloucester. Irish lost 29–22 (© Michael Peel)

Australian forward Nick Harvey, who has been so influential a figure for the Irish, in action against Gloucester in the Premiership (© Michael Peel)

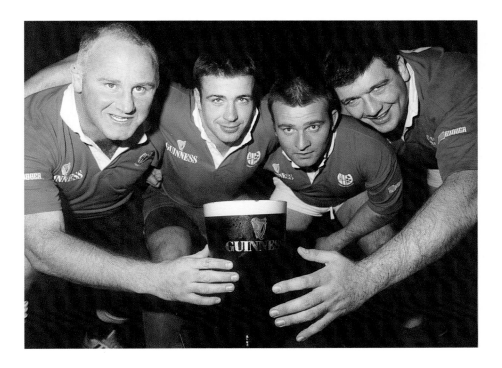

TOP: 'Oi, buy yer own!' Gary Halpin and pals protect valued property

BOTTOM: Kieron Dawson on the charge for the Exiles. The Bangor-born flanker has three international caps for Ireland (© Michael Peel)

The Exiles' international scrum-half Rob Saunders fires out a pass against Richmond in a club match at the start of the 1990s (© Phil Brown)

Scrum-half Kieran Campbell, who helped Ireland to victory in the Youth World Cup in France in April 1998, has already made his mark at Sunbury (© Michael Peel)

LEFT: Justin Bishop's form in the last couple of months of the 1997–98 season helped keep the Exiles in the Premiership and earned him his first Ireland international caps on their tour of South Africa in the summer of 1998
(© Michael Peel)

RIGHT: New Zealand-born back-row forward Isaac Fea'unati, who made a stirring impression immediately he arrived at Sunbury but suffered a severe knee ligament injury in the final match of the 1997–98 season and missed the early months of the following campaign
(© Michael Peel)

Catch 'em young: junior fans get a close-up view of the action at Sunbury (© Jack Kay)

Another win in the bag! A young Irish fan celebrates at Sunbury (© Jack Kay)

Robin Thompson (at centre rear of photo), later to lead the 1955 British Lions in South Africa, in action for London Irish against Trinity College, Dublin, at Blackheath.

national right wing, George Puil, who had joined the club that season. Paul MacWeeney wrote of him in the Lansdowne match, 'The Irish midfield backs were useful in attack and defence, but the best runner was the Canadian right wing G. Puil, who scored a gem of a try.'

Puil was no size at all, but he was a magnificent runner who had played American football and possessed a tremendous side-step. He scored six tries in his first 11 appearances in the Irish 1st XV, was awarded the honours cap for 1st XV backs in season 1953–54, and appeared in the final Irish trial, a very considerable achievement.

Colin Gibson, a qualified pharmacist who could also perform at outside-half, played four seasons for the club, himself winning the backs' 1st XV honours cap the season after Puil. He remembers London Irish at that time as a club filled with great characters, especially Bill Morgan.

'We went to the West Country one Saturday, I think to play Bath. Bill Morgan and John Donnelly used to stand at the ticket barrier at Paddington station and

Ronnie Thompson captaining the Irish. 'Bish' Gallagher is in the front row, extreme left.

count the players on to the train. When the whistle went, 14 had turned up but Michael Archer, the Cambridge blue who was a medical student, was missing. Morgan was beside himself with fury, smoke coming out of his ears the whole way down there. We eventually arrived, were walking out of the station and suddenly Archer appeared. He had dived into the guard's van, the last carriage, as the train pulled out of Paddington. But he couldn't get forward because it was not a connecting carriage. Bill Morgan was a delightful mixture of relief at seeing him and fury from three hours of saying what he was going to do to him!'

Results continued to be inconsistent. Season 1953–54 brought 14 wins, 14 defeats and three draws in 31 matches; 1954–55 ended with 16 defeats in 29 games, with only 11 wins. The club had three internationals on its books that season and, intriguingly, no mention whatsoever was made in Bill Morgan's end-of-year review of the honour awarded to a former London Irish player, Robin Thompson, who was invited to captain the British Lions in South Africa in 1955. The reason for that was simple – as soon as he returned, Thompson turned professional for a fee reputed to be £5,000, a decision which shocked the rugby establishment.

Years later, Sir David Orr said of Thompson, 'He was very good indeed as a captain and was an outstanding fellow, a really nice man. He was very happy at London Irish and it was a shame he disappeared from the game as he did. He made a great mistake in going professional; by doing so, he lost a lot of friends and influence.'

But by then the club had begun to acquire the nucleus of a squad of players who would come together and achieve the finest season London Irish Rugby Football Club would achieve in all its first hundred years. Just around the corner from the street where steady, dreary rain had fallen for some time, a bright sun was about to shine.

London Irish

R.F.C.

Programme

THE RECTORY FIELD, BLACKHEATH

Price 3d.

London Irish Rugby Football Club

Annual Dinner

at

The Connaught Rooms

on

Saturday, 2nd January, 1954

Chairman:
W. S. Foley, Esq., President

CHAPTER TEN

'Anything That Moves, Hit It!'

'I believe the right question to ask,
respecting all ornament, is simply this:
Was it done with enjoyment –
was the carver happy while he was about it?'

JOHN RUSKIN, 1819–1900

The building blocks for the near-impregnable castle London Irish erected at the end of the 1950s had been put in place as far back as the 1954–55 season, when certain players began to appear in the 1st XV lists. Principal among these was A.A. Mulligan, then an 18-year-old youngster just out of Gresham's school, Norfolk, a scrum-half about whom very good judges were becoming extremely excited. A slim, elegant scrum-half whose 5ft 10in, 11st 8lbs frame contained a strong heart and a readiness for the physical fray, Mulligan had forged a reputation on the schools circuit as a player who was a dangerous runner and breaker from the scrum with a fine, fast pass. There wasn't a lot he couldn't do, in fact.

And, of course, he had the passion for the sport from the start. Even today, he can remember plastering his bedroom wall at Gresham's with pictures of the great Jack Kyle. The dream was to come true, too: Mulligan played his first two internationals for Ireland inside the immortal Kyle, before the latter retired. 'He was still a magnificent player, had wonderful hands and incredible modesty,' remembers Mulligan.

It would be unfair to say that London Irish rushed Andrew Armstrong Mulligan into their 1st XV in those days. It was surely just mere coincidence that the Indian-born scrum-half (whose father, a specialist in tropical diseases, had been working on the subcontinent) made his debut for the club's senior side in the very first match of the 1954–55 season, against United Services, Portsmouth, at Blackheath, just a couple of months after he had finished at school. But then, he knew London Irish; he'd played in their Christmas holiday schoolboys' teams and had been noticed as a rare talent. 'From 16 to 18, I'd played in that schools side run by Bill Keegan, whose son John became a military historian. So my first year at Irish was 1952–53, when I was 16.'

Mulligan announced his arrival with the first London Irish try of the day in their 19–12 victory. He was one of those players who comes along once in a generation. An O'Reilly, an Edwards, a John, a Maso, a Gibson; players to make the heart race with excitement at their genius and quality. Footballers with class written all over them. From London Irish's point of view, though, they could never get enough appearances out of the man, because – roughly in this order – Cambridge University, Ireland, the British Lions, the Barbarians, Ulster, the Public School Wanderers and assorted others were always trying to persuade him to wear their shirt.

He went up to Magdalene College, Cambridge, in September 1955 and won his blue as a freshman, in a side that contained such renowned rugby international names as J.G.G. Hetherington, A.R. Smith, R.W.D. Marques, J.W. Clements and A.J. Herbert. No matter, Oxford beat them, and with the likes of M.J.K. Smith and D.O. Brace at half-back, J.D. Currie at lock and P.G.D. Robbins in the back row, maybe it wasn't a surprise. Such quality, though, such talent; Oxbridge rugby men nowadays would kill for half of them.

Mulligan won two blues and, by repute, his telephone would be ringing the morning after each Varsity match. It would be Bill Morgan on the phone from London Irish, asking him if he was available for the club that next Saturday.

They needed him, all right, this confident, polished young man who could play the flowing game but also dog it out on a mud-heap if need be and prove himself just as effective. Season 1955–56 brought 16 defeats and two draws from 30 games, yet the statistic was a shade misleading. Some fine players were beginning to make their mark, like a young full-back Micky Byrne, who had been born in London in 1933 but then sent to Dublin to be educated at Blackrock College. He had first appeared in the Exiles 1st XV on Easter Saturday 1953, but had gradually established a reputation as a fine footballer, solid enough in defence and sparkling when an attacking opportunity arose.

By then, too, Tom Reid had returned from the 1955 Lions tour of South Africa a proven Test-match lock forward. Micky Byrne remembered Reid as a former Gaelic footballer 'who handled so well, and did an awful lot of work. He was a lovely bloke, so kind-hearted.'

By then, Irish were denied Thompson's presence by his decision to turn professional, and they wouldn't have Tom Reid's services for too much longer either. He went on the Barbarians tour of Canada in 1958, seemed distracted about things towards the end of the tour, and when a team-mate put his head around his door on the morning of their flight home, expecting Reid to be all packed and ready, the big, genial lock was lying stretched out on the bed, examining the ceiling.

'Come on, get your things, we're leaving on the bus soon,' he was told.

'I'm not coming. Yer go without me.'

'Don't be daft. Get packed.'

'I tell yer, I'm not coming. I've met a woman, I'm in love and I'm staying here forever.'

And he did. But what a player he had been. And could have been, says Terry O'Connor, former rugby correspondent for the *Daily Mail* in London, and a visitor to London Irish whenever the opportunity arose. 'If Reid had played in this era he would have been a fantastic player. But he was never fit, although that changed briefly during that 1955 Lions tour. He was an unbelievable man and character.'

Ireland had, by now, also capped Jimmy Ritchie in their back row, making him captain on his debut, and Mulligan at scrum-half, the pair coincidentally making their international debuts in the same match, against France at Stade Colombes on 28 January 1956. France won 14–8 and Ritchie was to last only one more game, against England, that season. Mulligan, by contrast, was in the early spring of a magnificent international career.

There were others, too. J. Murphy-O'Connor, who had won an Irish cap in 1954 against England while with Bective Rangers, had come to London and joined the club; L. Crowe, the Old Belvedere wing who had three international caps from the 1950 season, was there, and so too was P.J. Kavanagh, a back-row forward out of UCD. Kavanagh's international debut, against England at Twickenham in 1952, was played on 29 March, having been postponed from 9 February owing to the death of King George VI.

There were plenty of other good players around too, forwards such as Brown, Gallagher, Brennan, McCarthy and the Cambridge blues McRoberts and H.D. Doherty, plus Tommy Tranter, a player with a tough reputation and the focus of many stories. But in later years Tranter insisted, 'I played a very hard, robust type of game but a fair one, which was the way I was taught during my school days in Warrington, Lancashire, where the popular game is rugby league. This was the basis of my rugby. I came from a very strong league family – my uncle was captain of Warrington, Lancashire and England – so you can see where my hard, robust game came from.'

There were, too, three-quarters like the 1955 Oxford blue T.J. Fallon, Archer, Craig, Creaven and Power, a strong, quick scrum-half who was invaluable when Mulligan was unavailable. But one other player at the club made as big a name for himself in that period as others who achieved many more caps. His name was Sean McDermott. A short, chunky, red-haired Irishman, McDermott was a fine player who was so versatile he could, and did, play class rugby at scrum-half, fly-half, centre and full-back. In the autumn of 1953, he made so good an impression while playing at scrum-half for the English Southern

Counties against the touring New Zealand All Blacks that the Irish national selectors were alerted to his talents. Within two years he had been chosen for the Irish team against Scotland and Wales. Andy Mulligan said of him, 'Sean was not a particularly good passer of the ball nor a great breaker, but he kicked very well with both feet, had plenty of courage and was a natural footballer.'

His debut against the Scots at Murrayfield in a losing Irish side contained some astonishing moments of classic 'McDermott-isms'. Herbie McKee, who was with the Irish from 1949 to 1958, remembers McDermott as a stickler for quick ball from his forwards. 'He would keep on at them to give him the ball as fast as possible; he felt he could only play with fast possession. The Irish pack at Murrayfield clearly hadn't got the message. They took an age to recycle possession at one breakdown, and when McDermott was at last fed it, he promptly booted it straight back into the mêlée of forwards, shouting at them, "That's useless! I don't know who picked you lot, but you're all hopeless."'

If there was someone around likely to do something completely irrational, then it was McDermott. In April 1957, London Irish went north for an Easter tour which included a match against Fylde. The home club had played Saracens the day before and put 45 points on them, which the Irish boys thought was in poor taste on an Easter weekend. Suddenly, a match which had little value assumed the importance of a full-blown international.

It wasn't the fact that London Irish put seven tries on the locals which caused such raised eyebrows. When McDermott stepped up to attempt the first conversion, he deliberately aimed low at the corner flag and sent the ball skidding into the crowd. He did it three more times, to astonished laughter from the locals. But the joke died on their faces when they realised Irish were taking the rise. They won 30–3.

Irish had lost seven of their first ten matches that season, but by a dramatic improvement from thereon, including victories over Richmond, Bath and the RAF, they finished the season strongly, winning 16 of their last 18 matches, for a points aggregate of 352–231. Overall, they achieved 22 wins from 33 matches, and Bill Morgan could write in his review of the season:

With an excellent pack admirably led by the captain T.A. Gallagher and containing three internationals, Robin Roe, T.E. Reid and J.S. Ritchie, and a young, fast backline including internationals S.J. McDermott at scrum-half and J.G.M.W. Murphy at full-back (he won five caps between 1951 and 1958), the whole side was an extremely good one.

In the 1955–56 season, London Irish lost a long and devoted servant of the club, one of their vice-presidents Harry Barry. His association with the club stretched back to those difficult early years after the First World War in 1920, and he served them as captain of the 'B' XV, team secretary and then fixture secretary. His influence in the last role was made obvious by the quality of opponents queuing up to meet London Irish. In 1956–57, the powerful Waterloo club from Lancashire intimated that a fixture was long overdue.

Jimmy Ritchie, captain in 1955–56, remembers, 'We had a very good team coming together, with some marvellous characters, like Sean McDermott, who was a headcase! Bish Gallagher, for example, might not have been a great player but, by God, he was such a character that he made the team gel. He could infuse a side with his own enthusiasm and players responded to him. He was also as strong as an ox, a really well-built fellow. With players like that, we played a fiery sort of game, and any forwards we met, we took apart. I'd give a team talk

Tom Reid (right, dark shirt), another of London Irish's 1955 Lions, in action for the club against Harlequins at Twickenham, 1956.

as captain and my favourite expression was, "Anything that moves, hit it!" The boys, in particular Tom Reid, usually did.

'And then you had Bill Morgan, who was in charge of playing matters in those days and would come out and watch you training. You'd be aching to get into the showers and finish and Morgan would stand there and say, "Do another circuit of the ground. I want to see you move!"

'It was a very happy side, and when I look back, I can only say to myself, "You were damn lucky to be there."'

Bill Morgan: ah, yes, remembers Brendan Quirke, with that familiar impish grin spread across his face. 'A tyrant, a benevolent despot. The only committee he believed in was a committee of one. He was a hard nut, no silver-tongued figure. He was blunt and took no nonsense.'

Quirke encountered the man with the best qualifications for the title 'Mr London Irish' when he joined the club in 1946. He was working in London, but became the first post-war deportee sent back to Dublin because he did not have a work permit. He reappeared 12–18 months later when his papers had been sorted, and remembers a unique welcome which Brendan Quin, who was secretary just after the war, always laid on for new members. 'He would take the trouble to seek you out, buy you a glass of beer and say how he hoped you would enjoy your rugby at London Irish. He was a wonderful man, with a marvellous stentorian voice, who would stalk the touchline.' Bill Pedlow remembers that voice to this day. 'When he shouted at Sunbury, I should think they heard it over at Twickenham.'

But Quin was a hugely popular figure, who became president in 1947–48. Tall and elegant, he would rap on the ceiling of Fitz's bar, the wooden shack at the bottom of the ground at Sunbury in those days, for the chattering classes to shut up when he had an announcement to make. He was the only one allowed to do so by Fitzy, who was a complete contrast to Quin in terms of size.

At one time, Brendan Quirke had played for every side in the club, at outside-half or on the wing, although a lot of the time he was in the Wild Geese. He got his big chance in the 1st XV one Saturday in January 1948, amid bizarre circumstances. There was a doubt about whether Kevin

A cartoon depicting Brendan Quin tapping the ceiling for silence in Fitz's bar. He was said to be the only one allowed to do so!

O'Flanagan would be able to play, although he had been on Bill Morgan's original team selection. O'Flanagan used to try and juggle the conflicting demands of rugby for London Irish and football for Arsenal. It was not always a successful trick, although he was a fine player at both codes. Bernard Joy, later to become soccer correspondent of the *London Evening Standard*, was one of his team-mates at Arsenal around that time.

THE WILD GEESE

Why was it necessary to put a name to a club's 2nd XV and what were the origins of the name 'Wild Geese'?

In 1951, a trend emerged at several clubs to name their reserve side. Richmond called theirs 'The Vikings', the London Welsh 2nd XV became known as 'The Druids' and Blackheath's were called 'The Blackheathans'.

The name 'Wild Geese' dates back to the late seventeenth century. Robert Kee's excellent book *Ireland: A History* records:

The raising of the siege [of Derry] then led to the eventual total defeat of James II in Ireland. William of Orange landed at Carrickfergus Castle the next year, 1690, and won great victories in battles at the Boyne and at Aughrim. In 1691 all the Catholic armies in Ireland totally surrendered at Limerick, under their Old English-Gaelic Catholic commander Patrick Sarsfield. He and thousands of his troops were allowed to go into exile to serve in the armies of Louis XIV and became known as 'Wild Geese'.

Bill Morgan had phoned up Quirke on the Friday evening and barked, 'Be at Waterloo station in the morning. If O'Flanagan doesn't arrive, you'll play.' Quirke remembers, 'I got there on the Saturday and we all waited around but O'Flanagan never appeared, so we got on the train for Aldershot and I assumed I was in the team against the Services side. But it turned out that O'Flanagan was waiting to join us at Surbiton. The only problem was, the train went straight through there, although we saw this extraordinary sight of O'Flanagan running down the platform, shouting and waving his boots.' Bill Morgan observed the unsavoury scene with complete distaste and snorted, 'Quirke, you're in!'

The match was a 6–6 draw, following a Todd try for Irish together with a Tommy Headon penalty goal. It wasn't the strongest London Irish side that day, but with characters such as Gallagher, Headon, McGuirk, Quirke and Pedlow, it was bound to be entertaining. Terry O'Connor said of Gallagher, 'He was an intellect, a man of

Lunch in New York: (from left) Andy Mulligan, Frank Shields (father of Brooke) and Tom Gallagher.

great distinction. He had a very deep, booming voice and was highly gregarious.'

Gallagher, whose father was a schoolmaster in Tullamore, formed a partnership for a PR/advertising agency in London, Gallagher Smail, that became highly successful. He was then head-hunted to become boss of the huge Doyle, Dane and Bernbach company in New York. He was such a fantastic personality that he went on to become the president of the company in the USA, became a millionaire and retired to the Bahamas.

O'Connor added, 'He was a personality beyond belief. He had one of the biggest houses in Bermuda but got himself excluded from a yacht club for being drunk. He was an unbelievable vodka drinker and during his days with London Irish could stay up drinking until three in the morning and then turn up sober for a meeting in the morning. Ollie Waldron, who knew a thing or two about the club and its characters, said that Gallagher was worth $10 million at one time.'

Alas, 'Bish' Gallagher was to die far, far too early, largely from alcohol abuse. It was to be a sad end for a great man. Andy Mulligan remembered one social occasion with 'The Bish': 'I think it was the Monday after my debut for London Irish's first team, a match in which I had scored a try. "Bish" was there with Patrick Campbell, that very funny Irish guy, and we met in a private room at a restaurant somewhere in Soho. That day I was introduced, at the age of 18, to my first five-hour lunch. That reflected the times we lived in, but also the personality of "The Bish". Most of the guys played rugby then to sweat the drink out. But all that changed in the late 1950s.'

Because he played for so many of the lower teams, Brendan Quirke came to appreciate deeply the social side of the club. 'Tommy Headon was a lovely singer and many others were too. The evenings were tremendous – nobody said "I'm going to dinner now" or "I'm taking my girlfriend out".'

Many of the songs emanated from the witty pen of Dr Cormac Swann, a GP who was also a gifted lyricist, writing plays and contributing wonderful lyrics for songs. The first verse of one of them, set to the tune of 'Galway Bay', ran:

I don't know why I joined the London Irish,
My mother was half Spanish and half Dutch;
I don't know if I ever had a father,
Mother doesn't talk about him too much.

Quirke swears blind that the subject of one of the best ever jokes told about London Irish was the Kerryman Michael O'Connor, a solicitor in London who was to become president of the club years later, from 1976 to 1981. The tale goes that many club members and officials gathered at Sunbury one Saturday afternoon, as they were wont to do in the 1960s once the new pavilion had gone up, to watch an Ireland international from Lansdowne Road live on television. The noise and general hubbub of the bar was making it difficult for some to hear the TV. At the height of the noise, Ireland were awarded a penalty and their kicker prepared for a pot at goal. The noise in the bar back in Sunbury was suddenly silenced when someone right beside the television stood up and shouted out excitedly, 'Would yer be kind enough to be quiet and give yer man a chance with his kick!'

What has London Irish meant to Brendan Quirke? 'I would never have thought of playing for another club. I was totally at home here. I took a year or two out in the mid-'60s to help run the Law Society RFC, a junior club, after I'd stopped playing around 1962. But I soon came back. It's difficult to imagine those times 40 years later. All the clubs were more "clubby", in a way, than they are today; people stayed on afterwards. It wasn't being anti-feminist, but for a while girlfriends were just regarded as being in the way.'

Quirke was asked one day if he would fill a role vacant because Jimmy Ritchie, who had by then retired, had fallen ill and could not attend a game. It was to be the start of an association which enhanced London Irish's reputation as a club forever with a broad smile upon its face. Quirke on the public address system was one of the afternoon's pleasures down at London Irish. 'I did it in the end for 20 years, and thoroughly enjoyed it.'

So did a lot of others, for his witticisms became legendary. But, mind you, it could be a tricky task too.

'We played Wasps five or six years ago down here. It was a nice day and there was a big crowd. They put 50 or so points on us, and when Rob Andrew

Irish at the Rectory Field, Blackheath, under 'Bish' Gallagher's captaincy.

converted a try, someone threw another ball on to the pitch. I said who had scored the try and converted it, and then added, "Some masochist has just thrown a ball on to the pitch." I was having a drink in the bar later when our full-back Jim Staples came up to me. "Listen," he said, his fist raised. "I'm not going to hit you because you're too old, but if you can't think of anything better to say than that, don't say anything." I didn't resent him saying it – what really hurt was him saying he wouldn't hit me because I was too old! But I think I was aware that you should never try to make a cabaret on the microphone. You can be too clever by half, and people out there can't answer back.'

Quirke was involved in the incident when a gunman tried to kidnap HRH Princess Anne in the Mall one evening in March 1974. He was in a taxi with the journalist Brian McConnell and some other friends when the car they were following was suddenly forced to stop by another. Shots then rang out. 'All hell broke loose,' remembers Quirke. McConnell was shot, as were the Princess's personal detective, the chauffeur and a police officer who was nearby. 'It wasn't very funny at the time, except that I remember the taxi driver, a man named Ian Pink, turning to me in the middle of it all, with a terrified expression on his face, and saying, "My God! What will the police say when they find I've had five up in the cab?"'

CHAPTER ELEVEN

A Crucial Meeting

'And broader still became the blaze, and louder still the din,
As fast from every village round the horse came spurring in;
And eastward straight from wild Blackheath the warlike errand went,
And roused in many an ancient hall the gallant squires of Kent.'

LORD MACAULAY, 1800–59

A dream move it might have seemed at the time, but the doubts concerning London Irish's residence at faraway Blackheath for all 1st XV home games were beginning to surface as early as 1956–57. It had become, by then, probably a question of moving the dream once again. David Orr, who had joined the club in 1950 when he came to London from Trinity College, Dublin, had played for Trinity against London Irish at the Rectory Field and had always had doubts about the venture.

'Unwisely, in my view, the club went to Blackheath for prestige reasons,' said Sir David in 1998. 'But it was rather unfortunate we were to stay there so long. Sunbury was way out in the sticks just after the war when the decision was made to relocate. But in a sense it didn't seem that critical.

'The *raison d'être* of the club was what mattered. It was always very good because people from all backgrounds and all religious affiliations mingled happily together under the London Irish jersey. It was a very good influence in the community, and we have all done our best through the years to boost that community spirit.'

Stan McRoberts shared criticism of the decision to go to Blackheath. 'In my view, it was a great mistake, both to share with another club and also to separate our junior sides from the 1st XV.'

They went to the Rectory Field for two basic reasons: the high cost of developing Sunbury into a ground worthy of a first-class club, and the opportunity to create that rugby centre of excellence. It was felt that the Rectory Field would become *the* centre for London rugby, which could only be beneficial to London Irish.

But in May 1957, Bill Morgan said in his review of the season:

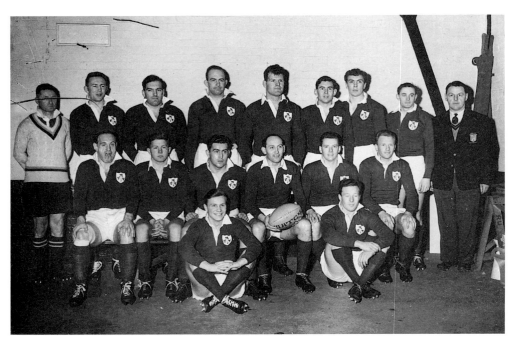

Four London Irish players in the 1956 Irish national side against England:
Jimmy Ritchie (captain), Robin Roe, Tom Reid and Andy Mulligan. The match ended
England 20, Ireland 0.

> *Our lease at the Rectory Field terminates at the end of April 1959. This means that we*
> *have two more full playing seasons at Blackheath. Your committee therefore have*
> *considered ways and means whereby our ground at Sunbury can be developed and*
> *made into a first-class playing condition with a stand and accommodation required to*
> *keep the club's present first-class standard a permanent one.*
>
> *A finance committee comprising our president with W.S. (Bill) Foley, T.A. Headon*
> *and P. Kelly has been appointed to deal with the financial problems which beset us here*
> *. . . So far it is estimated that it will cost £1,000–£1,200 to achieve what the club has*
> *in mind – a large sum of money to collect, and also a large sum to repay.*

So a very large, extremely deep begging bowl began to be passed around
London Irish RFC circles. Some members sniffed with a mixture of disdain and
delight. 'When we moved to Blackheath, we paid only £250 a year in rent. But
then the fee went up to £1,000 a year, and that was bad business,' said Albert
Hill.

Also, there was a feeling that bar profits on 'London Irish nights' were
keeping Blackheath in profit, because they were nowhere near as healthy for

their own home games. Blackheath chaps quietly sipping their G and Ts were unlikely to match the consumption of Irishmen lining up pint after pint of the black stuff, like attendants forever replacing skittles in a bowling alley. Some members had begun grumbling about giving all the profits to the Blackheath club. Terry O'Connor saw matches played by both clubs at the famous Rectory Field; you could tell which club was playing that week just by walking into the pavilion bar, he said. 'It was an amazing contrast, with Blackheath one week, London Irish the next. It was an entirely different scene: even a defeat, the Irish turned into a party.'

One of the prime movers for a relocation back to Sunbury, thereby enabling the whole club to settle together in one place, had been the Earl of Courtown OBE, who was president from 1956 to 1958. The crucial meeting which would decide the issue one way or the other was held in a room at the Crown pub in Brewer Street, in the heart of London's theatre land and close to the Windmill. But, in true London Irish tradition, an element of mystique hung over the outcome of that decision.

Colin Gibson, who was at the vital committee meeting, said, 'It was a simple choice. Did we accept the new, higher rent at Blackheath or return to Sunbury to redevelop? The decision was taken by a vote of 11–10 to go our own way. But I remember Paddy Kelly came down to the bar afterwards and said, "I don't know how we got that vote when there were 22 people up there." Bill Morgan went round the table and came up with a result that did not marry with the number of people there.' As that renowned London Irish member Spike Milligan used to joke during his Goon days when asked bleeding obvious mathematical questions, 'Ooh, the hard ones first!'

A BRAZIL NUT

London Irish men have laid claim to some astonishing feats through the years. But one of them, Colin Gibson, who played in the 1st XV in the early 1950s and was captain of the Wild Geese in season 1953–54, went on to become captain of . . . Brazil.

Gibson, who was working for Shell, led the South American country in a match against Uruguay in Montevideo after he had left the Irish in 1956. He was later moved to Hong Kong and also represented the British colony with whom he toured Vietnam in 1961, to play matches against the French. 'Saigon in those days was very sophisticated, like Lebanon before the civil war. The food was marvellous,' he remembers.

Had Morgan been in favour of relocation, you could have understood it. After all, as men like Des O'Brien and a succession of 1st XV captains after him wearily conceded, what Morgan wanted, Morgan usually got. Yet in this case he was in favour of staying at Blackheath. And you'd surely expect a bank manager to be able to count up to 22.

Cautious and conservative and a bank manager down to his thick, woolly winter socks, Morgan felt the economics of staying at Blackheath were more than satisfactory. He expressed considerable doubts as to whether the finances of building a new stand at Sunbury were practical, and he had a point. Raising the kind of money required – it was estimated to be around £20,000 but ended up being more than £25,000 – was no easy thing in those days, although a very great deal of donated Irish labour helped out on the project. Wimpey's were the official builders, and everyone held their breath about the finances once the project started. But at the RFU there was much angst over the money they eventually loaned the Irish for some of the project. 'It will prove to be our first bad debt,' sniffed one committeeman, laconically. Bill Morgan sensed it was too ambitious and told the meeting as much but, most unusually, what Bill Morgan said did not go. Not that night, anyway.

So it was decided to return to Sunbury, and frantic efforts ensued to raise some capital as the down payment for loans to build a stand which needed to be completed by the autumn of 1959. The design would be done by Des Hennessey, a club member. A brochure produced for the creation of the new stand explained:

Faced with the prospect of an increasing flow of young players from schools and universities in coming years, and with the need to cater for large numbers of non-playing members and supporters and also encouraged by the success of its teams in recent years, the club has decided that now is the time to establish a permanent home at its own ground at Sunbury-on-Thames, soon to be linked with the West End of London by a new arterial road. The object is to provide three well-drained playing pitches, a pavilion incorporating seating for 500 spectators and also a standing terrace, first-class changing and bathing accommodation, an adequate tea and supper room, and a bar and club-room which will be the envy of London. There will be a new car park.

The total bill will be over £20,000, but to budget for less at present-day prices would entail a legacy of inadequate and unworthy accommodation for the future London Irish, who will in any case have to share in repayment of any loans. At the moment, £4,000 is being spent under the draining and levelling contract for which the Rugby Union has generously provided a loan. The project will require by September a further £14,000. Donations from firms and individuals at present total about £1,000; in addition, £2,000 is due from loss of development rights, leaving £11,000 outstanding. The present income of the club is about £2,000 per annum but there is little doubt that this will rise when the club is settled at Sunbury, to about £3,000 per annum, which would justify further borrowing.

It is fascinating to compare such figures with those of today, such as the estimated £40,000 taken in bar receipts alone after the famous 62–14 Premiership win over Harlequins at the ground in May 1998. And, come to think of it, the estimated £5 million debt incurred by Harlequins in one of the early seasons of professionalism to erect their new stand at The Stoop.

In the meantime, season 1957–58, the second year under the captaincy of 'Bish' Gallagher, proved to be outstandingly successful for the 1st XV, with 20 wins and four draws in 30 matches, including good victories over sides such as Northampton, Richmond, London Scottish and London Welsh, Bath, Blackheath and Harlequins. Gallagher himself was injured in the match against Old Alleynians in January and could not play again during the season. McDermott took over as captain and, said Bill Morgan, led the team with skill and good judgement. Any club selecting two such extraordinary characters as 'Bish' Gallagher and Sean McDermott as its captains in a single season could scarcely be labelled boring or predictable. And slowly, inexorably, the bricks were being put into place for what would happen in 1959–60.

On the grand project for Sunbury, Bill Morgan told the Annual General Meeting in May 1958:

Sean McDermott, seated with ball, captains the talented Exiles side of the late 1950s.

This project is very ambitious, and we appeal to you to put your best foot forward towards assisting. Every member of this club is requested to do everything possible, and any suggestions will be greatly appreciated, especially towards the raising of capital which presents the outstanding difficulty at the moment. Our architect Desmond Hennessy has worked unsparingly on our behalf towards dealing with the difficulties presented by the various councils and the Ministry, and he has got over many of these difficulties with success. Without his assistance and excellent knowledge about these matters, it would not be possible to make any adequate progress, and as a mark of appreciation to him your committee have elected him an honorary life member of the club.

As the season closed, the club looked, as usual, for an increased number of members for the following season. Subscriptions were as follows:

- Country members £1.
- Non-playing members £3.
- Playing members £4.
- Playing members (Under-21) £2.
- Life members £15 15s.

Meanwhile, on the playing front, Micky Byrne had by now come through as a valuable member of the 1st XV. As a 19-year-old back in Ireland, Byrne had had the privilege of playing in a match against the great Jack Kyle. 'I was scared witless and quite overawed,' he remembers of a day of knocking knees and sweaty palms. Byrne went off for his National Service almost immediately after joining Irish and did not establish himself as a first-teamer until the 1954–55 season. Thereafter he was to play regularly, right through to 1966, when he finally finished, by then having made more than 320 first-team appearances and established himself as one of the club's greatest ever servants. The humble tankard with which he was presented in October 1965 on the occasion of his 300th appearance still stands proudly in his home back in Cork.

But by no means all of Byrne's games were at full-back, his usual position. The reason for this was the arrival of two other distinguished full-backs of the period. Paddy Berkery, the Lansdowne player who won 11 caps for Ireland between 1954 and 1958, was the first, and J.G.M.W. Murphy, first capped as Ireland's full-back in 1952 against Scotland while playing for Dublin University, also joined. Murphy ('He was full of initials,' jokes Byrne) had pursued his religious teachings in Africa but returned to Europe in the late 1950s and was recalled to the Irish national side in 1958 for the match against Wales. It was to be his sixth and last cap.

Juggling around three full-backs of high quality within the same team might have been expected to tax even the cunning and ingenuity of Bill Morgan. But, true to form, the man sorted it out. Byrne recalls, 'At one time, Gerry Murphy was the Middlesex county full-back, Paddy Berkery was Surrey's full-back and I was full-back for Eastern Counties. And somehow they used to fit us all into the Exiles side. When Gerry arrived, he got the full-back slot, Paddy was moved to the centre and I played on the right wing.'

Morgan, of course, remained a man not to be trifled with. But, as Byrne said, 'He was the mortar in the cement. The club would have gone way down but for him.'

THE REPORTER'S VIEW

Respected Irish rugby writer Ned Van Esbeck first saw London Irish in the 1950s when they visited Dublin. Van Esbeck, rugby correspondent for the *Irish Times* from 1968 until his retirement in 1997, remembers, 'There was an aura about them. They were known as "our friends abroad". And when I came to work in London for ten years from the late 1950s, I was always made so welcome at Sunbury.

'Bill Morgan, "Mr London Irish", was a real authoritarian. I had a good relationship with him but I'm not sure how he would have come across to people who didn't know him that well. But he lived, slept and drank London Irish. It was his life, and his contribution was immense.

'I remember reporting a London Irish match against Bristol and Irish got hammered 35–3 at Sunbury. My report appeared in the *Daily Telegraph*, and Bill phoned me up. "How unfair you are to London Irish," he said.

'Given that any score over 30 points was unbelievable in those days, and that it might easily have been 50, I said I thought it was perfectly fair. "The scoreline was totally false!" he replied.

'Sunbury was a great Irish centre and they served a great Irish purpose in that way. I always enjoyed my visits there. There was a great spirit and affinity at the club; the atmosphere was never too weighty. But I don't think the present London Irish club bears any relationship to the London Irish I knew. Don't get me wrong, there are still some great people there. But I believe professionalism has done irreparable damage to clubs like London Irish. The central ethic has been changed irrevocably, and we won't ever get it back. Rugby has lost something very special, in my view.

'But London Irish have made a great contribution to Irish rugby, and that must not be forgotten. They provided a real home for guys leaving Ireland, and they also produced some marvellous players.'

BLACKHEATH FIXTURES 1958-59

1958	K.O.	Opponents	
Sept. 20		OLD MERCHANT TAYLORS	Won 20-3 Away
27	3.00	GUY'S HOSPITAL	Won 44-0 Home
Oct. 4		BIRKENHEAD PARK	Lost 14-17 Away
11	3.00	NEWPORT	Won 6-5 Home
18	3.00	LONDON SCOTTISH	Lost 3-9 Home
25		LLANELLY	Lost 6-18 Away
Nov. 1	2.45	SWANSEA	Lost 3-5 Home
8		OXFORD UNIVERSITY	Lost 5-8 Away
15	2.45	CAMBRIDGE UNIVERSITY	Lost 3-12 Home
22		NEATH	Lost 6-17 Away
29		COVENTRY	Lost 3-15 Away
Dec. 6		HARLEQUINS	Won 44-3 Away
13	2.30	LEICESTER	Won 3-0 Home
20	2.00	RICHMOND (CENTENARY)	Lost 6-8 Home
26	2.30	OXFORD AND CAMBRIDGE	Won 17-14 Home
27		WASPS	Won 3-0 Away
1959			
Jan. 3	2.30	ROSSLYN PARK	Won 13-8 Home
10	2.30	HARLEQUINS	Home
17		LONDON SCOTTISH	Away
24	2.30	ROYAL NAVY	Home
31	2.30	ST. MARY'S HOSPITAL	Home
Feb. 7	2.45	LONDON IRISH	Home
14	2.45	RICHMOND	Home
21	2.45	ST. LUKES COLL.	Home
28		NEWPORT	Away
Mar. 7	3.00	NEATH	Home
14		LONDON WELSH	Away
28	3.00	BEDFORD (EASTER)	Home
		UNITED SERVICES (PORTSMOUTH)	Away
April 11	3.00	NORTHAMPTON	Home

LONDON IRISH v. BLACKHEATH

Saturday, 7th February, 1959

	LONDON IRISH		BLACKHEATH		
1 Full Back	† P. J. BERKERY	M. C. CLARKE	Full Back	1
2 R. Wing	G. W. HACKETT	M. STOKES	R. Wing	2
3 R. Centre	J. T. BAMBER	P. C. SIBLEY	R. Centre	3
4 L. Centre	D. A. POOLE	D. J. BLACKLOCKS	L. Centre	4
5 L. Wing	M. A. BYRNE	D. L. GUDGEON	L. Wing	5
6 Stand-off	†* S. J. McDERMOTT	R. VAN HEERDEN	Stand Off	6
7 Scrum	‡† A. A. MULLIGAN	P. J. DAVIES	Scrum	7
8 Forward	J. L. A. BROWN	P. T. WRIGHT	Forward	8
9 ,,	J. W. D. BARRY	D. G. WELLS	,,	9
10 ,,	S. M. McEVOY	A. D. NASH	,,	10
11 ,,	D. J. B. MICHAEL	H. R. MOORE ‡	,,	11
12 ,,	P. J. DONEGAN	C. L. J. BAILEY	,,	12
13 ,,	B. CUSSEN	J. B. WILLIAMSON *	,,	14
14 ,,	D. W. M. IRONS	E. JENKINS	,,	15
15 ,,	R. M. JOHNSTON	R. CHILDS	,,	16

* Captain † International ‡ Blue Referee : L. M. BOUNDY

Touch judge : D. G. KINSEY

To-day it is our pleasure to be "Host" to our co-tenants. Our games against Blackheath are always close encounters, as the results of the last two seasons show, when we won by 8 points to 3 and 3 points to nothing. Our opponents are enjoying a fairly good season in this their Centenary Year and though they may not have been very consistent, they have had some excellent results, such as the beating of Newport. We look forward to another hard game against them.

Since the New Year the weather has played havoc with our fixtures, but at least this has given an opportunity to some infrequent visitors to Sunbury to see the excellent work which has been done on the ground. The three pitches look in wonderful condition and should be second to none, when our 1st XV returns there next season. The building of the new stand, containing dressing rooms, bar etc., is to commence almost at once, but further funds are needed in order to complete the project as originally planned. The scheme, as set out in the Brochure, would give us one of the finest and best equipped grounds in the Country and those who wish to see this aim achieved in toto, now are asked for further financial assistance. The Treasurer Mr. G. S. Barry or any member of the Committee will be glad to give information as to how you can help by a donation or Deed of Covenant.

We congratulate A. A. Mulligan on being picked again to play for Ireland against England next Saturday.

Next Dance—14th February, 1959 at Chenil Galleries, adjoining Chelsea Town Hall.

Results: 2nd Feb. London Irish 10 points—Dublin University 6 points.

LONDON IRISH FIXTURES 1958-59

1958	K.O.	Opponents	
Sept. 6	3.15	OXFORD	Lost 1-4 Away
13	3.15	BEDFORD	Won 16-14 Away
20	3.15	UNITED SERVICES, PORTSMOUTH	17-5 Home
27	3.15	ST. THOMAS'S HOSPITAL	Won 20-3 Away
Oct. 4	3.03	BRISTOL	Lost 6-10 Home
11	3.00	WASPS	Lost 5-20 Away
18	3.00	NUNEATON	Lost 5-19 Away
25	2.45	METROPOLITAN POLICE	Won Home
Mon. 27	2.45	LANSDOWNE	Home
Nov. 1	2.45	NORTHAMPTON	Lost 14-24 Away
8	2.45	ROSSLYN PARK	Lost 3-12 Home
15	2.45	UNIVERSITY COLLEGE, DUBLIN	Won 13-3 Away
22	2.30	STREATHAM	Won 31-3 Home
29	2.30	LONDON SCOTTISH	Lost 3-5 Home
Dec. 6	2.30	RICHMOND	Won 9-0 Home
13	2.10	LONDON WELSH	Won 8-6 Away
20	2.10	RUGBY	Won 24-13 Rien's
27	2.10	BATH	Drawn 3-3 Away
1959			
Jan. 3	2.10	ALDERSHOT SERVICES	Won 12-0 Away
10	2.10	ROYAL AIR FORCE	Home
17	2.10	SARACENS	Home
24	2.45	MOSELEY	Away
31	2.45	GUY'S HOSPITAL	Away
Feb. 7	2.45	BLACKHEATH	Home
14	2.45	HARLEQUINS	Away
21	2.45	LONDON HOSPITAL	Away
Mar. 7	2.45	ST. MARY'S HOSPITAL	Away
14	2.45	OLD ALLEYNIANS	Home
28	3.00	ABERTILLERY	Away
Mon. 30	3.00	PONTYPOOL	Away
April 4	3.15	ABERAVON	Away
11	2.00	OLD MERCHANT TAYLORS	Home

One of the Exiles' last 'home' games at Blackheath. Note the combined quality of the two clubs' fixture lists.

The last London Irish season at the Rectory Field, 1958–59, under the captaincy of S.J. McDermott, produced more steady progress. Of 31 matches, 17 were won and three drawn, the best run of form coming from early December through to the end of March, when they won nine and drew two of their 12 matches. Early in the season, in September, the back-row forward Archer had broken his leg in the match at Bedford, a major loss to the side. But on the plus side, the 1955 Irish capped back-row forward D.A. MacSweeney, a strong-tackling, uncompromising player, had arrived and was becoming another valued member of the squad.

Near the end of the season there was a tough Easter tour of South Wales which produced a 3–3 draw at Ebbw Vale, a 29–8 defeat by an Abertillery side led by their British Lion Haydn Morgan and also including Alan Pask in the back row, and an upset 5–3 win at Pontypool. On the same day as the Pontypool game,

Andy Mulligan was helping the Barbarians follow their Easter Saturday victory at Cardiff with an 18–11 win at Swansea.

Mulligan's value to London Irish, whenever he could spare the time to play, was underlined by a report of the club's 10–6 win over Trinity College, Dublin, on 2 February 1959. Rugby writer Roy McKelvie said:

> *Trinity were six points up after seven minutes. London Irish did not overtake them until just before the end of this match at the Rectory Field, Blackheath. The winning score was a lovely piece of work by the Irish scrum-half Andy Mulligan. A Trinity man was forced over his own goal-line, and from the resulting five-yard scrum Mulligan broke diagonally to the open, across the goal. Jerking and jinking like a startled hare, Mulligan ended with a jack-knife dive that took his arms and the ball over the line. Sean McDermott converted, so the Irish won by two goals to a try and a penalty. Mulligan and McDermott were clever and occasionally brilliant.*

Just before Christmas that season, London Irish found yet another 'home', albeit for a single match and for a good reason. As their co-tenants at the Rectory

London Irishmen seriously socialising: from left, Sean McDermott, Colin Gibson, Jimmy Ritchie and 'Bish' Gallagher.

Field were using the ground for a veterans' game and then a fixture against Richmond, Irish played Rugby at Richmond, winning 24–13 with a much disrupted side. The Irish trial at Limerick robbed them of forwards Irons and Michael, while full-back Berkery was also unavailable, Byrne going to full-back. But Mulligan and McDermott again joined forces at half-back, a combination which would so often lead Irish towards victory with the skilful, inventive play of both men. A week earlier, the Irish had been to Old Deer Park and squeezed an 8–6 win over London Welsh.

At the start of 1959, W.E. ('Ernie') Crawford died at his home in Belfast at the age of 66. And, even closer to their hearts, London Irish lost Brendan Quin during the season, a man whose association with the club stretched back as far as 1910. Quin, player, honorary secretary, honorary fixture secretary and, finally, president in 1947–48, was deeply mourned by all who had known him.

The final London Irish match at the Rectory Field was on 11 April 1959, against Old Merchant Taylors. The 'home' side bade farewell to their 'home' with tries by McDermott, Berkery and Moore and a McDermott drop goal for a 12–8 win. But it had become an anomaly having the 1st XV the other side of south London. Six junior sides were now representing the club, and London Irish badly needed a home to call their own so that they could develop a ground for the future where every club team could be together.

Bill Morgan signed off the tenure at Blackheath by saying, 'It is not without regret that we are leaving the Rectory Field and we express thanks to the Blackheath club for making our co-tenancy such a happy one.'

Some members are said to have muttered quietly into their pints, 'Amen to it all.'

CHAPTER TWELVE

A Season to Remember

'Living well is the best revenge.'

ANONYMOUS

The stand was half-built, having only been started that summer, and was nowhere near ready for use on the big night. Builders' cement lay about; broken bricks were strewn around. The opening ceremony had to be performed in a tent beside one of the touchlines. Names from the past like Louis Magee, Des O'Brien and Tommy Headon had been replaced by Heath Robinson. But, for all that, Wednesday, 9 September 1959 was a lovely warm, sunny late-summer's evening at Sunbury-on-Thames, and no one seemed to care.

A festive occasion was enhanced by the presence of members and players from the three Exiles clubs in London, Irish, Scottish and Welsh, who came together to play a side raised by K.H. Chapman, a Harlequin chap but not a bad sort of egg for all that!

The *Manchester Guardian* ran a report the following day, stating:

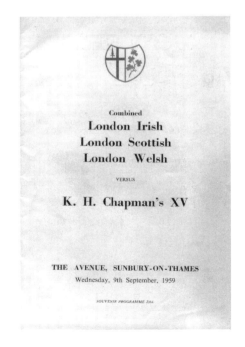

The wandering days of the London Irish rugby union club are over. Ever since their foundation 61 years ago they have been seeking a permanent home. Now, after sojourns at such widely differing places as Stamford Bridge and Wandsworth Common, they are back at Sunbury-on-Thames.

Last night's game, albeit with scaffolding still framing their half-completed stand, was staged to mark, after all, what was an historic occasion for

The programme for the grand opening of the new facilities at Sunbury.

121

Irish rugby exiles in London. A cheerful, cosmopolitan gathering saw a side raised by K.H. Chapman just beat a combined London Irish, Scottish and Welsh XV 11–10.

By coincidence, the score reflected exactly the voting figures which had approved the decision to return to Sunbury.

The deciding try was scored in the game's last minute against a combined Exiles team led by London Irish prop John Brown and which included only four other Irish players: Micky Byrne at full-back, Johnny Bamber at centre, A.T. Pearce the hooker and Marriott Irons in the back row. The *Guardian* went on:

So animated were the pre-match discussions in the well-patronised beer tents that the kick-off began, almost apologetically, 35 minutes late. From the start the game was in character with the evening, light-hearted and full of entertainment.

The sense of humour and good nature abroad on the ground that evening was confirmed when an over-enthusiastic fly kick scattered the thirstier onlookers still detained in a marquee. The *Guardian* reported, 'It evoked liquid shouts of "Well played, Chelsea."'

It added that at the conclusion of the match 'the beer tents rapidly filled again'.

And so they were off – up and running as a club with its very own ground, complete with proper facilities. Well, they would be soon, anyway, and after waiting 61 years, who was in that much of a rush? Delays in the process of planning approval (sounds familiar), concern over the raising of funds and interminable other frustrations meant that there had been serious delays before the building work could begin. And until it was finished, there was a great deal of make-do for a time. But when construction was finally completed, London Irish had exchanged an old wooden, wartime shack for a vast concrete edifice with changing accommodation for six sides, a first-floor tea room and a top-floor bar from one end to the other. Seating in comfort was another innovation.

The financial constraints meant that the club reluctantly had to omit the changing accommodation for junior teams and many of the planned interior finishes. Plainly, this was no luxury *Titanic* being constructed on the banks of the nearby Thames, but then this one did not sink ignominiously on its first proper outing.

Once the club had mortgaged itself up to the eyeballs simply to get the new stand up, it was reliant on individual donations or loans for any further monies. The club programme notes for that first evening suggested encouragingly, 'You might think your ten shillings a month is so small that it won't help. Don't you believe it . . . this scheme is already producing a very useful sum each year, but unfortunately it is still not enough.' All of which seemed to bear the firm, solicitous imprint of a man such as a bank manager. Perhaps even Bill Morgan, for example.

Everyone had helped or was helping, but all involved in the project recognised the magnificent efforts of Derek King, the club official who had led the ground committee, and George Barry, the honorary treasurer. Albert Hill called King 'a real stalwart, a man who did all the hard work'. But then the real heroes of the club, regardless of any work undertaken or tries scored, were those much-coveted, always-in-demand deviants known as car owners. If you had a car, you were king. Without one, you were consigned to scrambling around for lifts or joining the chugging train to and from Waterloo. Willie Lemon, who had arrived in London on business in 1959 and, like so many others down the years, had gone down to Sunbury unannounced, remembers, 'In those days there weren't many cars. I had an Austin A40 and we used to get seven or eight of the lads in it sometimes. God knows how, but we did. We were stopped by a policeman one foggy night on the A316, trying to find our way up to London after an evening at the club. The thing was, the car had fogged up as well, with so much breath inside it and the windows closed. The policeman flagged us down and said to me, "Hop out."

'These days, of course, you would fear the worst, but then nobody worried about drinking and you took risks. But all he said was, "I don't want to embarrass you in front of your friends, but you can't see out of your window like that." And with that he was on his way.'

So the good times began to roll at Sunbury. And most of the times that were good were staged in the immortal Fitz's bar, the old wooden shed at the end of the ground that had once been the tea and changing-rooms but became *the* place to drink at London Irish once the new stand had opened. Fitz's kept not only a tight ship but also a guest's book, which ended up being signed by rugby players, the good and great, from all over the British Isles and Ireland.

'Players would leave the clubhouse at 5.30 on the Saturday afternoon and walk out of the ground at about one o'clock the next morning,' says Willie Lemon. 'Some never got home at all and had to bed down in someone else's house for what remained of the night.'

It wasn't the rooftop bar on the Hilton, Quaglino's or the American Bar at The Savoy. But Fitz's bar quickly established a reputation as the best rugby watering-hole outside the capital. Visiting clubs used to talk about their nights in there for years afterwards. 'I remember Coventry coming down once and thinking they would leave at 7.30 on the Saturday evening,' says Albert Hill. 'They even picked up their bags and had walked out of the clubhouse to board their coach in the

Signing in: a player signs the visitors' book meticulously kept by Fitzy (left) in his bar.

car park.' The trouble was, Fitz's bar lay directly in their path, and it proved an obstacle quite beyond the negotiating skills of a bunch of rugby men. 'I think we saw them off shortly before 2 a.m.,' smiles Hill.

Mind you, Fitzy had his rules. He wouldn't tolerate the bawdy songs of those wretched, uncouth students from the medical schools, and you used foul language on pain of death. A large vodka bottle was kept on the bar and steadily accumulated coins, thrown in as fines for such language during the course of a season. And you had to watch your social airs and graces too; if Fitzy caught you with your hands in your pockets, you were fined sixpence. Swearing invoked a more severe penalty, usually five shillings. If you didn't say hello to Fitzy or take your cap off when you entered, that cost you one shilling. Des Egan, who ran the 'B' side known as 'Egan's Lions', pulled out a crisp five-pound note one night and said to Fitzy, 'Here, now take this and keep off my back.' Even members of the opposition would be fined. Half the money went to charity, and the other half towards the upkeep of the bar.

So Fitzy kept a nice, respectable house – although such standards were severely compromised the night Richard Harris turned up with a friend and two drop-dead gorgeous young women. Celebrities like Harris, Richard Burton, Dave Allen and others would frequent Sunbury whenever their commitments allowed. Len Dinneen recalled Richard Harris putting £50 behind the bar for the evening one day in the early 1960s, a not inconsiderable amount of money in those days. And the night Harris's female friends decided to entertain the assembled throng with an impromptu striptease down to bra and knickers entered the annals of folklore in the place. The 'entertainment' ended when someone threw a pint over one of the poor girls. Harris was subsequently fined ten pounds and threatened with banishment for life.

Comedian Dave Allen denies having been anywhere near the place on such an infamous occasion. 'Ah no, I'd have been saying Mass at the time,' he says. Finch's Bar in the King's Road was another famous place for the boys to gather. 'There used to be a line across the floor and anyone who wasn't Irish was banned from stepping across it,' remembers Allen. 'We were building borders even then, I suppose.'

But what was the intrinsic appeal of the place to men like Allen? 'The whole place has a wonderful relaxed feeling about it; it's what I have always enjoyed about an Irish rugby crowd. It is not an attitude of win at all costs. People today would say it's a very unprofessional way to look at rugby, but rugby was much more social in those days. You would meet people, have a few drinks and then go off for dinner and the evening somewhere. The rugby was of secondary importance. The game today is bound to lose something now it's become a professional game.

'It was always a great atmosphere down at the Irish. All the old-timers that used to play used to go down there, and you'd see some of the great players. It was very much a piece of Ireland.

'And if the game is played well, I don't much care who's winning it. There is nothing worse than a partisan crowd who can't see the good rugby being played. That's one thing I have always liked about the Irish: if they see good rugby, they applaud it.'

At Sunbury, they were such halcyon days that those involved sighed into their pints and silently wished they could last forever. And why not, for the fun just went on. No wonder worried parents in all corners of the land and across the sea back in Ireland fretted about their young men being exposed to such riotous goings-on at the London club.

'He'll still be there, you know.'

'Aye, love, but there's not a lot we can do about it now.'

For the parents of Jim McDonnell, it was all too much. McDonnell had been a priest but took the weighty decision to give it all up. His parents were so appalled at the news that they threw him out of the house he shared with them. 'Priests,' says Bill Pedlow, a grin writ large upon his face. 'They were worse than us with their language.'

Eventually, once the financial crises had been overcome, the supporters had been cajoled, begged, threatened or enticed to give their money in increasing amounts, and the grandstand had been finished, London Irish had a ground and a grandstand suitable for a top-class club. And that very first season, with a glorious Irishness about it, they produced the most successful team the club had known in its history. It was a good thing there were bars in both the new stand and in Fitz's wooden shed, such was the demand for celebratory drinks most match days. Once a year, too, Fitz's bar played a team from 'The New Buildings', as they came to be known.

London Irish started that famous season at Cheltenham on 5 September with a 9–3 win and played their first club game back at Sunbury seven days later, against Oxford on a sweltering early-autumn afternoon. They won that match 21–3, scoring five tries to one, and a bandwagon that was hitherto quite unexpected began its legendary roll towards glory.

Ronnie McCarten, a speedy, elusive wing three-quarter who had joined the club from Workington, scored two tries in the 21–0 win over St Thomas's Hospital that followed. In between, US Portsmouth had been beaten 14–5 on their own ground down by the dockyard in Pompey. Four matches, four wins – but a trip to Bristol offered the ultimate test of the Exiles' mettle. They passed it with a performance as near to their best as they would come, outscoring 'Bris' by five tries to two for a 21–15 victory, with Johnny Bamber (two) and Ronnie McCarten scoring tries early in the match which seemed to catch the home side cold. It was to be a seminal moment in their record-breaking season.

Speed and creativity in attack allied to solid tackling and energetic covering in defence was a handy combination for the Irish. There followed a home match with Wasps in which Mulligan made his first appearance of the season, and it was so physical a confrontation that some felt bruised just watching. Mulligan had been away with Ronnie Dawson's 1959 British Lions in New Zealand, after having been called out as a replacement, and the party had stopped off in Canada for two matches on their way home. To re-emerge in club rugby in a game as tough as this must have made Mulligan think he was back in New Zealand. The match, played in pouring rain, ended in a 0–0 draw.

Through the autumn and into mid-winter, the club kept going. No one, it began to emerge, could beat them – not in England, anyway. Nuneaton were

London Irish arrive at Dublin Airport, November 1959, for a match with Lansdowne. They lost 16–9, one of only two defeats they suffered all season.

beaten 18–3, New Brighton 24–3. A match report by Christopher Ford in *The Guardian* the next day said:

> *The new stand at Sunbury, all rattle, clatter, concrete and oxyacetylene, grew above and behind us. Once, a high and hearty touch kick threatened a man on a ladder; but otherwise all was well, Irishmen on and off the field imbued with the spirit of progress and building for the future.*

London Scottish were beaten 11–8 at the Athletic Ground, a game attended by King Olav of Norway, and then Loughborough Colleges were overwhelmed 18–6. In between, Irish faced a Rosslyn Park team at Roehampton who were similarly unbeaten and held them to a 6–6 draw, the irrepressible McCarten scoring again. It was a try described as 'near genius', and his fourth of the season by November. The game marked John Brown's 250th appearance for London Irish. The two teams launched a wave of attacks which threatened to leave one of them contemplating the end of a fine run, said Robin Marlar, writing in the *Daily Telegraph*. He went on:

Although the match was drawn, a try and a dropped goal against two tries, the accent was on whole-hearted attack. The Irish did have a brief spell of defence, after they had drawn level, during which McDermott judged it prudent to save his forwards from a rampaging Park eight by working the touchline, but the phase passed and gave way to a fabulous finale. As the contest drew to a dusky end, the ball was rushed from one end to another at an exhausting pace. Incredibly, both defences survived.

Then followed the first defeat of the season – but, what was this, London Irishmen crying 'No matter; it doesn't count'? After all, it happened in Ireland, against Lansdowne, and although it was a 16–9 defeat, subsequent wins back in England – 14–0 at Richmond, 8–0 at Old Millhillians and a 6–5 home defeat of London Welsh – followed by a 3–3 draw with Bath at Sunbury maintained the unbeaten record in England and took Irish into the New Year with the snatched breath of a gambler terrified his lucky run might break. It didn't look like it on 2 January 1960, Aldershot Services being thumped 42–3, with two of the nine tries from McCarten. It was a fair old record, not least because the captain Andy Mulligan had played just two of the 16 games in the first half of the season.

And it went on and on. US Portsmouth lost 6–3 and Moseley 11–6, by which stage only 15 games remained and some began to think the unthinkable. There had been good seasons for the club, occasionally a great one. But

Celebratory headlines from the record-breaking 1959–60 season.

LONDON IRISH SET RECORD

BY A SPECIAL CORRESPONDENT

London Irish 11pts Waterloo 5

THIS is a wonderful season for London Irish who beat Waterloo by a goal, a try and a dropped goal to a goal at Sunbury for their 23rd victory, their best record since the war.

As was exemplified in this exhilarating match, it has been a triumph for teamwork and fitness; a careful blending of youth and experience moulded into one of the best, and still to be beaten, sides in the country.

Waterloo made a rousing start, which realised a try by Carrington converted by Uren. This challenge only succeeded in bringing out the best in the Irish.

After Johnston had dropped a goal and Bamber had scored a try, the Irish went all out to establish a comfortable lead, and this came early in th. second half when Johnston rounded off a superb break by Mulligan for a try which McDermott converted.

London Irish.—M. A. Byrne; B. O'Hart, J. T. Bamber, G. W. Hackett, R. J. McCarten; S. J. McDermott, A. A. Mulligan; J. L. A. Brown, A. T. Pearce, S. T. Jones, J. P. MacDonnell, M. A. O'Flaherty, R M Johnston, D W M. Irons, W. Gahan.

Waterloo.—R. Uren; P. H. Thompson, C. R. Jennings, T. T. Critchley, R. Carrington; R. Lloyd Jones, R. I. Shuttlewor h; F. Gosling, N. Slack, M. Kirkup, J. C. Hutchison, J. J. Simpson, D. M. Roberts. A. Ashcroft. L. Barton.

Referee: R A B Crowe

Boat Race, April 2 (4.15)

HONOURS EASY ON TIDEWAY

TO MAKE IT HARD

Rugby Union

A DAY TO REMEMBER IN LONDON IRISH HISTORY

Two Worthy Feats : Northampton Outplayed and 400 Points Reached

By ROBIN MARLAR

Northampton .... 8 pts. London Irish 10

LONDON IRISH scored 10 pts. in the final 20 minutes of their floodlit match against Northampton on the well-appointed British Timken arena at Duston, where they gained an exciting victory by two goals to a goal and a try.

In the process they notched their 400th point when their sprightly left-wing threequarter McCarten sprinted under the crossbar for their second try, thus reaching a mark unknown in the club's history.

The start was delayed because the Irish became separated from

OXFORD UNIV.

an unbeaten one in England? No London Irish side had ever come close to that.

Still Mulligan didn't play that much (he captained Ireland that season, thereby becoming the fourth player from London Irish since the war to be national captain, after D.J. O'Brien, R.H. Thompson and J.S. Ritchie), yet still they kept on winning. They won and they won and they won . . . every one of those 15 matches right through to the end of the season. Their victims came from all over Britain: Abertillery, beaten 8–6, Blackheath 24–3, London Welsh 6–3, Harlequins 11–3, Old Alleynians 8–3, St Mary's Hospital 47–6, London Hospital 16–3, Waterloo 11–5, Northampton 10–8, Guy's Hospital 13–6, Rugby 9–0, Old Merchant Taylors 27–6, New Brighton 6–0, Fylde 16–6 and Sale 12–6.

They had done it against all the odds. Their last seven games had all been away from home and, perhaps even more of an impediment, Andy Mulligan had played in just nine of the 34 matches, an extraordinary statistic for a club captain. A man betting on that outcome from those circumstances would have been advised to seek medical help, as soon as the rapacious bookies had gleefully seized his wager.

But London Irish wouldn't be London Irish, lovely and charming and delightfully eccentric and masters of the unpredictable, without doing something unexpected. Having finished their scheduled season at Sale, they then agreed to a one-off extra match, a rerun of the original home fixture against Northampton which had been fogged off earlier in the winter. And what did the Irish do? Go and lose it, of course, 10–5, and so wreck a perfect story. Yet a brief look at the Northampton side indicates their power and quality at that time, with internationals past, present and future such as Hosen, Butterfield, Sykes, Jeeps, Jacobs, Taylor and White.

At Northampton during the first match between the clubs that season, there had been an explosion of anger involving Don White. Micky Byrne remembers, 'Ronnie McCarten had scored a try that night, making White look stupid. Don took it the wrong way and he laid Ronnie out. There was a tremendous surge on to the field by some of the boys not playing, led by Tommy Tranter. The referee had to intervene to calm it all down.'

The *Manchester Guardian* reported on the return game at Sunbury:

The precious record of not having been beaten in England which London Irish have guarded so jealously all the rugby union season was finally given up in their final fixture last night, when Northampton scored two goals to one before a large and excited crowd at Sunbury-on-Thames.

Nevertheless, it had still been a phenomenal achievement. Ronnie McCarten and Johnny Bamber in the backline scored a total of 39 tries in the season, 22 of

*Action from the Exiles' first game back at Sunbury, against a Combined XV,
September 1959.*

them going to Bamber, of whom a playing colleague remarked, 'From the moment he woke up in the morning to the moment he went to sleep at night, he was talking. He would always be instructing you where to put the ball.' Bamber eventually emigrated to New Zealand, perhaps working on the theory that with so many sheep there he could talk all day long and never be answered back, unlike at London Irish, where he'd had to suffer all sorts of quips and smart-arse comments!

Sean McDermott, who was Mulligan's outside-half when the captain played but his replacement at scrum-half inside Bill Hackett when the skipper was absent, masterminded the play and scored freely, amassing a total of 134 points from 40 conversions, 11 penalty goals, six drop goals and a single try. The 1st XV, in scoring 491 points in the season, achieved a magnificent total of 107 tries, testimony to the fine, enterprising play of a set of fast, elusive backs. Among them, Hackett was a small, lively player, quite fast and penetrative, a passer and runner with the ball. He had an outstanding season, but Bill Morgan wrote:

Many theories have been put forward for such outstanding 1st XV results. Some say it was due to a lack of stars in the team, but I do not agree, because we had 15 stars each Saturday. The team was not composed of 15 individuals (internationals or otherwise), but it is a club, a team. The art of producing this is the same in rugby football as in any other sport, namely club spirit.

A report in *The Times*, explaining the reasons for the excellent results, said:

The happy form of the Irish in their new surroundings this season is based on honest scrummaging in the tight, quickness to form round and heel from the loose, intelligent half-back play, a determined effort to get the ball to the wings and, above all, first-rate covering.

Yet there was another factor, one which did not emerge in the newspapers at the time. Andy Mulligan knew about it all along, but it wasn't apparent to opponents or the media. In 1998, on the morning of England's international with Ireland at Twickenham, almost 40 years after that extraordinary record-breaking season, Andy Mulligan sat at the breakfast table in a café in London's West End and recalled those halcyon days.

'The biggest advantage we had was our training; it had given us a significant lead on all the other teams we met because we were the first London club to get really fit. Ted Hammond, who was a serious, professional fitness trainer, was looking for something to do with his prowess as a trainer, and after seeing us train once, he told us that we could be twice as good as we were. He knew nothing about the game but saw a lot more could be made of the material available. He had coached Chris Chataway and Roger Bannister at Oxford, and the techniques he applied there were adapted to help us. We were introduced to things like interval running, and it had a profound impact. I should think we were 300 per cent fitter than we had ever been before.

'We used to train at the Duke of York's HQ at Chelsea in those days, and although there was a lot of resistance to Hammond's ideas at the beginning, we got into it. Simon Jones, who was an extremely good front-row forward, quite quick and a decent handler, was the guy who really started the idea of running as a prop, and that spread to most areas of the pack. Suddenly we had a pack that was "Irish" in its fierceness but hugely mobile and able to catch the ball. One mark of not being fit is that you drop the ball, but we got so fit, we stood out. We played against many heavier packs like Northampton but we would run others off the park. We preserved that "lead" for two years, until another Exiles club, London Scottish, followed us.'

Scottish then had their great time, the era of players like Shackleton,

The final match of a fantastic season: Northampton and London Irish players on the night of the Exiles' only defeat by an English club in the whole 1959–60 season.

Laughland, Rodd, Bruce, ten Bos, Wilson, Fisher and Campbell-Lamerton. That gave way eventually to the gifted London Welsh team which dominated the scene, sending a record seven players to New Zealand with the British Lions squad in 1971. Mulligan recalls, 'The difference between them and us was that they were really gifted rugby players. We were a mediocre team that achieved extraordinary things by being fitter. And there were two other things about that fine season: only about 18 or 20 players played – there were very few injuries – and the weather was good. We had a lot of dry grounds, which suited our style. But it didn't seem to matter who was in the team, it just clicked. Off the field, everything functioned because of Bill Morgan. He was known as Der Führer, but that was unfair because without him God knows what would have happened!

'He would work the telephones on Friday nights to find out if you were drunk, sober, injured or whatever. He would lasso anybody into joining and playing for London Irish. He once said "If you have an Irish setter dog, you qualify" – and I'm not sure he was joking!'

Always the jokes, forever the humour. Some of the Irish boys went on tour to Penzance with the Public School Wanderers one September, and 'Bish' Gallagher was there. He announced one morning in his booming voice that a competition was to be held to find the player seen in the company of the least good-looking woman during the tour. The winner (or should that be loser?) would be awarded a jockstrap known as 'the atrocity belt'. Gallagher then said, 'I won it this morning; I had a woman who had five o'clock shadow.' One wag at the back of the room shouted, 'The only people who had a woman in Penzance last night were Gallagher and the Royal Navy.'

'Bish' Gallagher had an appartment in High Street Kensington, above Bewley's shop. He shared with Tom Reid and it quickly became known as the Rockefeller Centre. Incredible parties took place there. When they were in London, Gallagher would go to Annabels for champagne, but a favourite watering-hole for most of the Exiles sides was the Queen's Elm pub in the Fulham Road. An Irishman called Sean Tracey owned it and it became a great haunt of sports people, but also of writers and actors. Mulligan remembers, 'Richard Harris drank there, as did Patrick Cavanagh, Stanley Baker and Richard Burton. Any of these people would drop in when they were in town.'

DUBLIN DELIGHTS

Andy Mulligan and Tony O'Reilly both represented London Irish and played together for Ireland, the 1959 British Lions and the Barbarians. Mulligan recounts a story O'Reilly told after an international match at Lansdowne Road in 1993 in which Ireland had shocked England 17–3.

O'Reilly was leaving the ground an hour or so after the game in a stretch limo, but as they passed a nearby pub, the car was stopped by heavy traffic. O'Reilly was on the mobile phone in the back of the car when there was a tap on the window.

O'Reilly wound the window down to be confronted by an Irish supporter who was already half drunk. The fan stuck his head into the car and slurred out, '734-8921. Phone the wife and tell 'er we won't be home for tree fookin' days!'

It was, insists Mulligan, the great Corinthian period of rugby. But it began to go as the 1960s unfolded. Levels of fitness and dedication began to be cranked up thereafter. God forbid, but others decided the sport might just be taken a bit more seriously.

For Mulligan, there would be only a brief time at Sunbury following the record-breaking season. He went to France in 1961 to become fluent in the language, playing for Paris University Club against the likes of the great Lourdes club of that era, Brive and Mont-de-Marsan. He did return to England from time to time, being married in the chapel of Magdalene College, Cambridge, by another ex-London Irish man Robin Roe, who became Chaplain General of the British Army.

Mulligan smiles warmly at the memories. 'Incredible times, remarkable people.' For sure, the salad days of their lives.

CHAPTER THIRTEEN

The Swinging '60s

'I've taken my fun where I've found it,
An' now I must pay for my fun,
For the more you 'ave known o' the others,
The less will you settle to one;
An' the end of it's sittin' and thinkin',
An' dreamin' Hell-fires to see.
So be warned by my lot (which I know you will not),
An' learn about women from me!'

RUDYARD KIPLING, 1865–1936

Given the fact that the swinging '60s became legendary in London, it is safe to assume that partying developed into an art form at London Irish.

Take the club's annual dinner, at most clubs an event as stuffy as a closed-up room on a hot summer's day. At London Irish, however, tickets for the event became – and remain to this day – among the most sought-after on the circuit. Writing years after his retirement as a player, Billy Doyle, a son of the '60s at Sunbury, remembers, 'One of the problems with these . . . London Irish . . . dinners was that the invitation would say, "Drinks 6 p.m., Dinner 6.30 p.m." However, we were often lucky to get the dinner started by 9 p.m., by which time some of the speakers (not to mention the guests) had difficulty staying up or . . . staying . . . aware, and the occasional one would have been despatched home by taxi in a comatose state before the second course – typical Irish, I suppose.'

The early '60s were lean times for the club. The great success in 1959–60 had not been sustained, even though Andy Mulligan had retained the captaincy for 1960–61, his last full season before departing to France late the next year. Of 31 matches that season, 18 were won and 13 lost. The most wounding defeat came shortly before Christmas when London Welsh beat the Irish 30–0 at Old Deer Park. Micky Byrne began to see a change in the recruits arriving at the club. 'The club had been well used to losing players. It seemed we constantly had guys coming over who had played for Ireland, but were coming to England for work with their companies for a few months or a year or two. They were always coming and going. In our day, one of the great aspects of London Irish was that in September you would still get a tremendous intake of players who were doctors, dentists or businessmen. But as times got better in Ireland, that intake dried up. Then we were depending on second-generation Irish sons to stay.'

Billy Doyle agreed. 'One week we would have a great team, the next it would be severely depleted because a lot of guys were out of town. It became a very transient situation at the club. And a lot of guys then joined other clubs.'

The Queen's Belfast outside-half Gerry Gilpin was an example, joining Harlequins when he came to London. He won three Irish caps in the 1962 season. The 1965 Oxford University captain, Freddie Craig from Campbell College, played for Richmond. Doyle remembered, 'When that happened, we began to fear that going to clubs other than London Irish would catch on and become a serious problem for us. But after the 1965 Varsity match, Mike [C.M.H.] Gibson turned out for a game with London Irish while he was in London briefly, and this started a more positive feedback to Ireland, with the result that from then on nearly all the internationals and good players from Ireland joined us.'

Billy Doyle joined the Irish in 1962 and stayed until 1971, seeing a host of players, famous faces and complete unknowns ply their sporting trade down at Sunbury. How seriously was it taken then?

'What was serious then and what is serious now?' asked Doyle. 'In general, those years of the '60s were not hugely successful. We had our good wins, but plenty of defeats too. When Ted Hammond was fitness trainer, the team was very fit. But when he quit, laziness set in. I suppose you would say that for those days we did take it seriously, when we could, but they were still fun times. And there was a great spirit even when things were going badly on the field.'

Like when Tommy Joy was on the charge. Joy, the sort of prop forward who suggested solidity for his scrummage and a sore neck for his opponent whenever he played, found himself in esteemed company against Saracens one day towards the end of the 1960s. Rumbling around the tail of the line-out, as he was wont to do, Joy proceeded – 'ran' would be an altogether misleading word – across the field in stately fashion. The faces of alarm belonged not to the opposition backline but to Joy's own three-quarters as they saw the big man approaching them, like a battleship bearing down on some elegant yacht off the Solent. Billy Doyle remembers standing watching with a curious mixture of horror and amusement as the scenario unfolded in front of him. 'Tommy had this habit of going straight – not at the opposition but across the field, without making a yard. Tony O'Reilly was on our wing and came flying up expecting a pass as he moved into position. The pass never came, but Tommy Joy did – straight into O'Reilly, with a crash that sent the pair of them falling into touch. O'Reilly climbed gingerly to his feet, shook himself and came up to me. "Who's that guy playing prop?" he asked. "I flashed him my identity card but the ******* ran me down."'

Dave MacSweeney was elected captain in the early 1960s, a time when Leicester and Coventry became new additions to the London Irish fixture list. Micky Byrne succeeded him in 1962–63, Ronnie McCarten was captain in 1963–64 and John McKenna was next in the 1964–65 season, followed by Len Dinneen in 1965–66, then Doyle himself in 1966–67 and 1967–68. Ollie Waldron was another great character of this era. Waldron was by then a renowned man of Oxford University following an incident during the university's match against the touring Australians at Iffley Road in 1966. A Wallaby forward took a fancy to one of Waldron's juicy-looking earlobes and bit it through. The Australian was promptly banned and sent home from the tour, while Waldron was despatched to the local hospital. 'No matter,' said a colleague later, with heavy sarcasm, 'Yer man looked as lovely as ever, a real pet, when he next appeared at Sunbury!'

MORGAN DEPARTS

At the club's AGM on 7 May 1964, Bill Morgan (or Phil Morgan, as the *Belfast Newsletter* somewhat disrespectfully referred to him in a diary article of 22 April) announced his retirement. Morgan had held the post of secretary for 19 years, been associated with the club since the 1920s and had at times held together all the component parts of a great rugby club almost single-handedly. His contribution could never be matched, still less replaced. 'It was a complete disaster when he left,' said Albert Hill.

Morgan bought a house for his retirement at Newcastle, Co. Down, after living in England for 40 years. 'But for the club I would have returned home long ago,' he admitted to friends. 'Rugby has been my life and it will be a terrible wrench to give it up after so long. But the time has come to make way for a younger man.'

At Morgan's retirement party at the bank, the chairman of Lloyds stood up and said, 'I think we have

A presentation to Bill Morgan on his retirement after more than 40 years with the club. Watching are (left) the legendary Fitzy and (second left) John Donnelly, president from 1969 to 1971.

supported London Irish very well through the years. I fully expect our telephone bill for the whole company to go down by half, now that Bill is leaving!'

Morgan's devotion to London Irish had been a passionate affair of love and respect for the better part of half a century. Men like him have been the true essence of rugby clubs since their inception, people prepared to serve loyally for year after year in a variety of roles. As player, captain, team selector, secretary and president, Morgan filled more roles than a sandwich-bar assistant, all of them vital to the well-being of the club.

They were known by a variety of names. After Bristol scored three tries in the last five minutes against a London Irish side in 1964, the *Daily Telegraph* reported the next day, 'The puffing paddies ran out of steam.' The nickname stuck.

In 1961–62, a rather notable wing three-quarter trading under the name Niall Brophy turned up at the club one weekend. Brophy had first been capped for Ireland as a UCD player against France in 1957 and scored a try on his debut as Ireland won 11–6 at Lansdowne Road. He qualified as a chartered accountant in 1961 and was sent to Berkshire on a training course with his new company. Joining London Irish seemed a logical idea, although clearly the programme editor had never heard of him before, his name appearing as 'N.B. Rophy' in the London Irish v. London Scottish match at Sunbury in September 1962!

Brophy, who was to go on to win 20 caps between 1957 and 1967, went on two Lions tours, Ronnie Dawson's 1959 visit to Australia, New Zealand and Canada, followed by Arthur Smith's 1962 tour of South Africa. In truth, he admits, they

weren't great days at London Irish, even though they also had another international wing at that time, L.P.F. L'Estrange, who had come from Dublin University and was one of nine new caps famously selected for the Irish team against England at Twickenham in 1962.

Three great Irish and British Lions players who represented the Exiles: Niall Brophy (left), Andy Mulligan (second left) and Tony O'Reilly (extreme right).

L'ESTRANGE ONE
Few London Irish rugby players have had a background as interesting as Larry L'Estrange, who won a single cap for Ireland against England in 1962. L'Estrange, who was born in Lytham, Lancashire, of Irish parents, was educated at Blackrock College, Dublin; the University of Chicago; and the Sorbonne in Paris. He then did National Service as a parachutist in Cyprus and Suez and was commissioned, before returning to Ireland to study modern history and political science at Dublin University.

Brophy remembers, 'I was living and working in Berkshire and just travelled up to Sunbury to play matches. I don't think I ever trained with London Irish. We weren't a very good side then. It was all friendly stuff but the really competitive element wasn't there. In Ireland we had cups in each province, which gave us a competitive edge that the English clubs never had at that time.

'I remember in one match, I had scored a try and was jogging back to halfway before the conversion attempt when I noticed that half my knee was hanging off. I had sliced it clean open, right back to the bone, by sliding on an icy ground. I had to cry off the Ireland match against France that was coming up and didn't play for three weeks. Then, in another game late in the season, in a desperate situation in defence I picked up the ball near my goal-line, looked up the field and said, "Here goes." I kicked ahead downfield, there was a terrific race for the ball, and although I just failed to score, I heard later that a selector saw it, and I got picked for the 1962 Lions tour after that.'

Of course, by no means every arrival at Sunbury had Irish international caps to his name. Some, it is true, were champions in the drinking stakes, and such men were always warmly welcomed by the Sunbury regulars. Others, like Len Dinneen, were well-respected, solid rugby players who were sure to enhance the playing strength of the Irish Exiles club. Dinneen went to live in Uxbridge, joined the club and one day foolishly raised the thought of travelling expenses with Bill Morgan. Given that one Irish player had grumpily confessed that Morgan, a bank manager, had even turned him down for a mortgage when he'd tried to buy a house, Dinneen's chances were, to say the very least, slim.

'He came up with a single sentence as a reply,' laughed Dinneen, these days living back in his beloved Limerick. '"You're playing for London Irish now." And that was all.'

Dinneen wanted a taste of the London life. He'd been a cub reporter on the *Limerick Leader*, earning the princely sum of £3 17s. 6d. a week. You had to serve five years before they gave you your stripes, but young Dinneen was impatient to see the wider world. London Irish was as good a place as any for that.

'The club became a home from home for me. When I walked through the gates of Sunbury, it was like a little bit of Ireland,' he said. He played his first match in the 4th XV, and his second in the 1sts. There he met the by now revered Andrew Mulligan, and promptly tapped him down a line-out ball which had a suicide note attached to it. Mulligan slowly picked himself up after the visiting forwards had left him, like lions feasting on a carcass, and sought out Dinneen. 'If I get a ball like that again, I'm walking off this pitch,' he said. Dinneen understood.

They called it social rugby, without the real competitive edge of playing for a cup or league title. But it was still as hard as nails. 'I got kicked in the kidneys playing against London Scottish one year,' Dinneen recalls. 'I needed an operation and was out for half the season. I was six and a half weeks in hospital. Brian Brolly took over as captain and I think we used about a hundred players. It was a disastrous season.'

One of the hundred was Kyle Mulligan, a pilot in the RAF who had played for Ulster and been a final Irish trialist. 'Second row, hard bastard, only six foot three but one of the best second rows I have ever played with. A very, very strong fellow,' was Dinneen's analysis. S.K. Mulligan never got a cap, in part, according to Dinneen, because the Irish national selectors weren't keen on picking players who played their club rugby in England. 'They wasted a lot of talent in those years,' he insists. Yes, probably true, but Ireland had by then unearthed a reasonably handy youth by the name of William James McBride to partner the venerable Bill Mulcahy. Ireland weren't short of a decent lock or two in those days.

Handling Bill Morgan until his retirement remained the trick. 'Sean McDermott couldn't stick it – he fell out with him,' said Dinneen. As for Brian Matthews, a real character, Morgan had his suspicions about his lack of fitness training, but he could never prove them. The players had little collective training at that time; it was up to each individual what he did. Matthews, 'a Brendan Behan-type Dubliner,' said Len Dinneen, was not the world's greatest trainer. Morgan marched up to him one day and barked out, 'Well, are you training?' Matthews, who was doing his best to conceal a rather large stomach, replied with a straight face, 'I do a few laps of Ealing Common every night. I prop up against a tree, too.' At which point Len Dinneen nearly lost his tongue, so hard was he biting it in an attempt not to explode into laughter.

The seasons came and went; matches were sometimes won but often lost. In 1964, about nine weeks of the season were lost because of the appalling weather in mid-winter. Len Dinneen recalled beating Coventry once, about 1966. 'We were leading 6–0 with 20 minutes to go and were knackered. They had a good side in those days, almost the full Warwickshire County Championship team, which was very powerful. We heard Peter Robbins winding them up, saying, "We're going to beat these bastards; they're no good." Well, the tiredness left us after that, we were so lifted.'

By the mid-1960s, with word of the Irish training difficulties becoming known,

London Welsh offered to let their exiled Celtic friends share the floodlights which had been installed at Old Deer Park. It helped immensely, once the initial grumbles by Irishmen concerned at the lack of drinking time available had been silenced.

'When you look back now,' says Len Dinneen, 'it is unbelievable how we prepared.' And how they celebrated. He remembers the night Dave Allen was down at the club after a match, having a drink with the players and enjoying the atmosphere. 'Things went on and we all had a great night with Dave. But when we came to go home, I could remember thinking, through a haze of Guinness, "The missus will kill me for going home this late. And she'll never believe I've been out with Dave Allen."'

Allen himself suggested a perfect solution. 'He said, "I'll write your missus a note and sign it, so she'll know it's genuine." The only thing I had to write on was my English driving licence, so Dave Allen wrote across one of the pages, "Sorry for keeping Len out so late. Best wishes, Dave Allen."

'Well, I remember stumbling up the path to my front door, letting myself into the house and then finding the wife. "Before you say anything," I stammered, "Read this."' At which point a driving licence was triumphantly produced from his pocket with an uncertain, but hopeful, flourish. His wife read the required page, put it down and promptly hit him. 'If you think I'm going to believe that, you've got another think coming!' she shouted.

London Irish Rugby Football Club, true to form, had enjoyed its 'less successful' era. After all, there were more important things in life than rugby. 'It was a unique club,' says Dinneen. 'You had all these characters and they always wanted to associate themselves with a member of the first team. They would come and buy you a drink, and although you didn't know the guy, eventually you would find out more about him. I look back with great memories. We lost the majority of our matches, but . . .'

And it paid to have your contacts. Dinneen was out in London one night, supping quietly until the small hours at hostelries such as the Bunch of Grapes in Kensington, a regular haunt for the London Irish boys. 'We left late and were making our uncertain way down the street singing, when a police car pulled up and two officers got out. "You're drunk and disorderly," they said. I think I was with Billy Doyle, or someone like that, and he said, "Who are you calling drunk and disorderly?" I said to them, "Do you know George Crawford [later to become a Chief Superintendent], your boss? I play with him at London Irish."

'Well, the policeman's tone changed so much in a flash that I thought it was all right to ask another question soon after. "You wouldn't give us a lift home, would you, boys?" There was an emphatic no to that, but no one was arrested.'

But things began to change from 1967 onwards. Or from about the time Al Moroney arrived in town. Moroney, square-necked, tough-jawed and squat, was greeted in a manner similar to that of an outlaw appearing in one of the old western towns: with very considerable caution. Yet he spent three years at Sunbury, the last two as captain, and had a profound impact on the way the club regarded both him and itself.

He knew the club because his brother, Mick, a hooker by trade, had played there. Al, an Army doctor at Pirbright Guards depot, was a front-row forward who deserved respect – and if others had not heard of him when they met, they quickly came to acknowledge his reputation on the field. And then off it into the twilight hours! Today, Dr Al Moroney, 57 years young with as fine a sense of humour as when he was a young man, is a Dublin GP and one of those human beings you encounter in life who makes you feel infinitely enhanced for the experience. Especially at two in the morning!

'We never had the time to do evening training in those days, so I told them they had to be fit to train. But with so many characters there, it was always trusting it to luck. There was a man called Des Quaid, and we played against London Scottish one season. Ian Robertson was playing outside-half for the Scottish and he tried a drop at goal. The ball never rose more than three or four feet off the ground and went straight through the uprights under the bar. The referee promptly gave the three points. Even London Scottish lined up for the 25 drop-out. The next minute, and I'll never forget the sight for the rest of my life, the referee was seen on the halfway line with Quaid dancing with fury beside him. Then he belted him in the jaw. The referee eventually got up, gathered himself together, gave a penalty and completely forgot to send our man off.'

One season, Irish met London Welsh at Old Deer Park and Moroney got wind of a £2,000 private bet laid with certain members of the Welsh committee. Both sides had players missing; Ollie Waldron, Mick Molloy and John Moroney were not available for Irish. The Welsh were building a fine side, the basis of which would contribute so much to the 1971 British Lions tour. But the Irish beat them that day, 14–6.

It then emerged, shortly before the return fixture at Sunbury in April, that the bet had been reactivated: it was double or quits. But again the Welshmen had chosen a poor investment. 'We were well organised, very fit by then and had a great defence which was hard to score against. We won 14–0,' smiles Moroney.

There was a ferocious battle with Moseley one season. 'Nigel Horton, the England lock forward who later played for the British Lions, was in their team, and out of the corner of my eye I saw him hit our hooker, Ken Kennedy, during the game. Quaid came up complaining about it, which puzzled me. I couldn't understand why he was defending Kennedy, because there was no love lost between them. Anyway, at the next line-out, Horton was hit in the small of his back and dropped. He got up after a bit, fair do's, and finished the match. But at the end, as we left the field, you could see he was looking for a fight, so I hit him again. He got up again, but wasn't looking for any more after that.'

Moroney helped Surrey to the County Championship title in that period, the epitome of the genteel English counties taking the field with eight Celts in its line-up! The coach was none other than Carwyn James, who was teaching in London at the time.

At Sunbury, Moroney had seen enough of the legendary London Irish 'politicking' off the field to know that it could be a hindrance to what he wanted to help them achieve on it. 'The playing talent was there but not the belief in the organisation off the field. But when Peter Whiteside took over and they spent money properly, the whole thing fell into place. Why is there always political in-fighting at the club? Because it's the Irish.'

But because it was the Irish, there were always the characters. Like Roy Croft, who played in some of Moroney's teams. 'Johnny Johnson came into our dressing-room one day before we played Harlequins to check our boots. He ran his hands over Croft's footwear and nearly had the skin torn off. Croft was wearing running spikes. "You can't wear those," said Johnson, a respected figure in the police force. "Oi'll be all right. Oi promise not to walk on anyone," Croft replied, in all seriousness.'

And then there was Kevin Lavelle, back-row forward *par excellence*, Royal Navy man and the source of more stories than most in the whole of London rugby. Lavelle was serving on the *Ark Royal* in the Bay of Naples when he was summoned to his captain's quarters one day. 'Ah, Lavelle, I have here a telegram from London asking that you be sent home to play for Ireland,' said the top brass. 'Now we don't really do this sort of thing, you know, but in these circumstances, to play for Ireland, well, we are willing to help.'

None of which would have come as a great shock to Lavelle, because he had engineered the crafty plot from its inception, arranging for a friend to send the telegram. Only trouble was, he wasn't playing for Ireland, just London Irish. No matter, a helicopter transported him off the ship and to an air base in Naples, from where he was flown to London. He played for London Irish and had a magnificent evening at Sunbury. Had it all been worth it?

'I was in irons for a month after they found out,' he later told Moroney. By which time Al Moroney probably knew everything there was to know about K. Lavelle, certainly after the Combined Services tour to the United States they had been on together. They stayed at the naval base at Rhode Island, and Moroney insisted everyone stayed together, officers and men. Lavelle was the only Able Seaman present.

'The officer of the naval base invited Lavelle to a big house party, and I went as his minder. I said he couldn't go without me, so off we trotted. Midway

The extraordinary Kevin Lavelle. 'The New Zealanders would have loved him,' said Al Moroney.

through the evening, Lavelle was to be seen with the Admiral's wife on her knees beside him, laughing her head off with his hand up her shirt. I thought we'd end up in the dungeon for it. But the Admiral apparently thought this was terrific form. I thought it was a sobering experience.'

Lavelle was fearless, with great skill and ability. Moroney once saw him drop a goal from the halfway line, and Billy Doyle went one better than that. 'Kevin dropped a goal right-footed before half-time in one game, and then another, left-footed, in the second half. You couldn't stop him after that; he was trying to drop goals from all over the field.'

Moroney was best man at Lavelle's wedding, and therein hangs a tale. Of course. 'I had to persuade him not to leave the church. He lost his nerve and went back in four times before going through with it. As a player, Kevin Lavelle was one of the most talented I ever saw. The New Zealanders would have loved him. He had such acceleration and power. He was a lovely guy, such a tough man, and unique, a one-off. He was an extraordinary human being. One late October evening in 1960, outside the Shelbourne Hotel in Dublin, I was with some friends and we spotted him biking the other way. We whistled, and when he saw us, he biked straight across two lanes of heavy traffic, with cars beeping their horns and drivers shouting. "Oh, is it yourselves?" he said, pulling up.

'In those days, though, you might have a hard match once a month. Today it's a hard match every week; it's so sapping. I played senior rugby until I was 42 and then social stuff until 48. Mind you, I'd switched from tight-head to loose-head by then. The pressure on your lower back as a tight-head is huge. At loose-head, you are holding things up rather than taking them down, which is the tight-head's job.'

Moroney took the London Irish captaincy on one understanding. 'I told them what I said went, that I would be the boss. They accepted it totally. I told them if they reneged on that, I would walk out. All I was interested in was the rugby and the team performing.'

He introduced a simple notion: the discipline of knowing that you have to pay for your fun. He brought in Sunday-morning training sessions, a move that was initially received with all the warmth and popularity of Fitzy closing his bar on a Saturday night. But it worked, and London Irish were one hell of a strong, committed, successful side under Al Moroney's influence.

September 1964, and Andy Mulligan is married to Pia. Another London Irishman, the Rev. Robin Roe, officiates.

By then, the barren years of the early '60s had been forgotten. London Irish had quality players such as Ken Kennedy, Johnny Moroney, a fine outside-half, Ollie Waldron, Al Moroney, Kevin Lavelle, and those renowned props Alex Newberry and Tommy Joy. Phil Douglas was another very useful player in the '60s. Mind you, being the Irish, there were always the unexpected slight disagreements over policy.

'We played a match down at Aberavon at the end of the 1960s,' remembers Billy Doyle. 'Alan Doherty scored a last-minute try in the corner and we needed to convert it to win. Johnny Moroney must have missed about 15 kicks at goal that day, but he picked up the ball to take the conversion. I said, "I'm taking this." He said, "You are not." The pair of us wrestled for the ball until the referee said, "Will you make your ******* minds up just who is going to take this?" I think I took it in the end and missed. Or kicked it. It doesn't seem to matter now.'

In Wales, too, London Irish's legendary touch judge Henry Hennessy distinguished himself. Henry, his stout figure a familiar sight on the touchlines of the leading rugby clubs in those days, was renowned for the generosity of his judgements when a ball went into touch. As long as it had been kicked by an Irishman. But trying to award penalties when they had missed by the proverbial country mile was also part of Henry's repertoire.

'I took a penalty kick at goal one Easter down in Wales, at Neath I think it might have been,' said Billy Doyle. 'The ball missed by about five yards and Henry promptly stuck his flag up. The referee, a local chap, ran up to him and said, "I'm warning you, boyo." About ten minutes later, there was a scene near one touchline, with one of their players and a lad from our team happily knocking six bells out of each other. Henry saw this, rushed on to the field and started wading into yer man, clobbering him with his touch flag. That was it for the ref – Henry had to go.'

```
                    ST.MARY'S HOSPITAL v. LONDON IRISH

ST.MARY'S HOSPITAL      Saturday, 5th March, 1966        LONDON IRISH

  15. D.J.THOMAS           Full back             ◊ 15. M.A.BYRNE
  14. R.EVANS              Right wing              14. J.MURRAY
  13. T.FLETCHER           Right centre            13. M.S.CUNNINGHAM
  12. R.PULLINGER          Left centre           ◊x 12. T.J.PALLON
  11. A.DALTON             Left wing               11. M.COLLINS

  10. P.COPLAND            Stand off             ◊◊ 10. C.M.H.GIBSON
  9. R.YOUNG               Scrum half              9. S.BINGHAM

  1. D.HURLE               Forwards             ◊ 1. D.RUSSELL
  2. H.O'DONNELL                                  2. A.SIMMONDS-GOODING
  3. G.ORR                                        3. T.M.CORRY
  4. J.WATSON                                   ◊◊ 4. .'.HILL
  5. J.SIMPSON                                    5. R.DUFFY
  6. W.WILLIAMS ..                             ◊ 6. J.H.McKENNA
  7. S.FERRIS                                     8. J.HAYNES
  8. K.TANSWELL                                   7. W.DOYLE

                  Referee: W.H.FISCHER Esq.    ◊ International
                                              ◊ County
                                              x Captain
```

The programme for the match between St Mary's Hospital and the Exiles. The game saw the sole appearance of C.M.H. Gibson for London Irish.

But if you had to award marks out of ten for genuine stories, then the saga of the Surrey seven-a-side tournament one year would take some beating. Billy Doyle tells it more than 25 years later, still struggling to keep a straight face.

'We'd had a series of late nights, four o'clock and worse. We had been to Taunton for the weekend for some match or a tournament or something, and we got back to London at around six or seven o'clock on the Sunday morning, having travelled by the milk train. We were hopelessly hung over, and someone suggested the only remedy was a drink. So we headed for our regular, the Bunch of Grapes in London, knocked up yer man and slumped down quietly, hoping to die. One of the guys was called Micky Collins, a small player but with a fantastic jink, a devastating side-step. Anyway, we were sitting there in the usual awful condition around ten in the morning when the door swung open and David Craig, who was team secretary, walked in, bright and breezy. He took one look at this assembled wreck of humanity and said in a shocked voice, "My God, don't you know you're playing in the Surrey Sevens at Sunbury today?"

'We were in a desperate condition but there was no alternative by that stage. So we played. The ball went down to our end, Collins picked it up near our dead-ball line and started jinking. The next thing was, he crashed into the goalposts with no one anywhere near him, the ball flew out of his hands and the opposition scored. The rest of us started laughing, an hysterical sort of laugh that we couldn't control. We just couldn't stop, it was so funny.'

It was, quite simply, a club that celebrated its good times and endured bad times too. But it enjoyed both. The very notion these days would be anathema even to most Extra 'B' XVs. Such is progress.

CHAPTER FOURTEEN

Strong Men at the Helm

'It was the best of times.'

CHARLES DICKENS, 1812–70

'We were known all over England. No one wanted to drop us from their fixture list,' said Tommy Joy, proudly. The devoted Exiles prop, who became an institution in the 1st XV during the 1960s and early '70s, went on, 'Everyone loved coming down for the craic.'

One year they played Lansdowne, and Henry Stevens was at outside-half. Tommy Joy remembers, 'The game was running late and Henry suddenly called out during the match, "What's the time?" Someone told him and he said, "Jaysus, I must be off. I've got a business meeting to attend and I'm booked on a flight." So he walked off the pitch, and, of course, in those days you couldn't bring on a replacement, so we had to finish the match with 14 men. We lost the game.' But it didn't seem to matter terribly.

In 1971, the Exiles had a front row of great repute: Al Moroney, the loose-head and captain, Ken Kennedy at hooker, and Dean Paddy, a New Zealander of impeccable Irish descent, who was a dentist. Programme writer Brian O'Hanlon revealed, 'When asked which side he [Dean Paddy] would prefer to prop, he is reported to have said, "I don't give a damn; it's all the same in New Zealand." "Which is why the 1971 Lions beat them," according to a voice not a million miles away from the throat of Al Moroney!'

And by the turn of the decade, the great Tony O'Reilly had joined the club, albeit desperately late in his career (he was by then 33), but was to play only eight matches before he decided that beanz meanz more to him than rugby football. In October 1969, 14 years after he had first represented Ireland, O'Reilly played his first match in first-class rugby for five years. There was a large crowd at Sunbury to see it, with Bath the opposition. 'Ah,' said a team-mate to a clearly bemused bystander, 'I'd say it's part of yer club's youth policy.' Bath won, comfortably.

O'Reilly's presence produced the best of Billy Doyle's humour when the young business executive arrived for training in the H.J. Heinz chauffeur-driven

Mercedes. 'Jaysus, Reilly,' said Doyle. 'There's no need for you to be getting fit – bring yer chauffeur, he can do the training for yer.'

And when O'Reilly played his final game for Ireland, against England at Twickenham in February 1970, having been called up as a late replacement (he was in Annabel's nightclub in London's West End, sipping champagne, as you do, on the Thursday night prior to the match when a call came through that he was needed), the wags had more rich pickings. The once flying but by then largely grounded wing went down, caught in a maul, and took a while to get up. As he lay dazed on the Twickenham turf, he remembers hearing a voice say, 'And while you're at it, why don't yer kick his ******* chauffeur, too.' Dave Allen, who was at that match, joked, 'O'Reilly was so large by that time, England couldn't run round him.'

Tony O'Reilly looks back on those days with that familiar mischievous sense of humour. 'At London Irish, there were some very nice, good-humoured fellows. By definition, the rugby was always mildly chaotic. When you saw the team sheet, you'd say, "Gee, look who's playing for us this week." There was an air of almost curiosity about not knowing which players would turn up. But then shifting personnel has always been their problem. It was always difficult for them to build the kind of loyalty and continuity which makes the great teams.'

And O'Reilly underlined the crucial significance for London Irish of the growth of the Irish economy in the Republic. 'That generation became the first among Irishmen never to have to emigrate involuntarily. In 1958, in my College year, 85 per cent of that year left Ireland. By that process, this overseas Irish diaspora was created. I believe the rules of qualification have to change to include all those who might loosely be part of that Irish diaspora. Ireland is a country of only five million and rugby is only the third game. But it could source its players from the best of the southern hemisphere.' Months later, Irish began to do precisely that.

Of course, wings stood around forlornly hoping for a pass in those days, but very often they only touched the ball during a match to throw in to the forwards. Or at the after-match dinner, to sign it. 'They used to say at Pontypool, where forward play was renowned, Lord Lucan had spent a season quietly playing on the wing,' joked O'Reilly.

O'Reilly was already inhabiting a different world from the likes of Tommy Joy when they played together. 'O'Reilly said we must have training at 5.30 p.m. because dinner was at 8 p.m.,' said Joy. 'But the rest of us were all broke and lucky to eat dinner. You wouldn't even get a bowl of soup or cup of tea after training.'

After one of O'Reilly's few appearances in an Exiles shirt, shortly before his

London Welsh v. London Irish: one of the classic battles against the outstanding Welsh Exiles teams of the 1970s.

LONDON WELSH
v
LONDON IRISH
SATURDAY, 15 DECEMBER, 1979
KICK-OFF 2.15 P.M.

LONDON WELSH R.F.C.
OLD DEER PARK, KEW ROAD, RICHMOND

PROGRAMME 15p

call-up for that final cap, Noel Henderson attended a London Irish match to see him play. Before the game, he strolled up to a group of players and enquired, 'How is O'Reilly playing?'

'With difficulty,' shot back Willie Lemon.

In season 1972–73, there were two high-quality contests with London Welsh. The first meeting of the old rivals, at Old Deer Park early in the season, brought a crushing 41–10 win for the Welsh. The return match at Sunbury again featured some glittering alumni: the captain Mick Molloy, Barry Bresnihan, Pat Lavery, Harry Rea and Ken Kennedy for the Irish, against J.P.R. Williams, John Dawes, Jim Shanklin, Jeff Young, Geoff Evans, Mike Roberts and the Welsh skipper John Taylor. Irish won a classic contest 16–12 – and to think they were only playing social rugby in those days . . .

If Bill Pedlow had been the rebel in the 1950s, then Tommy Joy emulated him in the next decade. 'They told me one day when I was 32 or 33 that I was too old for the first team and I had a row with them. They said I had to go down to the junior teams, but I wasn't having that. I left and got into the Richmond first team for two years. Then the Blackheath first team.'

Nor was that all. Joy, who hailed from Tipperary, even appeared briefly for Streatham, representing them against London Irish at Sunbury in September 1973, the Exiles' 75th anniversary year, before returning to Sunbury and resuming his 1st XV rugby for the next four or five years. And nobody seemed to mind at all. He was 41 when he finished. In the first team, anyway.

He then went off to terrify opponents in the lower ranks by captaining the 'B' XV. In November 1983, the 'B's lost for the first time in over a season, to the Richmond Heavies at Richmond. During the first 15 minutes of the game, an interesting verbal joust took place between Tommy Joy and Robin Robins. 'Don't breathe on me, ye'll asphyxiate me, yer big, fat *****' was Joy's gentle introduction. To which the referee took considerable exception and awarded Richmond a penalty. Afterwards, Joy was said to be so upset he wouldn't speak to anyone.

DEATH-DEFYING
In the autumn of 1973, following the announcement at the previous AGM of the death of Albert O'Carroll and Frank Whelan's letter to his relatives conveying the club's sympathy, Albert replied himself and, in the manner of Mark Twain, said that the rumour had been exaggerated. He added that it reminded him of another letter written by an Irishman which said, 'Let me know if you are alive, but don't bother if you're dead.'

To be sure, they were grand times. And a mite naughty, too, as Tommy Joy explained. 'There was a certain "lady" who was known to the boys at the club at that time, a very nice-looking air hostess. Depending on how well she considered you had "performed", you would get a little present afterwards from her duty-free treasure trove. If you'd been especially good, you'd get a bottle of Blackbush whiskey. If you'd done reasonably well, there would be some cigars. A few cigarettes were considered the lowest award on offer.'

They'd play on a Saturday afternoon, 'train' hard on Saturday nights and then return to Sunbury for a match with 'The Jackeens', a scratch invitation team on a Sunday which used to have games against anyone. 'You got accustomed to playing with a hangover,' remarked Joy, wearily. Easter tours were to South Wales, as usual, and the players had to pitch in their £12 each to help meet the costs.

'I have great memories of the club. Without it, what would a lot of Irish people have been doing over here? And they were from all walks of life. That was one of the attractions. There was no nonsense about some people from the north, others from the south. All that was left back in Ireland. True, the northern boys might sing the Orange song and then the lads from the south would sing an IRA song. But then we'd sing together all night. It has always been a great, welcoming place.

'I remember Dick Spring coming over; we shovelled concrete together on the building site in Hammersmith. He did it for a couple of days, then went off to New York. He was a very nice fellow. He liked his pint and his parties. But I'd have to be honest and tell yer, he wasn't much bloody good at shovelling concrete!'

The man who went on to play full-back for Ireland and then make a successful political career as Deputy Taoiseach in the Dáil would doubtless be interested to hear as much.

FAREWELL TO FITZY

In October 1973, Fitzy's farewell match was held at the club. The great man had held the position of London Irish bar steward for a quarter of a century and had long since become an institution in rugby circles everywhere. When he died in the mid-1970s, his ashes were scattered on the Sunbury ground in a special ceremony conducted by Father Mike Blackburn, a playing member of the club. Father Mike, fully dressed in his surplice, performed the ceremony an hour or so before the start of a home match against London Welsh. Two Welsh supporters arriving early for the game stumbled upon the scene, with Father Mike scattering the ashes and holy water on the ground and blessing the pitch. 'Blimey, boyo, the Irish lads are taking this one a bit seriously, aren't they?' one is said to have remarked.

Father Blackburn had run foul of the notorious Des Egan during his playing days for the 'B's at London Irish. He had damaged a wrist one day taking off his robes after saying Mass and told Egan he could not play the following week. Egan is reputed to have replied, 'Right, that does it, Father. I'm banning you from that Mass until the end of the season.'

By then, Father Mike was well used to hearing public confessions before matches. Jim O'Hara explained, 'As young lads, we would come into the dressing-room and talk about any girls we'd had a good time with the night before. Father Mike would hear this, so I suppose you could say he took confessions from most of the team before the games!'

Father Blackburn, Catholic priest and a lovely, gentle man, died in his mid-sixties in 1998 and was buried with a London Irish jersey on his coffin. The shirt belonged, ironically, to Terry Thompson, an Ulster Protestant. Jim O'Hara added, 'It was the only shirt we could find, but I'm sure Father Mike would have seen the amusing side of that.'

Spring spent two seasons with the club, 1974–75 and 1975–76. He was somewhat shocked by what he found on his arrival. 'The first year was a pretty sad state of affairs. Training was a mess, things were disorganised and there was not much club spirit. There was a sense that the team wasn't going anywhere and things fell off from that. At the end of the season, there was panic about the place. But then Ken Kennedy took over and we had a fairly successful season the following year because people gave it a go.'

Spring, who came to London from Cork Constitution, called it, intriguingly, 'a club of its time'. He went on, 'As ever, it fell to a few people to organise it, and it was as well organised as any other. It was always far more than just a rugby club; it was a home away from home. It is very important for Irish rugby to have a strong London Irish team. But in those days there was always the contentious issue of playing for London Irish; people playing for them were out of sight, out of mind in terms of national selection. But I think any sense of grievance has now gone.'

He recalls one trip north for a John Player Cup match in the 1974–75 season, against the Northumberland junior club Morpeth. 'We had sent our baggage man to Newcastle a week or two earlier to find a nice quiet hotel. We got off the train the day before the game and he said, "There's our hotel." It was right on the platform. We were awake half the night with the trains rushing through.'

It was a recipe for the disaster which duly followed. Exiles lost the second-round match 19–3, one of the biggest upsets in the competition's history. Yet they were not alone in their embarrassment by the end of that season. Morpeth promptly went to Bath and won in the next round before losing in the semi-finals to Rosslyn Park.

A POLICY OF YOUTH

In early 1974, there was a special celebration at London Irish when their wing three-quarter Pat Lavery was chosen for his first cap, against Wales at Lansdowne Road. Lavery had started with the club as one of Paul McCarthy's schoolboys and gone right through, up to the 1st XV and thence into international rugby, where he was to win two caps. It was testimony to the work put in at the junior levels by McCarthy, a long-term servant of the club.

Mick Molloy had joined Irish much earlier than Dick Spring, in 1969, but stayed for ten years and was captain in 1973–74. And the good doctor of the Irish Rugby Football Union ('I'd not let yer man near me, personally speaking,' said a former playing colleague in a not altogether serious vein) witnessed a unique sea change occurring at the club.

'It was an interesting situation. At universities, the students ran the show, and, to a great extent, the same became true at London Irish. After my first year at the club, there was a significant change and the players had a big say in what happened.'

Training continued to take place on Tuesday nights at the Duke of York's Barracks in the King's Road, and given that in the early 1970s the level of IRA activity in London was high, the sight of 25 Irishmen carrying large bags through the entrance to a high-profile British Army establishment building tended to raise the odd eyebrow here and there amongst those not familiar with the long-standing arrangement.

There were a lot of Services personnel at the Exiles club in those days: Molloy, Richard Rea, Al Moroney and Kevin Lavelle, among others. With the arrival of those players in that era, fortunes changed. The club began to cast aside the memory of those largely disappointing years of the '60s, in a playing sense at least, and become once more a force in the game in England. They did it, generally speaking, as the club had always done it: with a collection of quality forwards able to take on the best around. By 1969–1970, they could put out a pack containing the likes of Ollie Waldron (who had been captain in 1968–69), Kevin Lavelle, Billy Doyle, Mick Molloy and Ken Kennedy, quality players every one of them and, in the case of Waldron, Molloy and Kennedy, international footballers. 'Lavelle should have won an Irish cap. He was certainly good enough,' added Molloy.

With a quite glorious oxymoron, the club programme announced at the start of the 1968–69 season:

It is encouraging to see the greater amount of summer training our lads have done this year and Ollie's [Waldron] letter to playing members left nobody in any doubt about the basis of selection and qualification to play for the London Irish. The casual approach is out, and not before time. This year's club vice-captain Mansell Heslip is away on holiday but is back next week . . . Johnny Moroney is still in Ireland at the moment, Mike Miliffe is another happy holidaymaker this Saturday . . . Mick Cantrell is another holiday absentee . . .

Up to late 1969, the Sunbury club programme, price 1s., was complaining:

London Irish take the field this afternoon [against Saracens] knowing that a win is long overdue. The signs are that after the frustrations of recent weeks the side will show its capability, which has so far been a paper tiger, to the full. It is now six weeks since London Irish had a win. To be truthful, the club has not had a win to shout about this year. What matters is that we win over the clubs that matter. And, to this date, we have just not done so, as our bottom position in the Sunday Telegraph *table shows . . .*

Last week the club came back empty-handed from its annual Irish tour having been defeated 14–11 by Lansdowne at Lansdowne Road on Saturday and 12–8 by Clontarf on Sunday.

But whatever the failings on the field, the humour remained in place off it. The notes concluded:

To show that London Irish is ever alive with humorists, even if rugger players are maybe in short supply, I bid you look at the noticeboard in Fitz's. David Vance there has pinned a most reasonable letter stating that he has lost his rugger boots and wishes their return. Someone has scribbled underneath, 'C. Breeze has them for bedroom slippers.'

Life went on in Fitz's bar much as before. One Saturday night in February 1972, the lights suddenly died – a power cut. Brian O'Hanlon, who contributed some marvellous programme notes in that decade, wrote afterwards:

Every situation, however apparently disadvantageous, can sometimes bring unseen joy. Such was that of the power-cut situation last Saturday in Fitz's bar. The candlelight gave the old pavilion an aura of intimacy which was enhanced by there being a fiddler (a musical one) and a guitarist present to lead the singing. An impressive gathering sang far into the night, led, on occasions, by the corpulent (some would say fat) honorary assistant secretary of the club.

And, a couple of months later, O'Hanlon wrote:

Fitzy has now been running the building, our old pavilion which is affectionately known as Fitz's bar, for 21 years. The annual match between Fitz's and 'The Buildings' will take place on Sunday, 7 May, and it is Fitzy's wish that players from each side in the club play on both sides. It is also Fitzy's wish that those who play for 'The Buildings' show him a modicum of respect by getting beaten.

But gradually, as the '70s developed, things became different. Gradually, very few teams got the better of a powerful, experienced pack of forwards, although Al Moroney's injuries in 1971–72 prior to his return home were a blow. Nevertheless, the rugby improved, so much so that Molloy said in 1998, 'It was just as competitive then as now. There might not have been leagues, but the attitude was just as professional. A lot of guys were quite fit from that side and would have held their own in the modern game, I'm sure. We had our own PE instructor at the army barracks, and there was a lot of serious training.'

And there was once more a hum about the old place. Gerry Holland's 'B' XV won 20 out of 20 in season 1973–74, and things generally were on the up in all kinds of ways. By the early 1970s, lights had been installed at Sunbury, even though most people needed to be fitted with special night-sights to get a proper view of a rugby ball being thrown around in the gloom! On the training ground, too, there was a shock of near-electrical proportions when Tony Davis, a New Zealander, helped out with coaching one winter. 'It was a pretty different type of approach, bordering on the fanatical,' reported Molloy. 'Some training sessions got right over the top.' But the results improved in a way that was commensurate with that approach. In December 1970, Irish became the first non-Welsh club to beat the all-powerful London Welsh for three years. And they did it at Old Deer Park, giving them a tally of 15 wins in 17 games prior to Christmas that year. Al Moroney's tough regime was beginning to produce results.

Johnny Moroney was a highly able outside-half who hardly trained and would smoke up to the minute he went out on to the field, while at centre the international Barry Bresnihan, one of Ireland's most talented players, had come to London and joined the club. He was, inevitably, a crucial component in the club's revival.

For those travelling in the opposite direction at that time, to Dublin for international matches, there was a ruinously expensive offer from the Jury's group of a hotel room in Dublin at £9.50 single, £15 double. A pity the excellent Jury's couldn't have kept to such prices as we approach the millennium. Nowadays the price of a Guinness in there is almost the cost of a single bed back in 1974!

The selection committee of three contained two players, one of which was the captain, which meant that the players had control. And when the one in control was Ken Kennedy, everyone knew about it. Kennedy was organised, disciplined, hard; he wasn't there to fool around. He'd played rugby for Ireland and toured New Zealand with the 1966 British Lions. Furthermore, his lasting quality was demonstrated by the fact that he missed the 1968 and 1971 Lions tours but was then chosen for the 1974 tour to South Africa.

He might have been seen by some as the Devil incarnate, but he was exactly what London Irish

Ken Kennedy, another London Irishman who represented Ireland and the British Lions.

155

Northern Ireland politician John Hume, who was jointly awarded the Nobel Peace Prize in October 1998, at a fundraising dinner with Andy Mulligan and 'Bish' Gallagher in 1977.

needed after too many lean years. His tough, professional attitude, both as a player and then as a coach from 1972 onwards (after Al Moroney's return to Ireland early that year), with occasional interruptions, helped turn around the club, culminating a few seasons later in an appearance in the John Player Special Cup final of 1980. Kennedy brought in the first element of professionalism and the notion of demanding commitment from players and repaying it. He introduced structured 11.30 a.m. training sessions on Sunday and made sure some hot snacks were available for the players after training. It might seem tame enough these days, but then it was revolutionary stuff.

Kennedy's influence was timely: in 1976–77, the RFU introduced proper club Merit Tables, and in that season London Irish finished first in the London Division, with six wins from seven games and a commendable 85 per cent record. True, for the early, fledgling years of Merit Tables, including the John Smith's sponsored system in the mid-1980s, it was a flawed system, because not all the clubs played the same number of games. Nevertheless, the prosperity of the Exiles clubs was demonstrated vividly in season 1977–78, when London Scottish finished top of the table, London Welsh were second and London Irish third, with five wins and a draw from seven games. The

1978–79 season saw Welsh end up top, with Irish third, despite losing three of their seven matches.

Kennedy insisted that the days of optional training, ski holidays at Christmas and such like were all but over. Groans of disapproval and moans into a glass of the black stuff there might have been, but they accepted it. Andy Higginson, a back-row forward who had joined from NIFC and was in the Navy, made the 300-mile round trip from Plymouth twice a week for training and playing. Without a penny in expenses. Then came Les White, a highly durable prop forward who was living in Portsmouth and whose claim to fame would be a place in the Munster side which famously beat the 1978 New Zealand All Blacks and all but caused that part of Ireland to be drunk dry during that immortal night.

Noel Traynor, who captained the 'A's in the 1970s, became team secretary in 1976 in succession to John Hanaway, and is a long-standing observer of the Sunbury scene, said, 'We have always had a few strongmen who said, "This year we are going to train hard." Sometimes it worked, sometimes it didn't. The captain tended to be the man in control. If he was strong, it certainly made a difference.'

And Traynor was to detect a change in the social scene, too, when the 1980s arrived. 'In the 1960s and '70s, more people had flats in town and therefore the London Irish scene up there was very strong. Everyone would meet in the pubs we knew and drink together.'

But in the 1980s, a trend intensified to move out of London into the suburbs. Those players who had had bachelor pads in town got married and found suburban homes with gardens. The atmosphere at the London pubs wasn't the same; the scene had shifted closer towards the club's Sunbury base.

Mick Molloy was at Sunbury for 11 seasons. 'Ken Kennedy and I were the only two constant factors. Often we would pick up two guys late on before a game. It was quite difficult to cement a team under those circumstances, but gradually it came together.' Tony O'Reilly said that every time he saw Mick Galwey, the Shannon forward, he was reminded of Molloy: 'They were perhaps too small in height but with hearts bigger than any guys I have seen on the football pitch.'

Yet the social life and times had changed; the world was becoming a more serious place. Ye gods, it was the decade of Thatcher the milk-snatcher, and anyone living in England in that era must have understood the consequences of her creed. The more serious attitude towards training drastically reduced the opportunities for the kind of escapades that had hallmarked the 1950s. And a night's drinking followed by an unsteady path woven homewards up the A316 – or whatever direction the car followed on a Saturday night, normally by its own choosing – was becoming socially less acceptable. There was another problem, too. The number of doctors around at that time in the squad meant that frequent disruptions for work shifts at nights and on weekends often frustrated the best intentions of the Irish selectors. 'Even when I was captain in 1973, I would miss games or have to rush down to places like Bristol for a match after working throughout Friday night,' said Molloy.

They were times of occasional successes, frequent disappointments and a lot of hard graft to fit in the extra commitments. Yet Mick Molloy is like so many others who have had an association with this club: he retains a warmth and a respect for and a marvellous sense of gratitude towards London Irish for offering him so much. 'I had a great time. It was the most important club in my life. I enjoyed my time there very much and would have stayed involved had I remained in London.'

Molloy's quality was his play as a most valuable lock forward of the donkey variety. He was hard-grafting and a lot of his good work often went unseen. Only those who knew the game appreciated his qualities, which explains his 27 caps in a decade between 1966 and 1976. But at London Irish there was no doubt as to the seminal figure of that era – Ken Kennedy.

He had come to London in 1968 to undertake a two-year postgraduate course at Guy's Hospital. 'That time was politically interesting in Ireland because the Troubles had started. It seemed the correct thing to stay here until the thing finished, but in the event I didn't go back.

'It was always a very fun club, very amateurish. Initially you didn't know who was playing until they arrived at the ground on a Saturday afternoon. I was there in 1968–69–70 but had little input because I was playing international rugby and involved in my studies. But then I became captain when Al Moroney had to go back to Dublin, and we continued to pull the club round, saying things like, "You have to come to training if you want to play." But that was only the start. For me, the really vigorous time came when I finished playing international rugby in 1975 and became captain of the club again, intent on really changing attitudes. I was captain from 1976 to 1979 and I felt that if we were to exist, we had to change our attitude quite a lot.'

Under Kennedy, they endured such agonies as pre-season tours to the south of France, where visiting the likes of Beziers was as pleasurable as a wild, stormy night at Dracula's castle in Transylvania. You never knew which part would be bitten next. They went to South Africa, too, in 1977, becoming the first ever visiting club to play so many mixed-race teams. But the canvas had a wider spread: it was all part of the toughening-up process which enabled the club to build one of its best ever squads. In terms of results, what ensued may not quite have matched the exploits of the 1959–60 brigade, but, given the enhanced

Barry Murphy, who became an essential component of the London Irish sides of the late 1970s.

competitiveness of club rugby in England by that time, it was a highly meritorious achievement.

In 1976–77, there had been an RFU ruling that replacements would be permitted at all levels of rugby union, a small but significant step forward towards a more organised, manageable game.

Kennedy remembers, 'We won the London Merit Table in 1977 but the value of our tours was in developing players like John O'Driscoll, who then made his international debut in 1978, Hugh Condon and Freddie McLennan. And it also put us on the map as a club.'

Not that Kennedy was yet elevated to the rarified air breathed only in the committee boxes of rugby clubs in the land. Come summer, you would find him cutting the grass at Sunbury, helping to paint the changing-rooms and marking out the pitches. That was the way it was; everyone pitched in with a sort of wartime spirit. There were excellent people off the field, too, in higher circles, men like Paddy Forsyth and Herbie McKee. And others involved on the playing side. 'Without the boot-room staff, you couldn't do it, but especially at the start we had to do every job. We even had to go and buy the rugby balls and pump them up.'

But it began to pay off. Irishmen like Barry Murphy, a real livewire scrum-half, came 'home' after spells at Rosslyn Park and Blackheath, while Alistair and Roger McKibbin, three-quarters of rare quality, happened to be studying in London. Players like that were serious, top-quality rugby men; as Kennedy said, 'The jokes about Paddies and the Guinness stopped.'

Yet Kennedy knew what constituted a club atmosphere. He warmly welcomed the kiddies centre which Mick Molloy and others helped create for the club, a facility which meant families could go to Sunbury together. Twenty years later, London Irish remains the best club in London (and one of the best in the country) for providing facilities for youngsters to play while their parents enjoy the match or hospitality. It is a valued concept.

CHAPTER FIFTEEN

A Courageous Near Miss

'I think . . . that it is the best club in London.'

CHARLES DICKENS, 1812–70

1980 was a momentous year for rugby football in England. The English national team actually got to win a Grand Slam in the Five Nations championship by finally realising the potential of so much hitherto squandered talent. And London Irish reached the final of the John Player Cup and finished top of the RFU Club Merit Table for London.

Both achievements were of wondrous merit. England had been miserable failures for years, tormented by the Welsh and humiliated by Ireland, who fairly lorded it over them, winning Five Nations championship games in 1972, 1973, 1974, 1975, 1976 and 1979. Given what has happened in more recent times, it is clear the Irish missed a major trick by not abandoning the fixture and citing the understandable boredom factor of beating the English so often.

London Irish's march to the English cup final was a storybook happening, but without a storybook ending. They had started with a 29–9 victory over Maidstone, followed by a 15–9 win over Morley, both games at Sunbury. The quarter-final promised tougher fare, Bath away, yet they emerged winners, 6–3, to contest the semi-final at Rosslyn Park. It ended in a 6–6 draw, but in those days that was enough for the away team to go through. Two penalty goals by Clive Meanwell were all they could manage in a tight, dour semi-final, but it put them into their first ever final, against Leicester, the defending champions.

'We were probably the most aggressive defensive backline around in those days,' said Duncan Leopold, captain in 1978 and full-back in the cup final side. 'The whole way through that cup run, teams couldn't break us down for a try. Our approach was, if teams had the ball, hit them before they crossed the gain line and keep driving them back.'

But bodies were creaking under the pressure. Leopold was only playing with a couple of cortisone injections in a back in which he had two degenerated discs, Alistair McKibbin had a leg injury and a few others had aches and strains.

Clive Meanwell, top and below, whose scoring capabilities played a key role in the Exiles' journey to the 1980 John Player Cup final. Here, his penalty goal and try help Irish defeat Morley 15–9.

The final was unspectacular, in front of a record 27,000 crowd which paid a total of £55,000 to see it. Irish scored the only try, just before half-time, through second-row man Mike Smythe after Meanwell had burst through towards the corner before finding Smythe up in support for the score. Meanwell converted magnificently, left-footed, from the touchline to restrict Leicester's lead to 9–6 at the interval. He added a penalty goal in the second half, but by then Leicester had found the aerial route to success, Dusty Hare kicking four penalty goals and dropping a goal, with that impish little impresario of an outside-half Les Cusworth also dropping two goals. It meant that Leicester failed to score a try in the final and Irish had not conceded a try in their entire cup run, extraordinary statistics. Irish scored 65 points in the competition that season, with Meanwell accumulating 35 of them.

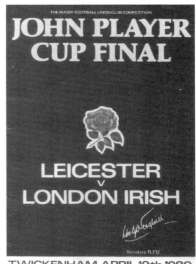

'Most of those matches were fairly tight,' recalls John O'Driscoll, a tough, industrious back-row forward who would win 26 Ireland caps between 1978 and 1984 and six Test caps for the British Lions in South Africa in 1980 and New Zealand 1983, as well as earning the universal respect of rugby men everywhere. He led Irish in that final and was captain from 1979 to 1981. A more quiet, yet determined and inspirational captain it would be hard to imagine.

'Everybody expected us to lose at Bath, but we always felt we were capable of beating them. We had a winning mentality that year, and it served us well. In the semi-final at Rosslyn Park we had a strong wind behind us in the first half, and when we reached half-time only three points up, I remember passing Andy Ripley, who said, "Well, that's it, then, isn't it?" But we gave a very gutsy performance in the second half to edge them out.

'Leicester were the better side in the final, no doubt. They put a lot of pressure on us. I think we were pretty philosophical about it afterwards. After all, Leicester were an extraordinarily good side, with seven internationals, and we had done well to get to the final. Only by playing out of our skins were we able to keep them under control, so it wasn't a major "downer" afterwards.'

London Irish might not have scored a hatful of tries *en route* to Twickenham that year, but they had plenty of ability and solidity. Leopold was full-back, the gifted Roger and Alistair McKibbin offered sublime talents in the backline, and Barry Murphy and Hugh Condon were wily and shrewd at half-back. The pack contained stout pillars of ability in props Les White and Alex Newberry, with Jim Sheehan and Smythe indomitable workhorses at lock and a back row of Walter Jones and O'Driscoll on the flanks and Kevin Short at No. 8. Plus the secret ingredient: team spirit. It brought them seven wins and a draw from eight London Merit Table matches, a points difference of 139–41 and a 93.75 per cent record.

O'Driscoll, who was at school at Stonyhurst, had been at Sunbury since 1973 when he had gone to London to attend medical school. He found a club of great vibrancy and atmosphere, from the players at 1st XV level taking it increasingly seriously to those in the most junior teams playing social rugby for the sheer fun of it all. 'Once the matches were over, you socialised together, with all those guys from the lower sides. That was the key thing at the club: it offered a warm welcome to everyone.'

O'Driscoll cites Michael O'Connor, president from 1976 to 1981, as a crucial figure in that era. 'He was someone who lent great stability to the club. He had the ability to encourage and maintain the atmosphere of the club while concentrating more on the rugby as well. And Mick Molloy was a very active club man on and off the field.'

Pat Parfrey became chief coach, ending his playing days and then helping to organise the senior side in a thoroughly proficient style. He loved to wander up and down the touchline in his overcoat, seemingly oblivious to most of the taunts of the locals in the crowd who enjoyed shouting well-intentioned abuse at him. Which was all part of the fun, really.

Ken Kennedy's fires of competitive zeal had been finally quenched by the time Irish reached that final, although he did sit on the replacements' bench – 'praying I wouldn't be needed,' he later joked. And then Kevin Short – he of that immortal phrase 'the days of training on Guinness are over' – finished playing and helped out with the coaching.

GONE FOR A BURTON

One of the most familiar faces at Sunbury through the 1960s and 1970s was that of newspaper reporter Charlie Burton, who contributed reports chiefly to *The Irish Times*. Burton, who became the inspiration behind the Public School Wanderers club, was a great old rugby man but a cantankerous character. He always demanded his favourite seat in the small press box and would not tolerate others inadvertently taking his place. He was one of the first journalists to be a regular visitor at Sunbury.

Burton was away with the team for a cup match at Redruth in 1981, staying overnight at a local hotel. As the players sat down to what the club programme notes the following week referred to as 'their gin and cornflakes', a scene ensued with Burton, flushed and angry, berating the hotel manager for the lack of loo paper in his room. The hubbub was too much for Freddie Williamson, who growled, 'Why the **** don't you use *The Irish Times*?'

O'Driscoll puts into words the fears of so many who have loved this game down the years. 'I had friends at medical school and they used to love coming down to Sunbury, playing and enjoying the fun. But I am not sure you can do that any more. I think it is a great pity for youngsters now.'

And, for sure, it will be a pity if that quality of unique comradeship is now compromised. In that respect, London Irish probably have more to lose than most clubs. Michael Flatley, the man given the onerous task, poor chap, of trying to accede to the whims, fantasies and ludicrous demands of the press corps for 17 successive seasons, joined in 1969 and speaks of the club with the kind of warmth and humility expressed so often by members in these pages.

'It was just nice to be there and be Irish. I played at the junior level and enjoyed it immensely. You went out and met people on the pitch, and they became lifelong friends.' Which isn't the worst testimony to what a sports club can offer men and women.

Flatley captained the Extra 'A's for five consecutive years, 'because I had access to a telephone and could get 15 men on the pitch on a Saturday,' he was told, with searing honesty! He insists that the Irish Exiles club is different from London Welsh or London Scottish. 'They're both still on the mainland. The Irish are true Exiles; they have come across the water to make their home in London. There is more of a kindred spirit amongst London Irish folk than the others.'

Flatley, like myriad others, saw and marvelled at players like Barry Bresnihan down the years: 'One of the best centres I ever enjoyed watching, the Jeremy Guscott of that era,' he says. 'His gliding and powerful running were superb.'

And they fitted in wherever they were needed, addressing whichever task was required, these servants of the club. Flatley and Ray McLennan, later fixture secretary and then chairman of the house and ground committee (in other words, the man with the keys), became accustomed to the midweek afternoon rush down to the printers of the match programme, D.C.W. Penrose in London Road, Staines, to make corrections, add the last up-to-the-minute team details and then stand back as the presses rolled. It all required free time generously donated, and such acts have been mirrored throughout Ireland, England, the northern and southern hemispheres – everywhere the game has been played, really. If you counted up the free time given by millions the world over to this sport, it would run into centuries.

Duncan Leopold was another who contributed handsomely, not to mention his wife, Helen, and the ladies of the social committee too. Captain in 1978, Leopold went on to become team secretary and selector before bowing out for a break in 1989. But in 1994–95, he was to return as chairman. He has seen countless good and bad seasons at Sunbury. In the 1980s, they fluctuated alarmingly.

The season after their 1980 cup final appearance, Irish were fortified by the arrival of internationals Moss Finn and Stewart McKinney, the latter a 1974 British Lion in South Africa but more recently incoming landlord at the Turk's Head, the London pub which vied with the Bunch of Grapes and the Antelope to see which hostelry could pour the most of the black stuff down willing young Irish rugby men's throats. The side finished seventh out of ten in the Merit Table London Division that season, with three wins and four defeats in seven matches. Perversely, the next year they ended up top with a 100 per cent record from seven matches, ahead of London Welsh second and the Scottish third. In one Ireland–England 'B' international that season, London Irish contributed two players to each side: Hugh Condon and Paul O'Donnell for the Irish team and Tony Watkinson and Peter Enevoldson, the Oxford blues, for England. This success was attributable to greater strength in depth, a consequence of the hard work put in over the previous ten years by people like Paddy Forsythe and others to attract London-born Irishmen to the club and see them develop through Schoolboy and Under-21 ranks.

When Paddy's wife Barbara passed away nine days before Christmas in 1983, the club paid tribute to their work for London Irish, saying, 'They joined the club in 1946 and Barbara, particularly, is remembered for her help in organising the Under-21s in the mid-'70s, sometimes ferrying carloads of players to and from games. She was always supporting from the touchline, and her presence will be very much missed by all at London Irish.'

In 1981, the club toured Canada, a hugely successful venture which was enjoyed by everyone. The following year, they went to the traditional rugby hotbed of Nigeria, a location London Welsh had visited the year before. 'We went up to the north of the country,' said Noel Traynor, 'and the group was split up to stay with local people. One of our props, who shall remain nameless, found quarters more African (unusual, that, in the middle of Africa) than European. The next morning, he was to be found sleeping on the dirt floor.'

THE WORLD OF MINI-RUGBY

1982 became famous as a splendid vintage – for red Bordeaux wine and the creation of the London Irish mini-rugby tournament. Amongst other things! The tournament has become an institution for a multitude of cheering, proud parents and screaming, mud-caked schoolboys from Under-8s upwards. From an indecently early hour in the morning until the late afternoon, hundreds of rugby-barmy kids ply their trade on the many fields London Irish commandeer for the day close by their Sunbury base. (If your son's team keeps winning, thereby extending your hours of duty on a sometimes cold, wet, bleak touchline, you know not whether to cheer robustly or curse privately.) The whole event is brilliantly well supported and organised, and a testimony to men like Paddy Hughes, Brian Gaule and many others who were instrumental in getting the whole thing up and running from the tiny seed of a committee-room idea. They did it by sheer hard graft, poring over details and arrangements for long hours of their time, all given on a voluntary basis. Such commitment has been the bedrock upon which much of the sport has been based.

'We still have one of the premier mini and junior sections anywhere at a European rugby club,' says Gaule. 'Alas, we perhaps just didn't have the foresight to retain some of the players we developed through this system.' From Under-8s upwards, they worked to bring on and develop literally thousands of young kids who might one day be invaluable to the London Irish club. Players like Paul Burke, the Hopley brothers, Sean O'Leary, Darren Molloy and Justin Bishop all came up through the ranks. All except for Bishop now have something else in common – none is still with London Irish. Which is deeply unfortunate for the club, although others have emerged and stayed.

As far back as 1985, as many as 720 boys from 13 clubs were battling it out all day on 15 pitches in 130 matches. Since then, the event has grown enormously in repute and appeal. The following letter, written in 1990, is one of many sent to chief organiser Paddy

Hughes over the years about the successful organisation of the mini festival.

> *Dear Mr Hughes,*
> *Just a note to thank you for a most enjoyable day at the mini-rugby tournament on Sunday. I thought the whole occasion was very well organised and please give my sincere thanks to all the people who put so much time and effort into the proceedings. It was the first time I have attended the London Irish Festival and I hope it will not be the last.*
> *Many thanks,*
> *Peter Sinclair*
> *(Hertford Under-9 Dad)*

Brian Gaule, who is now manager of the club's Under-9s, says, 'Back in 1983, I decided I wanted to get involved in the coaching of minis and juniors. This tournament was obviously the showpiece day of each season for the youngsters, but every Sunday morning at the club there were at least 400 running around in a variety of age-level teams. The organisation was all done by parents and coaches.

'The tragedy from the club's point of view was that for too long they didn't recognise the raw material that was there to be nurtured and developed for the future. They weren't forward-thinking enough. We weren't properly looked after; we were on the outside. Yet we had been among the front-runners of this huge growth the game eventually saw in mini-rugby. And, looking ahead, I am sure the club will benefit, because it realised that help was needed to put into place an infrastructure. In years to come, the benefit to the club will become very apparent. What is now needed is a fast-tracking system for the best youngsters. This is something that must be nurtured, and then we will get the benefits.'

The 1982–83 season saw Scottish top of the pile with Irish third, but 12 months later it was whoopsie-time again, Irish finishing eighth out of ten, with only two wins in nine games. They stayed in that lowly hollow the next year, too, with just three wins from eight games, and failure even to qualify for the John Player Special Cup. 'A very poor season by our standards,' rebuked Mr Flatley in the club programme. And the sense of gloom was deepened by the news that popular linesman Henry Hennessy would be hanging up his touch flag at the end of that season, after 17 years in the job.

OLLIE'S ODDITY

In April 1984, that delightful former Irish outside-half Seamus Oliver ('Ollie') Campbell accepted an invitation to come to London and present the prizes at the London Irish Mini-Rugby Festival. In telephone conversations prior to the trip, Campbell was anxious to ensure all would go smoothly.

'How will I recognise you at the airport?' he asked his London Irish contact. He was told what to look out for, and then said, 'Now, you'll want to know what I'll be in, so as to recognise me. I'll have on a green Ireland blazer with the shamrock, grey trousers and . . .'

'Ollie, Ollie,' interrupted our man, 'I think I know what you look like.'

Given that Campbell had helped Ireland to the Five Nations championship and Triple Crown in 1982 and joint championship in 1983, and the fact that he was one of the world's leading players, his modesty was wondrous to behold.

Yet, for all the lost matches and missed scoring chances, it remained a *real* club, vibrant and alive. Why, in 1986 even the club's 'B' team produced its own video, although whether we should term it a video special or a video nasty remains to this day a matter of some conjecture. International weekends were always special, with a visiting club over from Ireland, as Clontarf were in February 1984. And the same day, a London Irish 'casserole' side played St Luke's, while on yet another pitch the Under-19s were entertaining Galway.

'The dedication wasn't there at the top level at that time. Most of those years were just a void,' remembers Leopold. 'Players were looking after their careers far more.' Ah, the Thatcher influence once again.

When Leopold finally retired, he started up an Under-16s side with Alex Newberry, and they found huge interest among young players at several age levels, thereby providing another link in the valuable production line for the club's aspiring stars. Paul Burke, who started with the club, played outside-half for Ireland, then joined Bristol and is now with Cardiff, was coached by Leopold at Under-16 level.

THE PAVILION EXTENSION

The new pavilion at Sunbury, adjacent to 'The Buildings', or main stand, was officially opened on 6 September 1986. The facility greatly enhanced London Irish's capacity for corporate entertainment, providing a large upstairs dining area, next to which was a good-sized kitchen, plus a downstairs corporate entertainment bar, with adjacent toilets. It meant that the club could start to spread more decisively into the world of big-match hospitality at Sunbury, by offering companies a separate eating and drinking location before and after the match.

In 1985–86, the RFU in England introduced the John Smith's Merit Tables. Better than the John Thomas Merit Table, but every bit as daft in one sense, because it was lopsided, to say the least. In Table A, Leicester had ten fixtures in the season, Harlequins just four. But then, when did common sense ever intrude into those plush, exclusive committee rooms at HQ? At Sunbury, meanwhile, business commitments forced Paul O'Donnell to resign the captaincy, Michael Gibson, the international No. 8 who was first capped in 1979, taking over.

Hugo MacNeill, who had been loitering with educational intent at Oxford University for much of the 1980s up to that point and whose name was spelled incorrectly in the Twickenham programme for one England–Ireland international despite all the practice they'd had, joined the Irish in 1985. It was all very reminiscent of Oxford: there seemed to be loads of people lazing around not doing very much!

Hugo complained, somewhat ruefully, from the safety of his retirement armchair, 'I played for every club just before they became any good – Blackrock College, Trinity College, Dublin, Oxford University and then London Irish. It was a bit disorganised down at Sunbury in those days, before the Jim Staples, Simon Geoghegan era began. Results were up and down – and more down than up, for it wasn't a great squad of players. There was the occasional upset win, a great surprise result when we would suddenly beat one of the bigger clubs like Harlequins or Wasps. But that was pretty rare.'

Hugo, now clearly training for the diplomatic corps, chose his words carefully on the next topic. 'It was a lovely club to play for, but it was a funny club in the sense that you had various committees fighting over politics. The in-fighting there is legendary, and has put years on the lives of some people. But then it is a remarkable place, an amalgam of so many Irish people from different backgrounds.

'The political battles off the field probably held the club back from being as organised as it might have been, but the fact was that at the time we just didn't have the playing resources required to be a formidable club.'

You could hardly blame the delightfully friendly Hugo from harbouring some less than ecstatic memories about rugby in London in that era. In 1988, he was unfortunate enough to be chosen for Ireland (for the last time in a Five Nations match, quite coincidentally) against England at Twickenham, the day a 3–3 half-time score finished 35–3 to England. Twenty-four hours after the match, MacNeill was sitting in a London pub, the Turk's Head, when a character wandered over, stood right in front of him and asked the rhetorical question, 'What happened?' Memories of that day are painful in the extreme to all Irishmen. It's like asking British Army veterans about Dunkirk, or the Germans about Stalingrad. Very poor form.

He'll always remember his debut for the Irish, a match at Pontypool during which he was carried off, concussed and considerably under the weather. 'Staff' Jones (with whom he'd toured New Zealand with the 1983 British Lions) smirked afterwards and said, 'Welcome to Pontypool Park.' Funny sense of humour they have down in those valleys. Hugo laughed himself senseless while lying down in the back of the team bus all the way to London.

MacNeill encountered a similar difficulty to everyone else at Sunbury through the years. 'People came and then moved on. That was part and parcel of the place.' And he became the same as the rest of them, drifting off to America in 1988 (perhaps because word of the Twickenham débâcle hadn't got that far by then and, for all the muggings in New York City and Washington State, it was a hell of a lot safer than Pontypool Park) and finally finishing at Sunbury the following year. 'I passed through; it was a transition period for me.'

The second season of officially sponsored Merit Tables, 1986–87, saw Irish finish bottom of Table B with one win and eight defeats from nine matches. But the Yorkshire club Headingley, in the same table, only played six games, and many fixtures were arranged on days when the leading players like Brian McCall, the lock forward who was capped for Ireland in 1985 and 1986, were on representative duty. English rugby was still in the dark ages compared with the competitive structure long since established in a country like Ireland. That year, Irish went out of the John Player Special Cup in the third round, falling 9–3 at home to Richmond.

The beer was changed for the 1987–88 season, the Courage Leagues, largest competitions of their kind in the world, coming on tap, as it were. Irish were in National League Two and finished eighth out of ten, after four wins and a draw from 11 matches. In August 1988 there was a highly successful tour to Australia. But it ought to have been a better season at home. Brian Spillane, a hugely talented No. 8 forward, was in London studying sports medicine at the London Hospital in Whitechapel and joined the club once the inaugural World Cup had finished in Australia and New Zealand that summer, following a meeting with Paddy Forsythe in New Zealand. But Spillane was to suffer a cruel blow in a London Irish shirt.

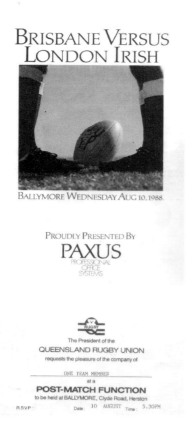

BRISBANE VERSUS
LONDON IRISH

BALLYMORE WEDNESDAY AUG 10, 1988.

PROUDLY PRESENTED BY

PAXUS
PROFESSIONAL
OFFICE
SYSTEMS

The President of the
QUEENSLAND RUGBY UNION
requests the pleasure of the company of

ONE TEAM MEMBER
at a
POST-MATCH FUNCTION
to be held at BALLYMORE, Clyde Road, Herston

R.S.V.P.:   Date: 10 AUGUST   Time: 5.30PM

Mementoes from the Exiles' highly successful 1988 tour to Australia.

'I played the first 12 weeks of the season but then suffered a serious eye injury in a match against Northampton. I caught a finger in one eye and was completely blinded. I lost the sight in it for six months. I was in hospital over Christmas at Moorfield's Eye Hospital, where they operated. They thought I might lose it altogether, for it had more or less exploded, but it was saved, although it took about a year to recover.'

Typically, London Irish folk rallied around. 'They were great to me, superb when I was in hospital,' recalls Spillane. 'They looked after us financially, too. My wife and I met a lot of great people at that club whom we are proud to call friends. It was only a reasonable side at that time, to be honest, but London Irish was a super place.'

Brendan Mullin, a beautifully balanced, classical centre three-quarter who had been playing international rugby since 1984 and had just won blues at Oxford University in 1986 and 1987, followed the Hugo MacNeill route down the M40 and then up the M3 to London Irish. He found a completely different culture from anything he'd known in Ireland. 'People travelled so far to play a match and then you'd never see them again until the next Saturday.' Which was quite unlike the Dublin rugby life. As was the work and training schedule. Anyone in the vicinity of the City of London around 5.45 p.m. on a Tuesday and Thursday was in danger of being cut down by a flying Irish rugby international centre dressed in pin-stripe suit and clutching umbrella and briefcase. Mullin would catch the 'Drain', local terminology for the tube direct from the City to Waterloo, where he would squeeze into a packed rush-hour commuter service down to Sunbury. Quality preparation for quality training, this, remember. 'I'd be absolutely exhausted by the time I got there,' he said. 'Then, after training, I'd get a lift back to town and get home by about 11.30 p.m., when I'd remember I hadn't eaten any dinner.'

And, after all that, he couldn't play that much anyway. Leinster had a series of warm-up matches for the inter-provincial season, and if he wasn't hurtling towards Sunbury, he'd be dashing out to Heathrow Airport and scrambling on to the flight for Dublin on a Friday night. But Mullin sensed what MacNeill had experienced. 'It was a very political club, and certainly in more recent years I could see the same issues arising between a strong, very opinionated committee and the playing side. Perhaps with Irishmen abroad there will always be arguments about how things should be run.'

But Mullin preferred to concentrate on playing matters. And one night in training he was intrigued by his first sight of a new player at the club. 'We were playing tip-rugby and this guy had real pace and power; he was the most dynamic guy I'd seen. But his hands were poor and he wasn't a footballer at that stage.' Enter one Simon Geoghegan.

Mullin was, like so many other notable players who joined the club, potentially an outstanding acquisition around whom an entire backline could be constructed. Except that he was so often away, involved in representative rugby, injured or simply unavailable. When you sat down at the end of a season and worked out just how many games a quality player of his ilk had played for London Irish, it made for depressing reading. And for Brendan Mullin, read Barry Bresnihan, Simon Geoghegan, Jim Staples, John O'Driscoll, Andy Mulligan . . . and so on and so on.

'A club with that problem can never really achieve its potential,' claims Mullin. 'With any club, you need a certain amount of time to structure a team or a squad, to get results three years down the line. It doesn't just happen. In my short time there – and I was gone after little more than one season – we had very good representative players from all the Irish provinces. But unless we played together, we struggled to get a team pattern going.'

Mullin remembers players like Paul Bell, with whom he'd played schools rugby, as among the most talented footballers he has ever seen. But business activities in the City meant that for Bell, like Mullin, work and rugby conflicted. Thus, says Mullin, Bell was never really recognised as being as good as he was.

That year, 1987–88, Rosslyn Park finished top of League Two, Leicester finished top of League One, and Irish crashed 16–3 at home to Sale in the cup. The final year of the '80s saw a marginal improvement, with Irish sixth that season after five wins and two draws from 11 games. They were, however, only two points behind promoted Bedford, champions Saracens dominating the division with 11 wins in 11 matches.

Michael Gibson had seen problems emerging as soon as he had become seriously involved at the club. The powerful, elegant No. 8 international forward had taken over as club captain in 1987–88 and soon had cause to remember his wife Mary's comment: 'If you want to lose friends, become captain of London Irish.' Gibson appointed Lyn Flye as the new coach, but it did not work as he had hoped.

'The problem was the old one pertaining to London Irish. So many players

The charismatic Simon Geoghegan, whose career at London Irish ended on a discordant note, through no fault of his own.

were so often unavailable. I doubt whether the same team was ever chosen in successive weeks. Worse still, you would never really have the team even to train together. There was this constant disruption because of inter-provincial matches followed by the international programme.'

But the malaise ran even deeper than that. 'The senior players were taking the piss, I thought. You would get a poor turn-out for training even when you knew sometimes they could have come. But we couldn't afford not to select them. However, I stood up to them, and maybe some noses were put out of joint. But I felt I had to do that.'

Neil Francis, the international lock forward, had come to London and joined the club in 1988–89. He found a club that was enjoying enormous playing talent around that time – Brendan Mullin, Michael Gibson, John O'Driscoll, Simon Geoghegan, Jim Staples, John Hewitt and plenty of others. 'Yet it just didn't work,' he conceded. 'It proved impossible to harmonise and galvanise even that amount of talent. People were working in the City and would turn up late at training, all kinds of things. And the training sessions were just ridiculous; you would have an unopposed game of tip, and unopposed line-outs. And everybody was off drinking in those days, particularly after the matches.'

The London scene amazed Francis. One night, he and Jim Staples ended up at a place called the Hibernian Club in Fulham Broadway and then moved on to a rave somewhere on industrial wasteland out in Essex. 'I was losing my mind with all this going on. I'd had a very settled environment in Dublin and was trying to build a career. The London scene was something else.'

They went to Orrell for the opening match of that season, a non-league affair, and Francis was marking Bob Kimmins, the big second-row man. 'I wasn't very fit when I was playing for London Irish, but I remember in that game I skinned Kimmins. Orrell were winning but I got the ball and got past Kimmins to score a try. That night, I got absolutely wasted. It was a great bender. By 11.30 p.m. I was absolutely gaga, and I slept most of the way back to London. Someone dropped me off at a tube station near Heathrow and I then fell asleep on the tube and woke up hours later in the sidings at Cockfosters station, with a Pakistani porter peering over me to see whether I was alive or dead. Anyway, I went outside the train, was sick and stumbled into a taxi they'd called because this was about four in the morning. It cost me about £35 to get back to my pad in London. I was called "Cockfosters" by the boys for months afterwards.'

League rugby was bringing a proper structure to English club rugby, and long overdue it was. And clubs like London Irish were struggling to grasp the growing realities and consequences of semi-professionalism.

Brendan Mullin and his fellow City workers decided that eating at around midnight after training twice a week was too much, so they sought out a club official and suggested some sandwiches and coffee might be laid on for the guys after training. And, by golly, those London Irish officials were spot-on in tackling the issue.

'The next week, Neil Francis and myself went to the bar and enquired as to the likelihood of some food. Lo and behold, about 15 minutes later, a couple of steak sandwiches arrived. We couldn't believe our luck. We ate them and were just getting up to leave when the club official I had spoken to walked up and handed me a bill for £14. I paid up and we never asked for sandwiches again.'

Some things were changing in the game, but the poor bloody infantry, the players, would be the last to know it.

CHAPTER SIXTEEN

Money Worries

'Money, money, money,
Must be funny
In a rich man's world.'

ABBA

Rugby union turned professional in 1995, but for several years prior to that momentous decision most clubs had been increasingly pressurised by financial concerns. But at London Irish, one figure had provided such substantial financial assistance over very many years that for a long time any financial strains had been eased.

Eddie Lawlor, owner of a land development company, had joined the club in the same week as Willie Lemon back in 1959 and had generously given money to London Irish for most of his life. Lawlor, who had also given financial assistance to Mother Theresa, may have made an overall contribution to London Irish in his lifetime of anything between £400,000 and £500,000. Or even more. He paid most of the cost of the pavilion, erected in 1986 at an estimated cost of £220,000, towards which the club raised no more than £40,000 over two years. He also paid for a complete new floodlighting system for the 1st XV pitch and many other things at the club, including a foundation scholarship scheme for Oxbridge through which players like Brendan Mullin, Charley Haly, Rory Moloney, Mark Egan and others went on to represent London Irish.

Lawlor became chairman of the club's development committee but at one point had his wrists slapped by the general committee for exceeding his powers, allegedly for bypassing the constraints of a club's rules, regulations and accepted structures in favour of getting things done. Lawlor, upset at being treated in such a way, briefly resigned from

One of the most sought-after items on the London rugby circuit: a ticket for the London Irish annual dinner.

THE
LONDON IRISH RUGBY FOOTBALL CLUB

President: Hugh Brady

ANNUAL DINNER

on
Friday 12th May, 1989
at
THE LONDON TARA HOTEL
Scarsdale Place, Kensington
London W.8.
7.00 p.m. for 7.30 p.m.

Dress: Black Tie   Ticket £27.00

the club. In the time of his absence, London Irish began to feel the cold wind of financial difficulties blowing into Sunbury.

The club overspent to the tune of £100,000, and a loan was raised for that amount. They were beginning to experience considerable difficulties. 'Like any club,' said Duncan Leopold, who was not involved on the committee at that time, 'London Irish were going through financial difficulties. They borrowed too much and things got difficult.'

But then, in season 1992–93, through a quirk of great fortune, another club member stepped forward with the wherewithal to ease troubled brows. Ray O'Rourke was the boss of a large construction company and had the funds to assist a club he had known for some years. He underwrote the £100,000 loan with the bank, and mighty grateful London Irish were too. Once O'Rourke arrived, heavy expenses such as the 1st XV squad's pre-season tour of France were met in full. The financial situation was eased, especially when, in the 1993–94 season, the Anglo-Irish Bank was brought in as the main club sponsor.

Except that things were not as easy as that. But then, they never are. Normally, having a situation where two wealthy patrons have agreed to pay most of your major expenses would seem like heaven on earth. But other concerns began to surface. Duncan Leopold explained, 'Gradually, many of the members in the club began to have the feeling that there was a hidden message, to the effect that "This is my ball. If you don't play with it my way, you can't have the ball."' As a result of which, four weeks before the AGM, in response to a widespread feeling of discontent among a majority of members, Brian Little, Duncan Leopold, Mike Gibson and Rob Alexander agreed to let their names go forward for selection in a variety of roles, to stand against Ray O'Rourke, Pat Barragry, Paul Collins and other O'Rourke supporters.

By now, O'Rourke and his supporters knew they faced a fight for ultimate control, and with a clear eye on winning hearts and minds they produced at the end of the 1993–94 season an infamous glossy brochure detailing their business plans for the future of the club. It was professionally produced and carefully prepared but its intentions and ambitions had left too many behind. When it landed on the doormats of club members and that section of the executive committee whose support could not be guaranteed, there was a seismic shock. Instead of rallying support, it had the reverse effect.

'Basically, it said, "Here is our plan for the next five years, and this is the way it is going to be,"' added Leopold. The trouble was, club members rose in dissent at what they saw as a takeover of London Irish. There was complete chaos, for half the committee knew nothing about it. The storm that broke threatened to do major damage to the British Telecom system as angry members scrambled to make calls at all hours of the day and night to all and sundry, discussing the events and pondering what tactics they should embrace at the following week's AGM.

That AGM, at the end of season 1993–94, was attended by over 300 members, a record. Those present were in grim mood, demanding to know what was going on. 'It was a wicked AGM,' said Kieran McCarthy who, together with Mike Gibson, survived from the committee. But several others went. Chairman Pat Barragry was forced to admit it had been wrong to send out the brochure without the approval of the full committee. Those on the committee who had put together the brochure had shot themselves in the foot; the coup was dealt a fatal blow. Besides, no one had seized the local radio stations, so it was never that well organised! It became an AGM famous for a rout, a complete whitewash which left O'Rourke and his associates no choice but to walk away. It also left Hika Reid vulnerable, and his tenure as coach ended soon after. AGMs at London Irish had always been eventful, but this was the most dramatic of all.

The departure of Ray O'Rourke and his allies meant that the committee then came back to people who had been involved in the executive committee of the club for some time. They were duly voted in, together with Alan McCartney, who became treasurer. Leopold was chairman, Little was president, Gibson was rugby co-ordinator and Alexander chairman of mini and youth rugby. 'I think if someone is prepared to put his hand in his pocket to give the club financial support, people should recognise that,' said Leopold in his acknowledgement and thanks to O'Rourke.

'People then feared the club would go down from Division Two and all the sponsors would walk away,' says Leopold. 'But in the event, the complete reverse happened. We increased our sponsorship over the next two years and went up to Division One. The Anglo-Irish Bank deal had been for one year only and the new club officials negotiated a new, improved deal with Guinness to become chief club sponsor. The new "Guinness Bar" was built and the balance sheet showed a healthy improvement.'

Eddie Lawlor eventually rejoined London Irish, and in April 1998 the club's stand was named after him. Lawlor, by then too ill to attend the ceremony, wrote the following letter to the club:

I am very sorry that I cannot be with you all today but this is, of course, due to my ill health. I do appreciate the honour you do me in naming the new stand for me. What I did for the club between 1985 and 1990 was done out of appreciation for what the club did for me when I first came to London in 1959. It literally became my second home and some of the friends I made during my playing days have become lifelong friends. Two in particular, Glen Keilty and Phil Douglas, shared flats with me, did business with me and we have become godparents to each other's children – lifelong friends indeed!

There are so many other people with whom I was involved when we were carrying out the improvements and rebuilding work at the club during the latter part of the '80s of whom I hold great memories, but I shall only mention Paddy Hughes. It was his enthusiasm and the enormous effort he put into the club that inspired me to do what I did, so – thank you, Paddy.

In the coming year the club will be celebrating its centenary. I hope that we do so in the Premier Division and in some style. I can only visualise what the coming centenary year and the millennium year that will follow it will be like. I shall be with you in spirit. Thank you once again for the honour you are doing me in naming this stand for me.

Professionalism had brought its own difficulties. Michael Watt, head of the TV rights company CSI Ltd, gave the club a handsome donation, telling them, 'This will help get you going.' But, as Leopold said, 'It was still like stepping off into a professional era knowing we had hardly any cash. We were just new to the First Division, we needed better players and we also needed to pay our best players very well just to keep them. You had to step off the cliff and hope there was a soft landing.'

When the RFU turned Twickenham into its futuristic reality from the old stadium of splintered wooden benches and rickety old chairs, it became a mutual and provident society, and promptly recommended to all its leading member clubs that they should do the same. London Irish officials assembled a team of solicitors and accountants and had various meetings before, in season 1995–96, becoming a limited company. This was an act which addressed the demands of professionalism in the game. And at the end of that season, the club returned to the First Division of the Premiership.

The board of the new London Irish RFC (Trading) Ltd company comprised David Jackson (chairman), Duncan Leopold (who had served as chairman on the executive committee for two years, stepped down from that role in 1995–96 and, starting from summer 1996, became chief executive of the new company), Alan McCartney (financial director), Jim O'Hara and Paddy Flynn. They maintained the club in the First Division with little money and put together a consortium of investors led initially by John Stackpoole, who had been wooed over a period of several months before accepting offers to come on board. Leopold stood down in September 1997, once the deal with the new consortium which was buying a controlling interest in the club had been finalised. Stackpoole became one of the directors of London Irish Holdings, the new consortium, an important move in further strengthening the club's financial potential.

The deal for the consortium, says Leopold, was unique. 'Some £1.6 million was put up by the consortium, £600,000 by mini consortia comprising blocks of £25,000, and the balance of £880,000 by the general body of membership. It was unique in that ownership did not rest with any one individual. No one person had more than 12.5 per cent, so the membership owned the club,' he said.

In the first year of professionalism, London Irish lost around £800,000. It was a sizeable sum, but a whole lot better than the alleged figures at some of their London neighbours: Richmond's deficit was said to be £3 million, Saracens' £2 million, Harlequins' around £1.5 million. Rugby clubs everywhere were finding the going tough.

Was all the grief worth it? Mike Gibson says, 'It was an evolutionary step. If we hadn't changed, we would have died out like the dinosaurs. There was a certain inevitability about the whole thing. But with any change there is pain.'

At London Irish, there had been plenty of other grumbles. In season 1993–94 the club had produced a new playing jersey for its first team which looked like a cross between a Pittsburgh Steelers American football shirt and a Zandra Rhodes fashion creation. The old school of members tended to blow their noses noisily when it was mentioned. Leopold remembers, 'That jersey had been suggested and created by certain individuals. It angered members who felt that it was no longer their club. The first thing we did when we had the opportunity in 1994–95 was go back to the original London Irish jersey.'

On and off the playing field, the changes in personnel during the late 1980s and 1990s have been frequent. Roger McKibbin, the son of Harry, the IRB member, had been rugby co-ordinator at the club and felt that George Hook should not stay as coach. He put forward his suggestion as a replacement, but there was a counter-proposal at committee level by supporters of O'Rourke to bring in Hika Reid, the former New Zealand hooker. Reid was eventually appointed, leaving McKibbin no choice but to stand down.

Roger's position of rugby co-ordinator on the executive committee was not immediately filled. Rugby matters were handled by Paul Collins, the 1st XV captain, and Hika Reid. The following February, the executive felt it necessary to appoint a replacement. Two candidates, Kevin Short, the 1st XV coach in 1990–91, and Michael Gibson, who had been club captain in 1986–87 and was Under-19 coach, were interviewed for the position, the latter being successful.

Mike Tewkesbury and then Lyn Flye had preceded George Hook's tenure as the first official paid club coach, and he was followed by Reid, who himself was replaced by Clive Woodward. The Leicester, England and British Lions player had been coach at the junior club Henley with conspicuous success, his philosophy based on experience gained while living and playing the game in Sydney, Australia.

Woodward sought a similar flat, attacking backline approach, with slick handling and the ball doing the work and creating the space. Alas, it took some time for Woodward's demands to work successfully, as Mike Flatley acknowledged. 'Clive was ahead of his time as a coach when he worked with us. His plans were too elaborate for the players he had available at the time at Sunbury.' Yet Irish were a most successful side in Woodward's second season at the club. 'It was a great achievement for an Exiles club to get into the First Division again, and everything was good that year on and off the pitch,' said Kieran McCarthy. 'When we clinched promotion, we had a big party. There were fireworks and bonfires and we decided that every home game thereafter would be a party.'

But Gibson had handed Woodward one hell of a task. 'Not only was he having to reshape our playing style, but he also had to drag the management and administration of the club into the new era. Clive took on a mammoth task and, looking back, he was a fundamental building block in our development in the modern game.'

Woodward himself had suggested recruiting a forwards coaching expert, and the club lured Willie Anderson, that highly charismatic former Irish international lock, from his Dungannon home to assist. In time, Woodward's spell weakened and Anderson took over. Then, midway through the 1997–98 season, he was replaced by Dick Best, the former Harlequins and England coach.

From 1987–88 and the inception of the Courage Leagues, London Irish's fortunes had fluctuated. That first season, they won only four of 11 league games; the next year, 1988–89, produced five wins and two draws in 11 games. It also produced a quite extraordinary climax. Irish needed victory in their last match, at home to mid-table Blackheath, to be in with a chance of clinching promotion to League One.

Neil Francis, the Irish international lock forward who played in the Blackheath match, traced the original problem to a sevens tournament the previous week. 'The club had entered us for the Oxford University Sevens, demanding London Irish be represented. I said, "What if someone gets injured?" They insisted we couldn't scratch and must be there. Then they picked me and insisted all the first-team players be there prepared to play.

'Well, Jim Staples and I were out on the Saturday night and didn't get home until six o'clock the next morning, the day of these sevens at Oxford. We woke up and everything was fuzzy, but we had to be in Oxford at 9 a.m. I remember someone driving us there, and I was sick in the car. We were groaning, we felt so ill. They took one look at Jim and me and put our match off until 11 a.m., at which news we promptly went back to sleep. They woke us at 10.30 and said we were playing Oxford in the first round. Then someone said Troy Coker, the Australian, was playing for Oxford and I said, "That's it, I'm not playing." I'd had some tough times against Coker; he was a hard bastard. The way I felt, there was no way I was ready to handle what I knew would be coming from him, even in a sevens match. Troy Coker doesn't play friendlies.

'They said, "We'll fine you." I replied, "You can't fine me, I have no money." And I didn't play. Ian Stevens, our other first-team lock, was called into the side, played in that first game against Oxford, was tackled by Coker and broke his leg badly in the first minute of the match.'

A team meeting was called on the following Tuesday night to ponder the make-up of the pack in Stevens's absence. It was decided that Michael Gibson would move from his customary No. 8 position to lock, and Dave Fitzgerald would play at 8.

Simon Geoghegan had scored 17 tries in the season prior to that well-attended game at Sunbury against Blackheath. He promptly added a first-half brace of tries, followed by one from Francis, of whom Mick Doyle once remarked, with cruel satire, 'He's jumping at 4 today, but will he jump at 3.30 as well?'

Francis, like the rest of his London Irish team-mates that day, was doing the business supremely well throughout the first half. So much so that at half-time, having played against the wind, Irish led 21–0, which prompted one supporter at the ground to jump in his car and drive round to the local supermarket for a case of champagne.

By the time he returned, it still didn't look bad. True, Blackheath had at last got on to the scoreboard and were starting to win a lot of possession from the back of the line-out, an area that was normally the domain of Gibson. Francis offered to move back and snuff out the threat from Blackheath's Micky Harris, but his offer was declined. The party still seemed imminent and only started to look imperilled when Blackheath scored another try and converted it, to close down the Irish lead to 21–19. But with just injury time remaining, an Irish win and, as it would show, certain promotion beckoned . . . until the Blackheath outside-half Jon King launched a 40-yard drop goal which sailed over the bar. The referee's whistle went, Irish had lost 22–21 and that kick had cost them promotion.

Ironically, King was studying at St Mary's University College at Strawberry Hill and his tutor was none other than long-term London Irish servant and supporter Jim O'Hara. One hour after the game had ended, with Sunbury like a wake, O'Hara summoned up some grim humour to tell King, 'If you think you've got any chance with those exams you're taking, you've got another think coming!'

Francis remembers, 'It was unbelievable, and someone said he thought we'd thrown the game. It was an incredible fluke of circumstances, because every other side going for the second promotion position lost. If we'd won, we would have gone up. But that summed up London Irish at the time, really. I left that summer, going back to Ireland. I felt that if they had been serious about building the club, they would have hung on to me.'

Kieran McCarthy still winces, to this day, at the painful memory of that match. 'I was standing watching the last ten minutes near the door by the entrance to the Four Seasons bar, holding a bottle of champagne. The referee, David Matthews of Liverpool, allowed about eight minutes of injury time and it was agony. When the Blackheath lad dropped that goal, the champagne dropped from my hand and crashed on to the floor.'

The Blackheath match catastrophe was followed by six victories in their 11 league fixtures of season 1989–90. That year, Ian Aitchison, who had joined the club from Waterloo as a points-accumulating outside-half, garnished a magnificent total of 261 points. But there was another disappointing Pilkington Cup exit, 17–13 to Plymouth Albion in the second round.

The 1990s could not have opened in better fashion. With Brian Mullen's boot to guide them from fly-half, Jim Staples's cool play to secure them at full-back and Simon Geoghegan's thrilling, penetrative play on the wing outside David Curtis (whose father had played for Ireland in 1950 and who was to follow the family line by representing Ireland in 1991 and 1992), London Irish had some exciting players. They won nine and drew one of their 12 Courage League games to win promotion as runners-up to Rugby. The pair replaced Moseley and

Brian Mullen releases Rory Moloney as Irish carve out an 18–18 draw with Richmond which clinches promotion in the final league match of the 1990–91 season.

Liverpool St Helens in the top flight. Irish also reached the Pilkington Cup quarter-finals, before losing heavily at Nottingham. They stayed in the top division the next season, 1991–92, winning three and drawing three of their 12 league games.

The first season back in the top flight of English rugby had begun with a bang. Bath were the visitors to Sunbury for the first league fixture of the season, and a large crowd turned up to see an Irish side laden with internationals like Geoghegan, Staples, Saunders and Curtis. A new-style glossy programme had been put together which was the envy of most Premiership clubs and which had advertising support worth a fantastic £30,000. Irish were only narrowly defeated by Bath, the reigning champions, 26–21, and optimism was high. Before too long, Brian Robinson, another talented No. 8 forward, would join the club. Alas, Irish could not build on that vibrant opening, failing to win any of their first six fixtures. But the second half of the season was much better, with wins over Wasps, Nottingham and Bristol and a draw against Rosslyn Park.

There was, however, the torturous embarrassment of losing to little Essex junior club Thurrock in the third round of the Pilkington Cup that autumn. Irish were 16–0 down at half-time, stunned by the determination of the locals and their own frequent mistakes. They managed tries by Paul Collins and Jim Staples in the second half, Brian Mullen converting one, but it was not enough to prevent what remains to this day one of the biggest upsets in the history of that competition.

However, it proved a relatively straightforward affair for Irish to retain their National League One status again the next year. They achieved a 50 per cent record with six wins and six defeats, and their 12-point total left them well ahead of the four clubs relegated: Rugby, West Hartlepool, Saracens and London Scottish.

A LOYAL SERVANT

In February 1997, the club lost one of its most distinguished old members, Sir James Holmes Henry CMG, MC, TD, QC 2nd Bart, a vice-president of the club in 1967. He passed away at the age of 85.

Sir James, a barrister and Military Cross holder, was Attorney General of Cyprus during the Eoka emergency. A native of Co. Londonderry, he played on the wing for London Irish before the Second World War and, once the conflict began, served as a company commander in the London Irish Rifles. He was wounded at Monte Cassino in Northern Italy in 1944 and was awarded the Military Cross for gallantry.

After a distinguished business career, he retired in 1984 and, together with Lady Hillary, who was also a life member, became once more a keen follower of the club's activities at all levels. When the duty scorer was absent at Sunbury, he would take over responsibility for the scoreboard at 1st XV matches.

But there were worse things to come, and the see-saw effect then came into play. Irish were relegated the next season, 1993–94, after managing just four victories in 18 league games, the home and away system having been introduced. Wing Michael Corcoran scored 110 points in the season but a run of seven straight defeats from early December to mid-March left them with too much to make up. Worse still, the star men quickly drifted away to pastures new back in the top division – and who could blame them? Well, some did, so much so that a nasty taste was left in the mouth. But, as Michael Flatley said, 'Who could blame a fine player like Simon Geoghegan for joining a top club like Bath? He went there to further his career, and you can hardly criticise anyone for seeking to do that.'

But there was a sadness about the final match in League One, a home game against Bath at which events off the pitch were even more dramatic than those on it – and it was a match of 63 points which Irish lost 32–31. Coach Hika Reid was persuaded by certain officials above him to change his original team selection and leave out Simon Geoghegan, knowing he was leaving for the West Country club. Others, like Staples and Gary Halpin, refused to play at the last minute in sympathy for Geoghegan. Kieran McCarthy, who had joined the club way back in 1979 and became junior players' representative in 1984, has served as an administrator in some form or another ever since. He remembers, 'We had a bit of cajoling to do to convince a lot of the senior guys to play.'

It was a sorry, unhappy episode the club could have done without. 'It was a bad atmosphere that day behind the scenes. It was the end of a fairly unhappy period off the park. The committee were getting too involved in rugby matters. What happened with Ray O'Rourke was a pity, because he not only put a lot of money into the club, he was also responsible for a lot of the commercial success. He was chairman of the sponsorship committee for two years and generated a lot of money. We had a period of excellent trading off the park: from 1991 to 1996 we had a very healthy five years. One year, we made a profit of £90,000, for we really hit the corporate entertainment side of things in a big way at that time,' said McCarthy.

The loss of Geoghegan, Jim Staples and Rory Jenkins (the latter pair to Harlequins), players who had followed others such as Paul Burke, the talented former Oxford University captain and No. 8 Mark Egan, John Hewitt and David

Curtis out of the club for a variety of reasons, meant that a mid-table finish in National League Two followed the next season. Yet it proved merely a temporary blip. Season 1995–96 saw Irish promoted again, together with Northampton, on the back of 15 wins in 18 games. There was, too, the pleasure of a long run in that season's Pilkington Cup, all the way to the semi-finals at a packed Sunbury where Leicester's superior experience and poise got them home comfortably enough, 46–21. By now, Gary Halpin's very considerable, reassuring frame was doing sterling service on behalf of the cause in the front row, although the eventual loss of Rob Henderson to Wasps and Michael Corcoran to Harlequins would be keenly felt in times to come.

The 1996–97 season saw Irish retain their coveted League One status, but only through a successful two-leg play-off contest with Coventry, to whom they lost narrowly 16–14 at Coundon Road before swamping them 28–7 at Sunbury in the return match. It would be the first of successive play-offs: season 1997–98 would end in identical fashion, except that this time Irish finished second bottom in the table and were saved relegation only by the ludicrously late decision to invoke once more the play-off system. There was a 16–13 win at Rotherham in the first match, but the return at Sunbury, once a nervy first half had been negotiated, was again conclusive, with Irish running out winners by 26 points to 14 for a 42–27 aggregate victory.

The club had gone some way along the road towards recruiting new players midway through the 1997–98 season, delving deep into the recruiting grounds of the southern hemisphere to bring to the club the influential and inspirational forward Nick Harvey from Australia, the classy Test centre Brendan Venter from the Free State in South Africa and a marauding Western Samoan back-row forward Isaac Feaunati from New Zealand. Feaunati, known instantly to one and all as 'Zac', was a powerful, highly industrious forward who, together with Harvey's example, lifted the pack and the entire team for a vastly improved second half of the season. It was deeply unfortunate that he should suffer severe knee ligament damage in the final moments of the last game of the season, against Rotherham. Brendan Venter's shrewd composure and experience in the midfield was another key factor in the side's improvement, and the acquisition of this trio must have indicated to the club the likely future trend required to ensure security and real prosperity in Premiership One.

Dick Best had replaced Anderson and was treated at once to a marvellous spectacle, the 38–23 crushing of Bristol which was more important in terms of the spirit and latent ability still clearly within the squad than anything on the scoreboard, welcome as the win obviously was.

There was another fine home win, 23–19 against Gloucester, and although they could not topple an ailing Bath side, the highlight of Irish's season followed

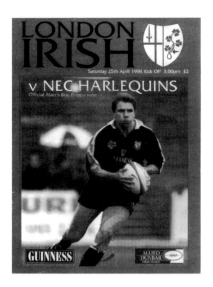

A famous day at Sunbury. The Exiles' 62–14 thrashing of Harlequins was easily their best ever Premiership win.

soon after. Dick Best had some unfinished business to attend to when Harlequins, the club that had sacked him following an unwise little dose of player-power at The Stoop, arrived at Sunbury for a crucial league match. Irish had reason to stoke up the fires, too; they had somehow squandered a vast half-time lead in the earlier fixture at The Stoop back in December to go down 26–24, a match they ought to have won in a canter.

The scene was set for something special, but few envisaged anything as remarkable as what happened. Harlequins must have felt like an army that had stumbled unsuspectingly into a minefield. They were blown to bits as Irish ran up a huge 62–14 winning tally, scoring eight tries to two, which represented by far their best ever win in league rugby.

The play-offs followed, securing another season among the best company. But it had been another very difficult season for Irish. Jeremy Davidson, their Ireland and 1997 British Lions lock forward, had damaged knee ligaments so seriously in his first game of the campaign that he never played another match all season. He then joined the French club Castres. In his absence, young Malcolm O'Kelly took the chance to confirm shrewd judges' opinions that he could become one of the great footballing second-row men of the modern game.

But Irish clearly needed more new men, and the summer was spent searching earnestly for fresh blood, particularly with outside-half David Humphreys, centre Mark McCall and lock Gabriel Fulcher, all internationals, having decided to return to Ireland to play their rugby. By the time of pre-season training, the huge southern-hemisphere influence had become apparent. Another departure was American chief executive Chuck Nelson, who had been with the club for just one season. The transient nature of London Irish was once more in evidence: Geoff Huckstep eventually replaced him.

Chairman Geoff Read makes no bones about the club's serious financial position when the new board took over at Sunbury. 'The club would have gone bust. There were significant liabilities which they could not meet, so there was no other option for it,' he says.

Under Read's chairmanship, the club has five quasi-executive directors: Maurice O'Connell (who has overseen facilities), John Finn (who has overseen finances), John Conlan (responsible for property development), Stephen Tye (merchandising) and Patrick Keily (chairman of the rugby committee). In addition, there are three other directors: John O'Neill, involved in the role of recruitment of sponsorships, Kevin Clancy, who also performed a role as executive in the rugby department in 1997–98, and John Stackpoole, who has been very involved in acquisitions, particularly with regard to land purchased adjacent to the club. Read says, 'Our strength is that everybody has taken an active role.'

Irish purchased seven acres of land originally owned by a convent at the rear of their Sunbury site, giving them 18 acres in total. Unfortunately, plans to develop a 15,000 capacity stadium with associated leisure facilities for the general public and more housing on the enlarged site have been turned down by the local council, making Irish's long-term future at Sunbury doubtful.

'We may be left with nothing else to do but move from Sunbury and develop the land here to enable us to fund a new home elsewhere,' says Read. 'The council say the infrastructure cannot handle such a development, but it leaves us with a problem. As things stand at Sunbury, we cannot meet the criteria of English First Division Rugby (EFDR) for Premiership clubs and their facilities.'

Especially when Read estimates that Irish need a 10,000 crowd for each match to break even, due to the alarmingly high costs of staging rugby at a non-modern stadium like Sunbury. 'Gates have been disappointing so far this season [1998–99],' he admits, 'but they have been everywhere. The potential for developing this game may well exist further down the track as long as the sport is properly and seriously marketed. No one quite knows to what extent that potential exists at present. Rugby has achieved a tremendous development on the pitch in terms of quality but people have not become aware of it. We have to be smarter in how we sell the game. Certainly, sponsorship will be increased significantly over the years, I am sure of that.'

Irish made significant progress in the summer of 1998, transforming the playing squad with the arrival of at least 15 new players, many from the southern hemisphere. In came Stephen Bachop from Wellington Hurricanes, Simon Berridge (Western Province), Jake Boer (Western Province), James Brown (Coventry), Jarrod Cunningham (Wellington Hurricanes), Kris Fullman (Bristol), Rob Gallacher (Manly), Michael Howe (Bay of Plenty), Matt Jones (Moseley), Richard Kirke (Bedford), Kevin Putt (Natal), Peter Rogers (Transvaal), Ryan Strudwick (Natal), Robert Todd (London Scottish) and Michael Worsley (Gloucester). Among 24 players departing were Sean Burns, Jeremy Davidson, Gabriel Fulcher, Gary Halpin, Niall Hogan, David Humphreys, Rob Kellam, Liam Mooney, Tony Redmond and Ken O'Connell.

Read says, 'Whilst some of the problems facing London Irish and the other Premier Division clubs have yet to be resolved, we should not lose sight of the considerable progress that has been made over the past two years.

'Given the investment made by the forward-looking clubs such as Saracens, London Irish, Richmond and Bath in the areas of marketing, stadium development (including ground share), sponsorship packages, merchandising and so on, allied to the impact the Rugby World Cup will make in 1999, we should look forward with confidence to achieving financial viability and profitability within the next two to three years.

'It is the intention of the board of directors and executive management team at London Irish to ensure this great club continues to be at the forefront of the development of the professional game in England and Europe in the years to come.'

CHAPTER SEVENTEEN

The Way Forward

'I have seen the future and it works.'

LINCOLN STEFFENS, 1866–1936

One thing alone is certain amid the rank uncertainty which passes for rugby in the northern hemisphere at this time. The future can be a bright, brash, breezy entity, and it is there ready to be embraced. The trouble is, those who want to go out and grab it believe they are being distracted by the traditionalists, a group in which some are fearful of the brave new world which rugby could become. Sorting it out has proved anything but straightforward.

Take London Irish. The impact made by non-Irishmen Brendan Venter, Nick Harvey and Isaac Feaunati in the second half of the 1997–98 season confirmed the judgement of those who had insisted that southern-hemisphere-based players would add a hard, knowledgeable edge to the club's play. Dick Best, who inherited the trio from his predecessor Willie Anderson, said, 'I would go so far as to say that without those three in the second half of last season we would have been preparing for the Second Division this past summer.'

'But they weren't Irishmen' was the cry of some traditionalists. Maybe not, but their value to a professional club was considerable, and people running a business – which, for better or worse, rugby had become once professionalism had been accepted – must make hard-nosed business decisions. Sentiment can play no part in such judgements.

Irish politician Dick Spring, a former London Irish player in the 1970s, says, 'It is inevitable you will get Australians, New Zealanders and South Africans coming into our teams and our game. A lot of them want to spend one or two years in this part of the world. And it's a good thing. I know a New

The Exiles' lock forward Aidan Higgins battles for possession in the 1990–91 Pilkington Cup quarter-final at Nottingham. Irish lost 46–9.

Zealand coach of an Irish school and he has transformed their rugby. They are playing a different game now. The New Zealand approach is so different in terms of keeping the ball in play. I think we need exposure to New Zealand rugby.'

Others take a similar view. Neil Francis, the ex-international lock forward who spent a season with London Irish in 1988–89, says, 'If they want to be successful, London Irish will have to lose a lot more of their Irish players. They have to be realistic for the future. It is the way life goes.'

Hugo MacNeill regards the future as 'very interesting', saying, 'The challenge is there for every club given the crazy economic structure they started this professional life with. The key question is, how do you get to a 15,000 attendance? How do you create that support? One problem at Sunbury, regardless of the make-up of the playing staff, is that it is a long way out, so perhaps they need to plug more into the local community. If you don't persuade fathers to take kids there, then this whole thing doesn't work. For any club. You have to create within the area a following. But can you do that in the Sunbury/Kingston area?

'London Irish are a little different from some professional clubs because they are not dependent upon one person as the chief investor. Others are, and that worries me. The Irish have a better economic base, too, and should become a centre of excellence for Irish rugby in England. It is a place with a wonderful atmosphere.'

And it offers magnificent hospitality, and always has done. As Brian Gaule, who joined in 1983, says, 'Times at the club were always a bit hit and miss. But that summed up the way the club was run and played over the years. That lies in the culture of the members. They were all for a bit of fun; it was never taken too seriously. And that still prevailed until a couple of years ago. Winning or losing didn't come into it that much; we wanted to put up some good hospitality. Which was right for the amateur game played in that spirit.'

As an abbreviated *modus operandi*, Gaule's words perhaps fitted the philosophy of London Irish better than any. But, as others have indicated, times move on, and rugby union football has undergone phenomenal change in the last two or three years – more, probably, than at any other time in its history. Adapting to that change is the challenge for all those now involved at the club, in whatever capacity.

The crucial decision, to vote the old members' club out of existence, was taken at a momentous meeting attended by more than 400 members in the Rose Room at Twickenham in the summer of 1997. The decision effectively agreed to end the club as it had been for 98 years, a club owned by its members, and allow the consortium to come in and take charge. As to the vote, it was carried overwhelmingly, with only a handful of members refusing to back the motion.

Geoff Read and his colleagues invested around £1.1 million to take charge at the club, but a shares issue, unique in British and Irish rugby at the time, among 340 members promptly realised a further £1.8 million, some of it through others brought in via the consortium. No single member owned more than 12.5 per cent of the club. Even allowing for significant debts incurred in the early, expensive times of professionalism, the two sums together represented a healthy investment in the future of the club.

When Duncan Leopold departed as chief executive of London Irish in the summer of 1997, he pointed out the promising state of the club. 'The new ownership structure at London Irish is unique in this country. The concept was a difficult one to achieve and, having raised £2.8 million, we can feel very pleased with our efforts. We also own our ground, which is another important factor for the future of this club.'

One year later, director of rugby Dick Best is similarly convinced that London Irish is a club with a bright future. 'At last I believe reality has come to Sunbury *vis-à-vis* the professional game,' he says. 'The reaction of the club's board to it is

Who leaps highest? International lock Malcolm O'Kelly is hoisted towards the heavens at a club training session (photo © Jack Kay).

in my opinion quite exciting. The major shareholders, the directors, are all winners in life, but they're also realists. They have rolled their sleeves up and got their hands involved in the business in an attempt to make it work. If this continues, if their involvement and expertise remain, I think we will do well. Knowledge of rugby is not a prerequisite for running a club successfully. It has taken clubs some time to understand that. Businessmen left their brains behind when they got involved with rugby in the past. Now it is a highly specialised business requiring particular skills.'

Best said that the actions of the IRFU in luring home, by dint of very lucrative contracts, as many of their English-based star players as possible had forced the hand of the London Irish club. He insisted the IRFU's action would probably

Action from the early 1990s. Rob Henderson's charge through the Bristol defence is halted by Ralph Knibbs. David Curtis, the international centre, hurries to assist.

deepen their problems in the long term. 'Players like Keith Wood and Paddy Johns improved so much by coming to play in England. Bringing so many back home and shutting the door to outside influences and overseas leagues will prove a retrograde step as far as Irish rugby is concerned, I am sure.'

There was a major clear-out at Sunbury in the summer of 1998, and Best knew he had to bring more players with southern-hemisphere experience to the club to provide the quality and power required even for survival in an increasingly competitive English Premiership. But Best insists London Irish can retain its Irish identity without necessarily having 15 Irish-qualified players in its first team.

'London Irish is an exiles' club but the sociological economic climate of what's going on back in Ireland and over here in England has changed. Therefore it is a natural evolvement to take players from a wider field. And, with the club having been in the play-offs for the last two years, even most traditionalists would probably recognise that the Irish players who have been based here have not been good enough.'

Therefore, Best began the summer with a large shopping list. He caught an early plane to South Africa to talk to potential recruits and did so convinced that it was the right way to ensure the club's future prosperity. The fact was, he insisted, had the full Ireland international team played in the English

Premiership last winter as 'London Irish', they still probably would not have beaten the likes of Newcastle or Saracens. Which is painful food for thought on both sides of the Irish Sea.

So although season 1998–99 and beyond into the beginning of the twenty-first century is seeing the London Irish 1st XV with just a handful of Irish players, a large part of the team being from the powerful southern hemisphere, men like rugby administrator Kieran McCarthy point to the rest of the club. 'Unlike clubs such as Harlequins and Wasps who have either disbanded or split from their junior teams, London Irish will be as Irish as ever before, with the sole exception of the first team. I know that is the flagship side, but we have to face facts. The club will continue to run six teams, including the social sides and a thriving junior section, and that provides a lot of the traditional Irish atmosphere. Others have long since jettisoned that, but it will remain an essential ingredient for this club.'

But hired hands wearing a green jersey in the 1st XV? McCarthy insists realism must prevail. 'We have no choice. Taking a commercial viewpoint, we need to have a team that's going to help us to fulfil our mission statement, which is to win the Premiership One title in three years' time. To do that you must have the proper resources. The fact is, the players we have had haven't been good enough. We have to be totally pragmatic, for we are an industry now. Commercial reality has to rule, and so unfortunately we have to leave behind one aspect of our past. But I will fight to help ensure that the ethos and spirit off the park and the members' enjoyment are retained.'

Club member Jim O'Hara joined London Irish back in 1966, played for many of its teams, was club secretary from 1985 to 1987, a committee member for many years and was a member of the former board of directors. All of which amply qualifies him to discuss the way forward for the club, to accept professionalism but not to disregard the club's roots.

O'Hara says, 'With so much emphasis now necessarily being given to the first-team squad, and with the inevitable increase in the number of non-Irish players, the role of the adult teams in the junior club becomes even more important. London Irish still turns out six adult teams and still offers a home for young, and not so young, Irishmen, be they first or fifth generation. This is in keeping with the original aims of the club's founding fathers, and it is with the junior teams and all their relatives and supporters, as well as the large pool of ex-players still around, that the fundamental cause of the club's Irish traditions are to be found. I believe it essential that this section of the club be maintained, supported and, indeed, increased in size. Like many things we take for granted, it is only when we lose them that we realise how important they are.'

CHAPTER EIGHTEEN

London Irish and the IRFU

'It is more shameful to spurn one's friends
than to be duped by them.'

DUC DE LA ROCHEFOUCAULD, 1613–80

It became, in a sense, the classic Richard Burton–Elizabeth Taylor love affair. Couldn't live with each other, couldn't live without each other.

London Irish and the Irish Rugby Football Union have been cohabiting partners for longer than most care to admit. The relationship has had its ecstatic highs and its bitter lows, but now, in the modern world of professional rugby, is it too late for a constructive relationship to exist whereby both club and union work together for the greater good of both? The stark answer is probably yes.

Hugo MacNeill sees it pretty clearly in terms of a path forward. 'I don't think the people at London Irish are being supported. And I think there's an attitude among some people in Ireland that they don't get the whole London Irish support.

'The IRFU should create a serious alternative in Ireland with provinces but also back London Irish by making it a focal point. They should realise a lot of Irish players will still want to come to London and play in the English league. London Irish will back Irish rugby more than any other English club; it would be very beneficial for Irish rugby as a whole if the IRFU really supported them. But sometimes you get a resentment syndrome from those people who have gone away. I believe London Irish have made tremendous strides, but the high-jump bar keeps being raised.'

Mick Doyle concedes that the IRFU have been put 'in a bit of a quandary' over their relationship with the club. 'The club is supposed to cater for all

Hugo MacNeill, another London Irish player who also represented Ireland and the British Lions.

PASSION IN EXILE

ex-pats in London, but it doesn't. That is a problem. But they don't seem to have created enough intent or colour about themselves like London Welsh have about Wales. London Irish perhaps doesn't seem to represent Irish rugby enough; it is a pity.'

Jim O'Hara insists there should still be a role for the IRFU as regards London Irish. It is his contention that some leading Irish players will continue to come to England, for reasons of career or rugby business. 'Where I believe the IRFU have a role to play is in persuading those players who do continue to come to England to join London Irish, for the good of Irish rugby, rather than any other English-based club.'

Ken Kennedy accepts the realities of Irish recruiting overseas players to their ranks. 'We have to be realistic; the club has to be opened a little. But I would despise us becoming like Richmond or Harlequins, who have almost no English players. We have to try to keep the idea of London Irish, which was to promote rugby for Irish people with Irish connections in London.

'I felt that the IRFU should have had a selector and committeeman based over in England to develop the London Irish idea. Then, about eight or nine years ago, they decided to start the Irish Exiles. I coached the Exiles for a year but the IRFU were still too parochially minded. I wanted to take the squad to South Africa for a tour; the IRFU said we should go to Ballinasloe. They didn't have the vision to develop the Exiles or the London Irish concept. And there has always been a bit of resentment, an attitude of "What are you doing in England – isn't Ireland good enough for you?" sort of thing. The problem remains because 40 per cent of the Irish international players have been based in England yet there was only one selector over here. The IRFU don't see the positive reasoning behind having more people over here to encourage, stimulate and watch players. There could have been a much better relationship between the IRFU and London Irish for many years.'

But veteran Dublin-based rugby writer Ned Van Esbeck puts the contrasting view. 'I don't accept that the IRFU have not used London Irish as they might have done, because the club had a very special position with the IRFU. They are the only club to have direct representation into the council AGM of the IRFU. No other club has.

'There was a feeling that players were falling through the net but then came the Exiles and that answered that. I think there was a little bit of a siege mentality among some London Irish people towards the IRFU. London Irish's attitude years ago was that they would stand on their heads to have their best players represent their provinces and the international team. But I am not sure that that is any longer the case, and I worry that the whole situation with London Irish will be gradually eroded. London Irish at the present moment are the same as

198

Jim Staples, a worthy servant for several years at London Irish.

any other English club. That is a force of circumstances rather than will, perhaps, but that is the reality. The IRFU have to take notice of that. The club has given colossal service to the benefit of Irish rugby. But that is eroding.'

Times have changed. Niall Brophy, former London Irish player, international wing and the 1997–98 season president of the IRFU, said, 'I think the London Irish scene has always helped Irish rugby but now it is counter-productive. The IRFU and London Irish have two separate agendas. The IRFU role is to develop rugby in Ireland and ensure we have the best international team. We have to compete effectively in the European Cup, but the problem in Ireland has been seeing players going to England. London Irish are not the sole culprits in that respect. It means that we suffered at club and inter-provincial level. So I feel the value of London Irish to Irish rugby will become less and less. But it is a club that has played its part in Irish rugby, and Irish people have always had a soft spot for it. Perhaps it is a fair criticism, though, that at times there was a sense of "out of sight, out of mind" as regards some London Irish players failing to make the national team.'

But now, with London Irish opening up their club more than ever before to non-Irish-qualified players, the value to the IRFU of a vibrant London-based club may have greatly diminished. If that proves to be the case, many will reflect on the long years when London Irish could have offered Irish rugby *per se* so much more, had stronger ties been forged with the union back home. The phrase 'a missed chance' might be more familiar in cricket, but it would appear appropriate in this instance.

CHAPTER NINETEEN

That Unique Spirit

'Be not drunk with wine,
wherein is excess;
but be filled with the Spirit.'

EPHESIANS, THE HOLY BIBLE

On Saturday, 4 January 1986, Richard Cross was playing full-back for London Irish Extra 'A's against London Scottish. Some way into the game, he went in for a tackle from which he fell to the ground injured. He was taken to Ashford Hospital, where a broken neck was diagnosed. Paralysed, he was transferred to Stoke Mandeville, where he slipped into a coma.

Richard, who had played for Cheltenham 1st XV, Newcastle University 1st XV (with another future London Irish man Paul O'Donnell) and the Teddington-based club Antlers had joined London Irish only that season. But he had already, in the space of just a few months, become a highly popular member. Perhaps a measure of his character was his reply to the doctor who told him he was very seriously injured: 'Okay, but tell me the important news – did we win today?'

Complications set in and he was transferred to Oxford Royal Infirmary. Despite every effort to save him, he died on the following Monday night. His death stunned the London Irish club. His friends, team-mates and club officials were deeply saddened by the tragic loss of a young man from their midst as he played a sport he loved. But his young wife Clare and 20-month-old son William bore the greatest loss.

Accordingly, the rugby club and rugby players from all parts rallied round. As they do. A memorial match was held on Sunday, 27 April that year at Sunbury to commemorate Richard Cross. Star players came from England, Ireland, Scotland, Wales and France to participate in the game and help swell the funds to assist his young family. And today, more than 12 years later, the name of Richard Cross is still remembered with affection, and sorrow, at Sunbury.

Some seven months after Cross's tragic accident, another London Irish rugby player also suffered a severe injury, albeit not on the rugby field. Roger

THE RICHARD CROSS MEMORIAL MATCH
(Sunday, 27th April 1986 - K.O. 3 p.m.)

	LONDON IRISH RFC INTERNATIONAL XV	v	A SELECT INTERNATIONAL XV	
15	HUGO MacNEILL (Ireland & British Lions)	FULL BACK	JEAN-BAPTISTE LAFOND (France)	15
14	TREVOR RINGLAND (Ireland & British Lions)	RIGHT WING	DAVID TRICK (England)	14
13	MICHAEL KIERNAN (Ireland & British Lions)	RIGHT CENTRE	SIMON HALLIDAY (England)	13
12	HUGH CONDON (Ireland)	LEFT CENTRE	RICHARD CARDUS (England)	12
11	ROGER ANDERSON (London Irish)	LEFT WING	CLIVE REES (Wales & British Lions)	11
10	PAUL O'DONNELL (London Irish)	STAND OFF	NICK PRESTON (England)	10
9	BARRY MURPHY (London Irish)	SCRUM HALF	MARK DOUGLAS (Wales)	9
8	MICHAEL GIBSON (Ireland)	LOCK	DAVID COOKE (England)	8
7	JOHN O'DRISCOLL (Ireland & British Lions)	WING	PETER WINTERBOTTOM (England & British Lions)	7
6	FERGUS SLATTERY (Ireland & British Lions)	WING	WILLIE DUNCAN (Ireland)	6
5	WILLIE ANDERSON (Ireland)	SECOND ROW	BILL CUTHBERTSON (Scotland)	5
4	DONAL LENIHAN (Ireland & British Lions)	SECOND ROW	JEREMY CAMPBELL-LAMERTON (Scotland)	4
3	PAUL KENNEDY (Ireland)	PROP	IAIN MILNE (Scotland)	3
2	CIARAN FITZGERALD (Ireland & British Lions)	HOOKER	IAN KIRK (London Scottish)	2
1	TOMMY HENNESSY (London Irish)	PROP	JIMMY McCOY (Ireland)	1

Referee: HARRY NICHOLL (London Society and London Irish)

Today's Match Balls are kindly sponsored by BRIAN and LIZ HORNE of the MAGPIE HOTEL, SUNBURY

RICHARD CROSS

On Saturday 4th January, Richard Cross was playing full back for London Irish 'Ex A's' against London Scottish. Some way into the game he went in for a tackle from which he fell to the ground injured. He was rushed to Ashford Hospital where a broken neck was diagnosed. Paralysed, he was transferred to Stoke Mandeville where he slipped into a coma. Complications set in and he was transferred to Oxford Royal Infirmary. Despite every effort to save him, he died on the following Monday night.

Richard who had played for Cheltenham 1st XV, for Newcastle University 1st XV with Paul O'Donnell and for Antlers in Teddington had only joined London Irish this season. But already he was a popular club member. Perhaps a measure of his character was his reply to the doctor who told him he was very seriously injured, "O.K. but tell me the important news - did we win today?"

With Richard's death we're all losers - rugby as a whole, London Irish, his team mates and friends. But the greatest losers are his young wife, Clare, and his twenty-month old son, William. So today, particularly, we must help them and show that we care. There will be a blanket collection during the afternoon. Please give generously, cheques to 'LIRFC Richard Cross Appeal'.

We thank everyone — guest players, entertainers, officials, organisers, and you, the spectators, for making this benefit possible.

Richard and Clare

Richard and William

The programme for Richard Cross's memorial match, following his tragic death in January 1986.

Anderson was a highly talented wing three-quarter who had climaxed an impressive season with London Irish by scoring a try in the Irish trial at Lansdowne Road. He was 23 and seemed certain to win international honours, such was his great ability. Then came the accident which was to end his days of playing rugby.

Anderson was on holiday in Greece when he lost control of the motorcycle he was riding and crashed into a steel barrier. He suffered terrible head injuries, including five hairline fractures of the skull and internal damage to the brain, and was in a coma for ten days before eventually coming round.

Doctors told Anderson his career was over, but the determined youngster was hopeful he could prove them wrong. Alas, their prognosis proved correct and the enormous talent of the young man from Coleraine who had represented Ulster was never fulfilled.

Also warmly remembered at the club is Lieutenant-Commander Denis Patrick Kelly, who was killed in a flying accident in Sussex in 1957. Kelly, a wing forward, had last played for London Irish in the 1955–56 season, his appearances restricted by his Services commitments. He also played for Dartmouth Naval College and the British Navy, played for Co. Dublin in a representative match and was a playing member of London Irish for six seasons. Aged 31 when he died, Commander Kelly was the son of Mr Pat Kelly of Cooraclare, Co. Clare.

Denis Kelly was a tough, robust flank forward who played the game with that envied combination of steely determination and a ready smile. He had been pilot to the Duke of Edinburgh and was navigating pilot attached to *Britannia* shortly before his death. In the Korean War in 1951, he became the first man to ditch a plane from the carrier *Theseus*. At the time, the carrier's Sea Furies were attacking camel and mule trains supplying communist forces. Commander Kelly was rescued from the bitterly cold sea by a Canadian destroyer.

He died when the single-seater Sea Hawk plane he was piloting crashed on the railway line between Arundel and Littlehampton, hit the live rail and burst into flames. He was greatly missed down the years by his many friends and playing colleagues at London Irish.

In December 1969, London Irish lost another dear friend, Jimmy Monahan, who died suddenly at his home in Wiltshire. He was just 21 years of age. James

We London Irishmen mourn this week the tragic death of Jimmy Monahan who died suddenly at his home in Wiltshire Tuesday week last, December 2nd., 1969. To Mrs. Monahan, Jimmy's brother and their entire family we send our very much heartfelt condolences. James Dermot Monahan was just 21 years of age. He came to London Irish three seasons ago whilst still at Cambridge where he obtained two Blues. He obtained an Irish Trial and played inter-pro for Ulster. Jim was the regular London Irish tight head prop for all of last season and recently returned to his place in the side when he came back from Ireland. His last game for the Club was against the Scottish at the Athletic Ground, three days before his death. Jimmy himself was born in Bishopstone near Swindon. His father was born in India, the son of a clergyman from Donegal. To say Jimmy Monahan was a very popular fellow as well as being an extremely quiet, likeable one is not just to pay lip service to the dead. It is a fact with which nobody who had ever met him would disagree. The Club was represented at the funeral by Messrs. H. R. England, J. M. Moran and D. H. Craig.

London Irish player Jimmy Monahan, who died aged just 21.

Dermot Monahan was a fine young prop forward who won two blues at Cambridge and joined Irish while still at the university. In season 1968–69 he was the club's regular tight-head prop, played for Ulster in the Inter-Provincial Championship and appeared in an Irish trial. Jimmy had been born near Swindon, but his father, himself born in India, was the son of a clergyman from Donegal. Jimmy's last game for London Irish was against London Scottish at the Richmond Athletic Ground three days before he died, through suffocation, on 2 December 1969. He was mourned by the many friends he had made during his time at London Irish.

Tragedy befell another London Irish member, although he lived to tell the tale. In 1980, Jim Sheehan had been a member of the London Irish side in the John Player Cup final against Leicester at Twickenham. He had joined the club in 1979 and stayed until 1986–87, winning the 1st XV forwards' honours tie in his final season before returning, briefly, to Ireland. Sheehan was a players' player. Industrious and devoted to the team, his contribution was occasionally missed by those who did not know the game. But his team-mates never underestimated Sheehan's ability. He wasn't a man to make a fuss, as was confirmed by a delightful story he told of his earliest times at London Irish.

Sheehan, who had played for University College, Cork, joined the club and was put into the redoubtable Tommy Hynes's 'B2's. He played five or six matches for them and was put down under the name 'Liam or Jimmy Murphy'. Hynes was notorious for keeping quiet about any talented players in 'his' team. 'Ah, now, I only have average players in my team,' he would say to anyone inquiring about personnel. But Hynes's plot was blown apart when Sheehan attended the English Universities v. Irish Universities match in London. London Irish first-team coach Pat Parfrey, another ex-UCC man, was there and spotted his old Cork acquaintance. 'What on earth are you doing here?' he asked Sheehan. The reply took him aback somewhat. 'I'm living in London and playing for London Irish.'

'Well, why don't I know about it?' asked an incredulous Parfrey.

Sheehan says, 'We never trained together, the lower teams and the 1sts, and just gathered on Saturday mornings. So there was no reason for Pat to know I was there. Tommy was very, very protective of his team. The story then grew at Sunbury that Tommy had played me in the "B2"s for the last year, but in fact it was only for eight weeks.'

The next week, Sheehan was 'promoted' to the 3rd XV, but the match was cancelled. No matter, the next week he was in the Geese, then, two weeks later, the 1st XV. And as the London Irish cup run gathered pace, Sheehan played a valuable role, appearing in the quarter-final tie at Bath before losing out to Dave McCracken for the semi-final when Irish felt they needed a bigger presence in the line-outs.

But he won back the place for the final, becoming the fittest he'd ever achieved in his life through training sessions of two to three hours, three days a week. And he remained a faithful club servant through those early years of the '80s, the kind of devoted player who is the backbone of any club. 'I was the newcomer to that side for the final, as enthusiastic as hell. But I gave away a couple of penalties, two of many we conceded on the day, and Leicester scored from them both. The hour's silence in the dressing-room after was the longest I had known. No one wanted to leave. But every guy had given his best, and we had a good night in London.'

The first time Sheehan was on first-team duty, as a sub, he set off from his Kilburn High Road flat and spied a guy waiting at a bus stop with a London Irish bag. 'It turned out to be John Casalaspro. I came to understand he was one unbelievable guy for Guinness. It would have no effect on him. We would succumb after five to eight pints, but he could drink ten and it would have no effect. And he'd always know somebody to take him home.'

Eventually, Sheehan returned to Ireland, seeking a quieter life than the London scene. But he did not settle, returning to England and Nottingham, for whom he played a few 2nd XV games, before joining Ilkeston as player-coach.

By 1994 he was 38, married to Joanna and they had a young son, Conor. One icy February day, they set out for Rosslare to catch the ferry over to Pembroke on the Welsh coast. It was a day that changed his life. 'We hit black ice and slid across the road, into the path of an articulated lorry. It was all over in ten seconds.'

Joanna was killed in the crash; little Conor, still strapped into his baby chair, survived. Jim Sheehan was cut out of the wreckage, flown to Wexford hospital and was in intensive care for five weeks, and in traction for eight weeks. He spent six months in the national rehabilitation hospital at Dun Laoghaire. He had broken his neck at the sixth and seventh vertebrae and was paralysed. Today he is living with his sister and her family at their home outside the small village of Bandon, 17 miles from Limerick. There, as his little boy runs around and does all the scampish things all little boys do, he has shown the same incredible spirit and determination which served him so well in his rugby career to rebuild his shattered life. He greets you with a cheery wave, smiles a lot and is simply outstanding company. You are filled with wonder at such human spirit and how it prevails, such courage in the face of adversity. You are humbled by the marvellous experience of meeting him, as is the case with so many paralysed people.

Jim Sheehan told me, 'As I was carried into the helicopter, someone told me, "Your wife did not make it." After that, the shock of eventually realising I would be in a wheelchair was small.'

Sheehan was treated by Martin Walsh, medical officer for the Irish national soccer team. 'Do you want the full story?' he challenged Sheehan one day, after being asked for the truth. Jim Sheehan nodded and was told he would never walk again. 'Once I knew, I thought, "Right, life begins from here again."'

But where does such courage come from, and how can such a shattering experience be answered by the emergence of vivid willpower? 'It was the way we were brought up. My parents were always very practical people. As children, we were told, "If you are down, get back up on your feet again very quickly." I needed plenty of help from my family but they gave it to me. My mum would say, "Come on, Jim, pull through."'

If the crash and mental trauma were not enough, Jim Sheehan then had to endure the physical agony of months of physiotherapy in an attempt to regain some movement in his arms. 'The physiotherapist would push me through hell. It was only because I had done rugby training at a high level that I could handle it. It was really hard work. But rugby taught me the phrase "No pain, no gain". It is a true saying.'

And the brotherhood of rugby football that had taught him the value of real friendships then emerged to help Jim Sheehan. London Irish men Noel McCulla and Paddy Byrne met in New York and decided something needed to be done. They settled on a bike ride, not down to your local pub for a pint or two, but a five-day jaunt covering 405 miles from Malin Head, the northernmost tip of Ireland, to Mizen Head, the furthest point in the south. They had some willing assistants for the ride: Hugh Condon, Brian Spillane, Peter Rolls, Des Fitzgerald and his wife Andrea, Jim Sheehan's brother John, Mick Condon, John Donovan and Paddy's wife Grainne Barnett Byrne.

Mind you, Paddy Byrne was in fearful trouble by the end of the first day. The first leg was scheduled from Malin Head to Sligo, and Byrne, well, slightly miscalculated the distance. Not, of course, overestimating, but underestimating – by a painful 30 miles. 'But I called the AA and they told me,' he pleaded to his critics. 'Well, that explains everything. Fancy ringing Alcoholics Anonymous – no wonder you got the wrong distance!' they snorted with derision.

Together with a fundraising evening at Twickenham, they collected the considerable sum of £65,000. Not for the self-satisfaction, of course, but to help a rugby mate in trouble. It helped inspire Jim Sheehan to his memorable fightback, which today sees him taking part in wheelchair rugby and other sports.

And it has been that way, especially at this unique club called London Irish, throughout the years. All rugby clubs have great servants; most have a *bonhomie*, a spirit that is special for sport in general. But if you were searching for a club to epitomise these outstanding qualities, this generosity in giving time, care, money, commitment, whatever it may be, then it is hard to think of a club that better illustrates such wonderful elements of the human spirit than London Irish.

It has brought together men of radically different backgrounds, some of whom back in Ireland were not fortunate enough to know peace and friendship with complete strangers. They witnessed it, in many cases, only when they ventured into this club for Irishmen living away from home. Rugby itself inculcates qualities such as discipline, spirit and willpower, as Jim Sheehan demonstrates every day of his life. Others, for less painful reasons, have similarly had cause to reflect upon time spent at this unique sporting club and allow a smile to flicker across their faces.

At the conclusion of a hundred years of London Irish RFC, some may seek their triumphs in matches won, cups lifted, international or provincial caps earned or similar achievements. But to do so would be to miss the fundamental point of what this rugby club has stood for. Throughout its history, it has introduced strangers and made them friends, nurtured the injured and offered comfort and concern, shown life as a sparkling, smiling affair, a cause for joy, when given the slightest opportunity. And it has spawned a multitude of characters, all of whom have contributed so handsomely to the life and times of the club. These, surely, have been the true achievements of London Irish rugby club.

It has been a fascinating hundred years. Front-row seats to watch the next hundred are going to be at a premium, whichever world one happens to be inhabiting at the time.

Bibliography

Rothmans Rugby Union Yearbook (assorted years), edited by Stephen Jones, Mick
     Cleary and John Griffiths (Headline)
One Hundred Years of Irish Rugby, Edmund Van Esbeck (Gill and Macmillan)
The History of the British Lions, Clem Thomas (Mainstream)
The International Rugby Championship, Terry Godwin (Collins Willow)
The Giants of Irish Rugby, John Scally (Mainstream)
The Luck of O'Reilly, Ivan Fallon (Warner Books)
Playfair Rugby Union Annual (assorted years) (Headline)
Assorted national daily newspapers in Ireland and England
Rugby World magazine (assorted editions)